Ethics and Action

by
PETER WINCH

London
ROUTLEDGE & KEGAN PAUL

First published 1972
by Routledge & Kegan Paul Ltd
Broadway House, 68–74 Carter Lane,
London EC4 5EL
Printed in Great Britain by
C. Tinling & Co. Ltd, Prescot

ISBN 0 7100 7438 7

Contents

		Page	
	ACKNOWLEDGMENTS		vii
I	INTRODUCTION		I
2	UNDERSTANDING A PRIMITIVE SOCIETY		8
3	NATURE AND CONVENTION		50
4	HUMAN NATURE		73
5	MAN AND SOCIETY IN HOBBES AND ROUSSEAU		90
6	WITTGENSTEIN'S TREATMENT OF THE WILL		IIO
7	TRYING		I30
8	THE UNIVERSALIZABILITY OF MORAL JUDGMENTS		I5I
9	MORAL INTEGRITY		I7I
IO	CAN A GOOD MAN BE HARMED?		I93
II	ETHICAL REWARD AND PUNISHMENT		2IO
	INDEX		229

Acknowledgments

The essays in this volume first appeared in the following publications and the author wishes to thank the editors and publishers concerned for permission to reprint them here.

'Understanding a Primitive Society' first appeared in the *American Philosophical Quarterly*, Vol. 1, 1964. 'Nature and Convention' and 'Can a Good Man be Harmed?' appeared in the *Proceedings of the Aristotelian Society*, 1959-60 and 1965-6 respectively; 'Trying' is adapted from a symposium on 'Trying and Attempting' held at the Joint Session of the Mind Association and Aristotelian Society at Nottingham in 1971 (the first symposiast being Professor Peter Heath) and published in the *Proceedings of the Aristotelian Society*, Supplementary Volume XLV, 1971. 'Human Nature' was a lecture to the Royal Institute of Philosophy, delivered in 1969 and published in *The Proper Study*, edited by G. N. A. Vesey (Macmillan, 1971). 'Man and Society in Hobbes and Rousseau' appeared in *Hobbes and Rousseau*, edited by M. Cranston and R. S. Peters (Doubleday, 1971). 'The Universalizability of Moral Judgments' was first published in the *Monist*, Vol. 49, 1965; 'Wittgenstein's Treatment of the Will' in *Ratio*, Vol. X, 1968; 'Ethical Reward and Punishment' in *The Human World*, Vol. 1, 1970. 'Moral Integrity' was an inaugural lecture, delivered at King's College, University of London, in May 1968, and published by Basil Blackwell in the same year.

The author also wishes to thank the very many people from whom he has learned, both through their writings and through discussion; and particularly Mr Rush Rhees, whose colleague he had the privilege to be for many years and who, to put the debt at its very lowest, first showed him where the really important issues in moral philosophy are to be found.

1
Introduction

These essays have been written over a period of about ten years and have already been published separately in various places. With some misgivings I have allowed myself to be persuaded that there would be a point in having them printed together in one volume on the grounds, first, that some of them are rather inaccessible and, second, that they deal with a sufficiently interrelated set of topics and from a sufficiently stable point of view to be looked at together. They were not composed as part of any large-scale plan to work out a systematic 'position'. Each subject for discussion has been treated on its merits as I conceived them, though it is true that there has been a sort of progression of thought in that I have found one topic arising naturally out of what I have wanted to say about another. As a result there are many loose ends and much is inconclusive. I dare say too that there are inconsistencies. However, the state of moral philosophy at present seems to me such that any attempt at formulating conclusive and definitive positions is more likely than not to lead to distortion and dogmatism. As for inconsistency, where this is the outcome of the tangled nature of the subject matter and of the tensions which certainly do obtain between various ways of thinking about ethical questions which arise out of the varied conditions of our lives together, I believe that the fact that one is led, sometimes, into saying (at least apparently) inconsistent things about the same questions, when one looks at them from different points of view, can itself be instructive.

Very roughly speaking there is a broad division of interest between essays 2 to 5 and the rest. In this first group of essays the main emphasis is on the social conditions which make moral conceptions possible (or equally, one could say, the moral conceptions which make social life possible); correspondingly, I am mainly, though not exclusively, concerned here—especially in essays 2 to 4—with questions about the nature of one man's understanding, in moral terms, of the lives and actions of *others*. In the other essays the emphasis tends more towards the application of moral concepts in the lives of individual men; and, correspondingly, the discussions here centre on the way in which moral concepts may enter into a man's understanding and assessment of his own life. I will try to say a little more in this Introduction about the relations between these points of view and, at the same time, to sketch some of the lines of connection which hold between the various essays.

'Understanding a Primitive Society' raises questions about the relation between the ways in which men may try to understand the world they live in and the ways in which they try to understand *each other* in the context of the lives they lead together. The main body of the essay does not concern itself directly with specifically moral dimensions of life, but apart from the fact that these moral dimensions receive some attention towards the end of the essay, its argument is relevant to the issues discussed in subsequent essays. For these issues have to do with ways in which certain actions having moral significance for the agent have a bearing on his understanding of himself and his life; the notion of understanding which is employed here cannot, I believe, be separated from the place which the agent conceives himself to occupy in the world in which he lives his life. 'Understanding a Primitive Society' criticizes some forms of the idea that there is, or can be, a conception of 'a world' to be understood, which conception is independent of forms of social life and can provide us with criteria by reference to which we can criticize as 'irrational' certain ways in which men do live. I argue, rather, that any such conception of a world to be understood is intelligible only against the background of a way (or ways) in which men live together and understand each other. If one wants to talk about 'priority' at all here, I should regard it as less misleading to say that men's understanding of each other is more fundamental than (and in that sense prior to) their understanding of the world. But it is probably less misleading not to put the matter like this: to say rather that either sort of understanding is inconceivable apart from the other. In view of various criticisms which have been made of this essay since it was first published, I ought perhaps to emphasize that its argument is not, absurdly, that ways in which men live together can never be criticized, nor even that a way of living can never be characterized as in any sense 'irrational'; still less do I argue in it that men who belong to one culture can 'never understand' lives led in another culture. The argument is rather against certain kinds of account of the criticisms which are possible and of what is involved in such 'cross-cultural' attempts at understanding.

Another prevalent form of the idea that there is a datum given independently of particular forms of social life by reference to which these can be assessed and criticized is the appeal to human nature, in some of its manifestations. This topic is taken up in the essay on 'Human Nature', where it is suggested that ideas of what human nature consists in are themselves expressions of moral ideas which can only be understood in a context of social life, and where some of the implications of this suggestion are discussed. Again, the argument is not that notions of human nature are either senseless or useless; it is only against certain misconceptions about their sense or use. And in 'Man and Society in Hobbes and Rousseau' there is what is intended as a sympathetic discussion of some of the ways in which Rousseau uses such a notion.

In each of the essays I have mentioned so far there is some discussion of what is involved in, and what are the conditions of, a man's attempting to arrive at a moral understanding of his *own* life and of the relations between this and his understanding of his relations with his fellow men. This topic, however, becomes much more central in the later essays in this volume. I should like now to try to explain why this is. Consideration of a serious deficiency in essay No. 3, 'Nature and Convention', may help in this. I argue there that not *all* standards of behaviour accepted in a context of social life can be conceived as matters of convention in the sense that they could be thought of as absent, while social life were thought of as continuing. The example there discussed is the standard of truthfulness in speech, concerning which I argue that there is an incoherence in the thought that there could be a society in which this were not, in some sense, the norm. I also argue that the significance of truthfulness in a society could not be a purely utilitarian one in the sense that it were generally regarded as to be adhered to only for the purpose of getting other people to behave as one wanted them to behave. I persuaded myself, mistakenly,[1] at the time of writing that essay, that an argument along these lines was sufficient to establish that truthfulness must be regarded as a *moral virtue* in any possible human society.

I think that an important part of the diagnosis of my mistake here lies in the obscurity of the project. What exactly is one trying to prove in proving that a certain standard has the status of a 'moral' standard? And this obscurity in its turn springs from the fact—which brings great difficulty into moral philosophy—that people, besides disagreeing on the rights and wrongs of particular moral issues agreed to be such, may *also*, and perhaps more fundamentally, disagree on what is to be counted as a moral issue at all. This complication receives some attention in both 'Human Nature' and 'Moral Integrity'. But another source of the mistake is that on one important conception of what is involved in attaching moral significance to a standard of behaviour, I was looking for an account of such moral significance in altogether the wrong dimensions. R. F. Holland brings out the point so well that I shall quote him at length:[2]

Consider . . . the life-form argument in the version which concludes that it is impossible to conceive a human life in which truthfulness would not generally be regarded as a virtue. This conclusion is soothing to the intelligence as long as you do not enquire into the concept of virtue that is being employed. But ask what concept it is—or to put the question in another way, ask what sort of truthfulness might be at issue—and immediately your attention is caught by what the argument does not do. For the argument neither claims nor implies that truthfulness must exist to the same degree and have the same significance in all societies or among all the people in a particular society. Well then, if the concern of some of them for truth be such that they would hazard all their prospects for it there is something as yet to be accounted for. For the only truth thus far explained is the sort that is told in the degree to which it supports the existing organization or gets you by without disrupting the existing social pattern. All that is necessary for this is a modicum of truth or something that approaches it yet keeps its distance, a conventional sort of standard truthfulness but anyway a relative truthfulness —even if it be arguable that in some society, in view of the advanced state of commerce say, the standard might have to be very precise or very subtle. I should be sceptical about '*the* standard', but anyhow my point is that alongside it there could co-exist for at least some people in the society a concern with truth of an altogether different character, in which *not to falsify* became a spiritual demeanour. Where then could this spirit come from?

Holland goes on to point out that the possibility of such a demeanour will have to be sought not in what he calls the 'life-style' of a community but in that of the individual in whom it is manifested. Naturally, it must not be lost sight of, and Holland does not lose sight of it, that there are intimate conceptual connections between the possible ways in which individuals may live their lives and the institutions of societies.

In the series of essays beginning with No. 6 I am mainly concerned with questions about the kind of moral significance which a man can attach to his own acts, as distinct from the significance to him of other men's acts. Questions of this sort obviously involve the notion of the human will. This notion is already central in essay 5, 'Man and Society in Hobbes and Rousseau', where I discuss some problems concerning the relation between citizen and state. The main topic of discussion here is the way in which the notion of 'legitimate government' depends on a certain disposition of the will on the part of citizens; the essay is also concerned with the way in which a certain quality of social life is a necessary condition for such a disposition of the will. But 'Wittgenstein's Treatment of the Will', which follows, is more directly concerned with the way in which the notion of the will enters into our understanding of the actions of individuals. Some of the issues here which are most important for moral philosophy seem to me to be brought out by the difficulties which Wittgenstein had with the notion of will at the time of writing the *Tractatus Logico-Philosophicus*; and also by his way of meeting these difficulties in *Philosophical Investigations* and other of his later writings. Wittgenstein's abandonment of his earlier conviction that the will (in one sense of the term which he recognized) must be understood as a sort of causal principle from which actions spring is also the starting point for the essay on 'Trying', which attempts to open out some questions about the different kind of moral significance born by a man's completed actions as compared with what he has merely attempted.

The arguments of these last-mentioned two essays already lean rather heavily on the radical distinction in significance for a man of his own acts as distinct from those of others. Failure to recognize this distinction, or at least to give it sufficient prominence, is responsible, in my view, for some of the main shortcomings in those currently popular accounts of morality which insist on that notion of 'universalizability' which would have it that a man who thinks that a given action is the right one for him to perform in certain circumstances is logically committed to thinking that the same action would be right for anyone else in relevantly similar circumstances. Essay No. 8 on 'The Universalizability of Moral Judgments' is a direct criticism of such a notion, while No. 9 'Moral Integrity' explores closely connected issues.

Wittgenstein's discussion of the will in the *Tractatus* involved a distinction between the will as the putative cause of particular human actions, 'the will as a phenomenon', and what he called 'the will in so far as it is the subject of ethical attributes'. His way of conceiving the relation between these two notions led him into great difficulties and the distinction virtually disappears in his later treatments of the notion of human action. I believe, however, that something analogous to his notion of 'the will as the subject of ethical attributes' is indispensable in the treatment of certain fundamental problems of moral philosophy and that some place must be found for it there. Essays 10 and 11, 'Can a Good Man be Harmed?' and 'Ethical Reward and Punishment', are intended as a contribution towards finding such a place. It goes without saying that a great deal more needs to be said about this subject; and the same applies, of course, to all the other subjects treated in this book.

NOTES

[1] See R. F. Holland, 'Is Goodness a Mystery?', *The University of Leeds Review*, May 1970, Vol. 13, No. 1; and Richard Norman, *Reasons for Actions* (London: Basil Blackwell, 1971), pp. 135-9.

[2] Loc. cit., p. 70.

2

Understanding a Primitive Society

This essay will pursue further some questions raised in my book, *The Idea of a Social Science.*[1] That book was a general discussion of what is involved in the understanding of human social life. I shall here be concerned more specifically with certain issues connected with social anthropology. In the first part I raise certain difficulties about Professor E. E. Evans-Pritchard's approach in his classic, *Witchcraft, Oracles and Magic among the Azande.*[2] In the second part, I attempt to refute some criticisms recently made by Mr Alasdair MacIntyre of Evans-Pritchard and myself, to criticize in their turn MacIntyre's positive remarks, and to offer some further reflections of my own on the concept of learning from the study of a primitive society.

1. *The Reality of Magic*

Like many other primitive people, the African Azande hold beliefs that we cannot possibly share and engage in practices which it is peculiarly difficult for us to comprehend. They believe that certain of their members are witches, exercising a malignant occult influence on the lives of their fellows. They engage in rites to counteract witchcraft; they consult oracles and use magic medicines to protect themselves from harm.

An anthropologist studying such a people wishes to make

those beliefs and practices intelligible to himself and his readers. This means presenting an account of them that will somehow satisfy the criteria of rationality demanded by the culture to which he and his readers belong: a culture whose conception of rationality is deeply affected by the achievements and methods of the sciences, and one which treats such things as a belief in magic or the practice of consulting oracles as almost a paradigm of the irrational. The strains inherent in this situation are very likely to lead the anthropologist to adopt the following posture: *We* know that Zande beliefs in the influence of witchcraft, the efficacy of magic medicines, the role of oracles in revealing what is going on and what is going to happen, are mistaken, illusory. Scientific methods of investigation have shown conclusively that there are no relations of cause and effect such as are implied by these beliefs and practices. All we can do then is to show how such a system of mistaken beliefs and inefficacious practices can maintain itself in the face of objections that seem to us so obvious.[3]

Now although Evans-Pritchard goes a very great deal further than most of his predecessors in trying to present the sense of the institutions he is discussing as it presents itself to the Azande themselves, still, the last paragraph does, I believe, pretty fairly describe the attitude he himself took at the time of writing this book. There is more than one remark to the effect that 'obviously there are no witches'; and he writes of the difficulty he found, during his field work with the Azande, in shaking off the 'unreason' on which Zande life is based and returning to a clear view of how things really are. This attitude is not an unsophisticated one but is based on a philosophical position ably developed in a series of papers published in the 1930s in the unhappily rather inaccessible *Bulletin of the Faculty of Arts* of the University of Egypt. Arguing against Lévy-Bruhl, Evans-Pritchard here rejects the idea that the scientific understanding of causes and effects which leads us to reject magical ideas is evidence of any superior intelligence on our part. Our scientific approach, he points out, is as much a function of our culture as is the magical approach of the 'savage' a function of his:[4]

> The fact that we attribute rain to meteorological causes alone while savages believe that Gods or ghosts or magic can influence the rainfall is no evidence that our brains function differently from their brains. It does not show that we 'think more logically' than savages, at least not if this expression suggests some kind of hereditary psychic superiority. It is no sign of superior intelligence on my part that I attribute rain to physical causes. I did not come to this conclusion myself by observation and inference and have, in fact, little knowledge of the meteorological processes that lead to rain. I merely accept what everybody else in my society accepts, namely that rain is due to natural causes. This particular idea formed part of my culture long before I was born into it and little more was required of me than sufficient linguistic ability to learn it. Likewise a savage who believes that under suitable natural and ritual conditions the rainfall can be influenced by use of appropriate magic is not on account of this belief to be considered of inferior intelligence. He did not build up this belief from his own observations and inferences but adopted it in the same way as he adopted the rest of his cultural heritage, namely, by being born into it. He and I are both thinking in patterns of thought provided for us by the societies in which we live.
>
> It would be absurd to say that the savage is thinking mystically and that we are thinking scientifically about rainfall. In either case like mental processes are involved and, moreover, the content of thought is similarly derived. But we can say that the social content of our thought about rainfall is scientific, is in accord with objective facts, whereas the social content of savage thought about rainfall is unscientific since it is not in accord with reality and may also be mystical where it assumes the existence of supra-sensible forces.

In a subsequent article on Pareto, Evans-Pritchard distinguishes between 'logical' and 'scientific'.[5]

> Scientific notions are those which accord with objective

reality both with regard to the validity of their premises and to the inferences drawn from their propositions . . . Logical notions are those in which according to the rules of thought inferences would be true were the premises true, the truth of the premises being irrelevant . . .

A pot has broken during firing. This is probably due to grit. Let us examine the pot and see if this is the cause. That is logical and scientific thought. Sickness is due to witchcraft. A man is sick. Let us consult the oracles to discover who is the witch responsible. That is logical and unscientific thought.

I think that Evans-Pritchard is right in a great deal of what he says here, but wrong, and crucially wrong, in his attempt to characterize the scientific in terms of that which is 'in accord with objective reality'. Despite differences of emphasis and phraseology, Evans-Pritchard is in fact hereby put into the same metaphysical camp as Pareto: for both of them the conception of 'reality' must be regarded as intelligible and applicable *outside* the context of scientific reasoning itself, since it is that to which scientific notions do, and unscientific notions do not, have a relation. Evans-Pritchard, although he emphasizes that a member of scientific culture has a different conception of reality from that of a Zande believer in magic, wants to go beyond merely registering this fact and making the differences explicit, and to say, finally, that the scientific conception agrees with what reality actually is like, whereas the magical conception does not.

It would be easy, at this point, to say simply that the difficulty arises from the use of the unwieldy and misleadingly comprehensive expression 'agreement with reality'; and in a sense this is true. But we should not lose sight of the fact that the idea that men's ideas and beliefs must be checkable by reference to something independent—some reality—is an important one. To abandon it is to plunge straight into an extreme Protagorean relativism, with all the paradoxes that involves. On the other hand great care is certainly necessary in fixing the precise role that this conception of the independently real does play in men's thought. There are two related points that I should like to make about it at this stage.

In the first place we should notice that the check of the independently real is not peculiar to science. The trouble is that the fascination science has for us makes it easy for us to adopt its scientific form as a paradigm against which to measure the intellectual respectability of other modes of discourse. Consider what God says to Job out of the whirlwind: 'Who is this that darkeneth counsel by words without knowledge? . . . Where wast thou when I laid the foundations of the earth? declare, if thou hast understanding. Who hath laid the measures thereof, if thou knowest? or who hath stretched the line upon it . . . Shall he that contendeth with the Almighty instruct him? he that reproveth God, let him answer it.' Job is taken to task for having gone astray by having lost sight of the reality of God; this does not, of course, mean that Job has made any sort of theoretical mistake, which could be put right, perhaps, by means of an experiment.[6] God's reality is certainly independent of what any man may care to think, but what that reality amounts to can only be seen from the religious tradition in which the concept of God is used, and this use is very unlike the use of scientific concepts, say of theoretical entities. The point is that it is *within* the religious use of language that the conception of God's reality has its place, though, I repeat, this does not mean that it is at the mercy of what anyone cares to say; if this were so, God would have no reality.

My second point follows from the first. Reality is not what gives language sense. What is real and what is unreal shows itself *in* the sense that language has. Further, both the distinction between the real and the unreal and the concept of agreement with reality themselves belong to our language. I will not say that they are concepts of the language like any other, since it is clear that they occupy a commanding, and in a sense a limiting, position there. We can imagine a language with no concept of, say, wetness, but hardly one in which there is no way of distinguishing the real from the unreal. Nevertheless we could not in fact distinguish the real from the unreal without understanding the way this distinction operates in the language. If then we wish to understand the significance of these concepts, we must examine the use they actually do have—*in* the language.

Evans-Pritchard, on the contrary, is trying to work with a conception of reality which is *not* determined by its actual use in language. He wants something against which that use can itself be appraised. But this is not possible; and no more possible in the case of scientific discourse than it is in any other. We may ask whether a particular scientific hypothesis agrees with reality and test this by observation and experiment. Given the experimental methods, and the established use of the theoretical terms entering into the hypothesis, then the question whether it holds or not is settled by reference to something independent of what I, or anybody else, care to think. But the general nature of the data revealed by the experiment can only be specified in terms of criteria built into the methods of experiment employed and these, in turn, make sense only to someone who is conversant with the kind of scientific activity within which they are employed. A scientific illiterate, asked to describe the results of an experiment which he 'observes' in an advanced physics laboratory could not do so in terms relevant to the hypothesis being tested; and it is really only in such terms that we can sensibly speak of the 'results of the experiment' at all. What Evans-Pritchard wants to be able to say is that the criteria applied in scientific experimentation constitute a true link between our ideas and an independent reality, whereas those characteristic of other systems of thought—in particular, magical methods of thought—do not. It is evident that the expressions 'true link' and 'independent reality' in the previous sentence cannot themselves be explained by reference to the scientific universe of discourse, as this would beg the question. We have then to ask how, by reference to what established universe of discourse, the use of those expressions *is* to be explained; and it is clear that Evans-Pritchard has not answered this question.

Two questions arise out of what I have been saying. First, is it in fact the case that a primitive system of magic, like that of the Azande, constitutes a coherent universe of discourse like science, in terms of which an intelligible conception of reality and clear ways of deciding what beliefs are and are not in agreement with this reality can be discerned? Second, what are we to make of the possibility of understanding primitive social institutions, like Zande magic, if the situation is as I have outlined? I do not claim to be able to give a satisfactory answer to the second question. It raises some very important and fundamental issues about the nature of human social life, which require conceptions different from, and harder to elucidate than, those I have hitherto introduced. I shall offer some tentative remarks about these issues in the second part of this essay. At present I shall address myself to the first question.

It ought to be remarked here that an affirmative answer to my first question would not commit me to accepting as rational all beliefs couched in magical concepts or all procedures practiced in the name of such beliefs. This is no more necessary than is the corresponding proposition that all procedures 'justified' in the name of science are immune from rational criticism. A remark of Collingwood's is apposite here:[7]

> Savages are no more exempt from human folly than civilized men, and are no doubt equally liable to the error of thinking that they, or the persons they regard as their superiors, can do what in fact cannot be done. But this error is not the essence of magic; it is a perversion of magic. And we should be careful how we attribute it to the people we call savages, who will one day rise up and testify against us.

It is important to distinguish a system of magical beliefs and practices like that of the Azande, which is one of the principal foundations of their whole social life and, on the other hand, magical beliefs that might be held, and magical rites that might be practised, by persons belonging to our own culture. These have to be understood rather differently. Evans-Pritchard is himself alluding to the difference in the following passage:[8]

> When a Zande speaks of witchcraft he does not speak of it as we speak of the weird witchcraft of our own history. Witchcraft is to him a commonplace happening and he seldom passes a day without mentioning it ... To us witchcraft is something which haunted and disgusted our credulous forefathers. But the Zande expects to come across witchcraft at any time of the day or night. He would be just as surprised if he were not brought into daily contact with it as we would be if confronted by its appearance. To him there is nothing miraculous about it.

The difference is not merely one of degree of familiarity, however, although, perhaps, even this has more importance than might at first appear. Concepts of witchcraft and magic in our culture, at least since the advent of Christianity, have been parasitic on, and a perversion of other orthodox concepts, both religious and, increasingly, scientific. To take an obvious example, you could not understand what was involved in conducting a Black Mass, unless you were familiar with the conduct of a proper Mass and, therefore, with the whole complex of religious ideas from which the Mass draws its sense. Neither would you understand the relation between these without taking account of the fact that the Black practices are rejected as *irrational* (in the sense proper to religion) in the system of beliefs on which these practices are thus parasitic. Perhaps a similar relation holds between the contemporary practice of astrology and astronomy and technology. It is impossible to keep a discussion of the rationality of Black Magic or of astrology within the bounds of concepts peculiar to them; they have an essential reference to something outside themselves. The position is like that which Socrates, in Plato's *Gorgias*, showed to be true of the Sophists' conception of rhetoric:

namely, that it is parasitic on rational discourse in such a way that its irrational character can be shown in terms of this dependence. Hence, when we speak of such practices as 'superstitious', 'illusory', 'irrational', we have the weight of our culture behind us; and this is not just a matter of being on the side of the big battalions, because those beliefs and practices belong to, and derive such sense as they seem to have, from that same culture. This enables us to show that the sense is only apparent, in terms which are culturally relevant.

It is evident that our relation to Zande magic is quite different. If we wish to understand it, we must seek a foothold elsewhere. And while there may well be room for the use of such critical expressions as 'superstition' and 'irrationality', the kind of rationality with which such terms might be used to point a contrast remains to be elucidated. The remarks I shall make in Part II will have a more positive bearing on this issue. In the rest of this Part, I shall develop in more detail my criticisms of Evans-Pritchard's approach to the Azande.

Early in this book he defines certain categories in terms of which his descriptions of Zande customs are couched.[9]

> MYSTICAL NOTIONS ... are patterns of thought that attribute to phenomena supra-sensible qualities which, or part of which, are not derived from observation or cannot be logically inferred from it, *and which they do not possess.*[10] COMMON-SENSE NOTIONS ... attribute to phenomena only what men observe in them or what can logically be inferred from observation. So long as a notion does not assert something which has not been observed, it is not classed as mystical even though it is mistaken on account of incomplete observation ... SCIENTIFIC NOTIONS. Science has developed out of common-sense but is far more methodical and has better techniques of observation and reasoning. Common-sense uses experience and rules of thumb. Science uses experiment and rules of Logic ... *Our body of scientific knowledge and Logic are the sole arbiters of what are mystical, common-sense, and scientific*

notions. Their judgments are never absolute. RITUAL BEHAVIOUR. Any behaviour that is accounted for by mystical notions. *There is no objective nexus* between the behaviour and the event it is intended to cause. Such behaviour is usually intelligible to us only when we know the mystical notions associated with it. EMPIRICAL BEHAVIOUR. Any behaviour that is accounted for by common-sense notions.

It will be seen from the phrases which I have italicized that Evans-Pritchard is doing more here than just defining certain terms for his own use. Certain metaphysical claims are embodied in the definitions: identical in substance with the claims embodied in Pareto's way of distinguishing between 'logical' and 'non-logical' conduct.[11] There is a very clear implication that those who use mystical notions and perform ritual behaviour are making some sort of mistake, detectable with the aid of science and logic. I shall now examine more closely some of the institutions described by Evans-Pritchard to determine how far his claims are justified.

Witchcraft is a power possessed by certain individuals to harm other individuals by 'mystical' means. Its basis is an inherited organic condition, 'witchcraft-substance' and it does not involve any special magical ritual or medicine. It is constantly appealed to by Azande when they are afflicted by misfortune, not so as to exclude explanation in terms of natural causes, which Azande are perfectly able to offer themselves within the limits of their not inconsiderable natural knowledge, but so as to supplement such explanations. 'Witchcraft explains *why*[12] events are harmful to man and not *how*[12] they happen. A Zande perceives how they happen just as we do. He does not see a witch charge a man but an elephant. He does not see a witch push over the granary, but termites gnawing away its supports. He does not see a psychical flame igniting thatch, but an ordinary lighted bundle of straw. His perception of how events occur is as clear as our own.'[13]

The most important way of detecting the influence of witchcraft and of identifying witches is by the revelations of oracles, of which in turn the most important is the 'poison oracle'. This name, though convenient, is significantly misleading insofar as, according to Evans-Pritchard, Azande do not have our concept of a poison and do not think of, or behave toward, *benge*—the substance administered in the consultation of the oracle—as we do of and toward poisons. The gathering, preparation, and administering of *benge* is hedged with ritual and strict taboos. At an oracular consultation *benge* is administered to a fowl, while a question is asked in a form permitting a yes or no answer. The fowl's death or survival is specified beforehand as giving the answer 'yes' or 'no'. The answer is then checked by administering *benge* to another fowl and asking the question the other way round. 'Is Prince Ndoruma responsible for placing bad medicines in the roof of my hut? The fowl DIES giving the answer "Yes" ... Did the oracle speak truly when it said that Ndoruma was responsible? The fowl SURVIVES giving the answer "Yes".' The poison oracle is all-pervasive in Zande life and all steps of any importance in a person's life are settled by reference to it.

A Zande would be utterly lost and bewildered without his oracle. The mainstay of his life would be lacking. It is rather as if an engineer, in our society, were to be asked to build a bridge without mathematical calculation, or a military commander to mount an extensive co-ordinated attack without the use of clocks. These analogies are mine, but a reader may well think that they beg the question at issue. For, he may argue, the Zande practice of consulting the oracle, unlike my technological and military examples, is completely unintelligible and rests on an obvious illusion. I shall now consider this objection.

First I must emphasize that I have so far done little more than note the *fact*, conclusively established by Evans-Pritchard, that the Azande *do* in fact conduct their affairs to their own satisfaction in this way and are at a loss when forced to abandon the practice—when, for instance, they fall into the hands of European courts. It is worth remarking too that Evans-Pritchard himself ran his household in the same way during his field researches and says: 'I found this as satisfactory a way of running my home and affairs as any other I know of.'

Further, I would ask in my turn: *to whom* is the practice alleged to be unintelligible? Certainly it is difficult for us to understand what the Azande are about when they consult their oracles; but it might seem just as incredible to them that the engineer's motions with his slide rule could have any connection with the stability of his bridge. But this riposte of course misses the intention behind the objection, which was not directed to the question whether anyone in fact understands, or claims to understand, what is going on, but rather whether what is going on actually does make sense: i.e., in itself. And it may seem obvious that Zande beliefs in witchcraft and oracles cannot make any sense, however satisfied the Azande may be with them.

What criteria have we for saying that something does, or does not, make sense? A partial answer is that a set of beliefs and practices cannot make sense insofar as they involve contradictions. Now it appears that contradictions are bound to arise in at least two ways in the consultation of the oracle. On the one hand two oracular pronouncements may contradict each other; and on the other hand a self-consistent oracular pronouncement may be contradicted by future experience. I shall examine each of these apparent possibilities in turn.

Of course, it does happen often that the oracle first says 'yes' and then 'no' to the same question. This does not convince a Zande of the futility of the whole operation of consulting oracles: obviously, it cannot, since otherwise the practice could hardly have developed and maintained itself at all. Various explanations may be offered, whose possibility, it is important to notice, is built into the whole network of Zande beliefs and may, therefore, be regarded as belonging to the concept of an oracle. It may be said, for instance, that bad *benge* is being used; that the operator of the oracle is ritually unclean; that the oracle is being itself influenced by witchcraft or sorcery; or it may be that the oracle is showing that the question cannot be answered straightforwardly in its present form, as with 'Have you stopped beating your wife yet?' There are various ways in which the behaviour of the fowl under the influence of *benge* may be ingeniously interpreted by those wise in the ways of the poison oracle. We might compare this situation perhaps with the interpretation of dreams.

In the other type of case: where an internally consistent oracular revelation is apparently contradicted by subsequent experience, the situation may be dealt with in a similar way, by references to the influence of witchcraft, ritual uncleanliness, and so on. But there is another important consideration we must take into account here too. The chief function of oracles is to reveal the presence of 'mystical' forces—I use Evans-Pritchard's term without committing myself to his denial that such forces really exist. Now though there are indeed ways of determining whether or not mystical forces are operating, these ways do not correspond to what we understand by 'empirical' confirmation or refutation. This indeed is a tautology since such differences in 'confirmatory' procedures are the main criteria for classifying something as a mystical force in the first place. Here we have one reason why the possibilities of 'refutation by experience' are very much fewer than might at first sight be supposed.

There is also another closely connected reason. The spirit in which oracles are consulted is very unlike that in which a scientist makes experiments. Oracular revelations are not treated as hypotheses and, since their sense derives from the way they are treated in their context, they therefore *are not* hypotheses. They are not a matter of intellectual interest but the main way in which Azande decide how they should act. If the oracle reveals that a proposed course of action is fraught with mystical dangers from witchcraft or sorcery, that course of action will not be carried out; and then the question of refutation or confirmation just does not arise. We might say that the revelation has the logical status of an unfulfilled hypothetical, were it not that the context in which this logical term is generally used may again suggest a misleadingly close analogy with scientific hypotheses.

I do not think that Evans-Pritchard would have disagreed with what I have said so far. Indeed, the following comment is on very similar lines:[14]

> Azande observe the action of the poison oracle as we observe it, but their observations are always subordinated to their beliefs and are incorporated into their beliefs and made to explain them and justify them. Let the reader consider any argument that would utterly demolish all Zande claims for the power of the oracle. If it were translated into Zande modes of thought it would serve to support their entire structure of belief. For their mystical notions are eminently coherent, being interrelated by a network of logical ties, and are so ordered that they never too crudely contradict sensory experience but, instead, experience seems to justify them. The Zande is immersed in a sea of mystical notions, and if he speaks about his poison oracle he must speak in a mystical idiom.

To locate the point at which the important philosophical issue does arise, I shall offer a parody, composed by changing round one or two expressions in the foregoing quotation.

> Europeans observe the action of the poison oracle just as Azande observe it, but their observations are always subordinated to their beliefs and are incorporated into their beliefs and made to explain them and justify them. Let a Zande consider any argument that would utterly refute all European scepticism about the power of the oracle. If it were translated into European modes of thought it would serve to support their entire structure of belief. For their scientific notions are eminently coherent, being interrelated by a network of logical ties, and are so ordered that they never too crudely contradict mystical experience but, instead, experience seems to justify them. The European is immersed in a sea of scientific notions, and if he speaks about the Zande poison oracle he must speak in a scientific idiom.

Perhaps this too would be acceptable to Evans-Pritchard.

But it is clear from other remarks in the book to which I have alluded, that at the time of writing it he would have wished to add: and the European is right and the Zande wrong. This addition I regard as illegitimate and my reasons for so thinking take us to the heart of the matter.

It may be illuminating at this point to compare the disagreement between Evans-Pritchard and me to that between the Wittgenstein of the *Philosophical Investigations* and his earlier *alter ego* of the *Tractatus Logico-Philosophicus*. In the *Tractatus* Wittgenstein sought 'the general form of propositions': what made propositions possible. He said that this general form is: 'This is how things are'; the proposition was an articulated model, consisting of elements standing in a definite relation to each other. The proposition was true when there existed a corresponding arrangement of elements in reality. The proposition was capable of saying something because of the identity of structure, of logical form, in the proposition and in reality.

By the time Wittgenstein composed the *Investigations* he had come to reject the whole idea that there must be a general form of propositions. He emphasized the indefinite number of different uses that language may have and tried to show that these different uses neither need, nor in fact do, all have something in common, in the sense intended in the *Tractatus*. He also tried to show that what counts as 'agreement or disagreement with reality' takes on as many different forms as there are different uses of language and cannot, therefore, be taken as given *prior* to the detailed investigation of the use that is in question.

The *Tractatus* contains a remark strikingly like something that Evans-Pritchard says.[15]

> *The limits of my language mean the limits of my world.* Logic fills the world: the limits of the world are also its limits. We cannot therefore say in logic: This and this there is in the world, and that there is not.
>
> For that would apparently presuppose that we exclude certain possibilities, and this cannot be the case since otherwise logic must get outside the limits of the world:

that is, if it could consider these limits from the other side also.

Evans-Pritchard discusses the phenomena of belief and scepticism, as they appear in Zande life. There *is* certainly widespread scepticism about certain things, for instance, about some of the powers claimed by witch-doctors or about the efficacy of certain magic medicines. But, he points out, such scepticism does not begin to overturn the mystical way of thinking, since it is necessarily expressed in terms belonging to that way of thinking.[16]

> In this web of belief every strand depends on every other strand, and a Zande cannot get outside its meshes because this is the only world he knows. The web is not an external structure in which he is enclosed. It is the texture of his thought and he cannot think that his thought is wrong.

Wittgenstein and Evans-Pritchard are concerned here with much the same problem, though the difference in the directions from which they approach it is important too. Wittgenstein, at the time of the *Tractatus*, spoke of 'language', as if all language is fundamentally of the same kind and must have the same kind of 'relation to reality'; but Evans-Pritchard is confronted by two languages which he recognizes as fundamentally different in kind, such that much of what may be expressed in the one has no possible counterpart in the other. One might, therefore, have expected this to lead to a position closer to that of the *Philosophical Investigations* than to that of the *Tractatus*. Evans-Pritchard is not content with elucidating the differences in the two concepts of reality involved; he wants to go further and say: our concept of reality is the correct one, the Azande are mistaken. But the difficulty is to see what 'correct' and 'mistaken' can mean in this context.

Let me return to the subject of contradictions. I have already noted that many contradictions we might expect to appear in fact do not in the context of Zande thought, where provision is made for avoiding them. But there are some situations of which this does not seem to be true, where what appear to us as obvious contradictions are left where they are, apparently unresolved. Perhaps this may be the foothold we are looking for, from which we can appraise the 'correctness' of the Zande system.[17]

Consider Zande notions about the inheritance of witchcraft. I have spoken so far only of the role of oracles in establishing whether or not someone is a witch. But there is a further and, as we might think, more 'direct' method of doing this, namely by post-mortem examination of a suspect's intestines for 'witchcraft-substance'. This may be arranged by his family after his death in an attempt to clear the family name of the imputation of witchcraft. Evans-Pritchard remarks:[18]

> To our minds it appears evident that if a man is proven a witch the whole of his clan are *ipso facto* witches, since the Zande clan is a group of persons related biologically to one another through the male line. Azande see the sense of this argument but they do not accept its conclusions, and it would involve the whole notion of witchcraft in contradiction were they to do so.

Contradiction would presumably arise because a few positive results of post-mortem examinations, scattered among all the clans, would very soon prove that everybody was a witch, and a few negative results, scattered among the same clans, would prove that nobody was a witch. Though, in particular situations, individual Azande may avoid personal implications arising out of the presence of witchcraft-substance in deceased relatives, by imputations of bastardy and similar devices, this would not be enough to save the generally contradictory situation I have sketched. Evans-Pritchard comments:[19] 'Azande do not perceive the contradiction as we perceive it because they have no theoretical interest in the subject and those situations in which they express their belief in witchcraft do not force the problem upon them.'

It might now appear as though we had clear grounds for

speaking of the superior rationality of European over Zande thought, insofar as the latter involves a contradiction which it makes no attempt to remove and does not even recognize: one, however, which is recognizable as such in the context of European ways of thinking. But does Zande thought on this matter really involve a contradiction? It appears from Evans-Pritchard's account that Azande do not press their ways of thinking about witches to a point at which they would be involved in contradictions.

Someone may now want to say that the irrationality of the Azande in relation to witchcraft shows itself in the fact that they do not press their thought about it 'to its logical conclusion'. To appraise this point we must consider whether the conclusion we are trying to force on them is indeed a logical one; or perhaps better, whether someone who does press this conclusion is being more rational than the Azande, who do not. Some light is thrown on this question by Wittgenstein's discussion of a game,[20]

such that whoever begins can always win by a particular simple trick. But this has not been realized—so it is a game. Now someone draws our attention to it—and it stops being a game.

What turn can I give this, to make it clear to myself?— For I want to say, 'and it stops being a game'—not: 'and now we see that it wasn't a game.'

That means, I want to say, it can also be taken like this: the other man did not *draw our attention* to anything; he taught us a different game in place of our own. But how can the new game have made the old one obsolete? We now see something different, and can no longer naively go on playing.

On the one hand the game consisted in our actions (our play) on the board; and these actions I could perform as well now as before. But on the other hand it was essential to the game that I blindly tried to win; and now I can no longer do that.

There are obviously considerable analogies between Wittgenstein's example and the situation we are consider-

c

ing. But there is an equally important difference. Both Wittgenstein's games: the old one without the trick that enables the starter to win and the new one with the trick, are in an important sense on the same level. They are both *games* in the form of a contest where the aim of a player is to beat his opponent by the exercise of skill. The new trick makes this situation impossible and this is why it makes the old game obsolete. To be sure, the situation could be saved in a way by introducing a new rule, forbidding the use by the starter of the trick which would ensure his victory. But our intellectual habits are such as to make us unhappy about the artificiality of such a device, rather as logicians have been unhappy about the introduction of a Theory of Types as a device for avoiding Russell's paradoxes. It is noteworthy in my last quotation from Evans-Pritchard, however, that the Azande, when the possibility of this contradiction about the inheritance of witchcraft is pointed out to them, do *not* then come to regard their old beliefs about witchcraft as obsolete. 'They have no theoretical interest in the subject.' This suggests strongly that the context from which the suggestion about the contradiction is made, the context of our scientific culture, is not on the same level as the context in which the beliefs about witchcraft operate. Zande notions of witchcraft do not constitute a theoretical system in terms of which Azande try to gain a quasi-scientific understanding of the world.[21] This in its turn suggests that it is the European, obsessed with pressing Zande thought where it would not naturally go—to a contradiction—who is guilty of misunderstanding, not the Zande. The European is in fact committing a category-mistake.

Something else is also suggested by this discussion: the forms in which rationality expresses itself in the culture of a human society cannot be elucidated *simply* in terms of the logical coherence of the rules according to which activities are carried out in that society. For, as we have seen, there comes a point where we are not even in a position to determine what is and what is not coherent in such a context of rules, without raising questions about the point which following those rules has in the society. No doubt it was a realization of this fact which led Evans-Pritchard to appeal to a residual 'correspondence with reality' in distinguishing between 'mystical' and 'scientific' notions. The conception of reality is indeed indispensable to any understanding of the point of a way of life. But it is not a conception which can be explicated as Evans-Pritchard tries to explicate it, in terms of what science reveals to be the case; for a form of the conception of reality must already be presupposed before we can make any sense of the expression 'what science reveals to be the case'.

2. *Our Standards and Theirs*

In Part 1, I attempted, by analysing a particular case, to criticize by implication a particular view of how we can understand a primitive institution. In this Part, I shall have two aims. First, I shall examine in a more formal way a general philosophical argument, which attempts to show that the approach I have been criticizing is in principle the right one. This argument has been advanced by Mr Alasdair MacIntyre in two places: (*a*) in a paper entitled 'Is Understanding Religion Compatible with Believing?' read to the Sesquicentennial Seminar of the Princeton Theological Seminar in 1962;[22] (*b*) in a contribution to *Philosophy, Politics and Society (Second Series)*,[23] entitled 'A Mistake about Causality in Social Science'. Next, I shall make some slightly more positive suggestions about how to overcome the difficulty from which I started: how to make intelligible in our terms institutions belonging to a primitive culture, whose standards of rationality and intelligibility are apparently quite at odds with our own.

The relation between MacIntyre, Evans-Pritchard, and myself is a complicated one. MacIntyre takes Evans-Pritchard's later book, *Nuer Religion*, as an application of a point of view like mine in *The Idea of a Social Science*; he regards it as an object lesson in the absurd results to which such a position leads, when applied in practice. My own criticisms of Evans-Pritchard, on the other hand, have come from precisely the opposite direction. I have tried to show that Evans-Pritchard did not at the time of writing *The Azande* agree with me *enough*; that he did not take seriously enough the idea that the concepts used by primitive peoples can only be interpreted in the context of the way of life of those peoples. Thus I have in effect argued that Evans-Pritchard's account of the Azande is unsatisfactory precisely to the extent that he agrees with MacIntyre and not me.

The best point at which to start considering MacIntyre's position is that at which he agrees with me—in emphasizing the importance of possibilities of *description* for the concept of human action. An agent's action 'is identified fundamentally as what it is by the description under which he deems it to fall'. Since, further, descriptions must be intelligible to other people, an action 'must fall under some description which is socially recognizable as the description of an action'.[24] 'To identify the limits of social action in a given period', therefore, 'is to identify the stock of descriptions current in that age.'[25] MacIntyre correctly points out that descriptions do not exist in isolation, but occur 'as constituents of beliefs, speculations and projects'. As these in turn 'are continually criticized, modified, rejected, or improved, the stock of descriptions changes. The changes in human action are thus intimately linked to the thread of rational criticism in human history.'

This notion of rational criticism, MacIntyre points out, requires the notion of choice between alternatives, to explain which 'is a matter of making clear what the agent's criterion was and why he made use of this criterion rather than another and to explain why the use of this criterion appears rational to those who invoke it'.[26] Hence 'in explaining the rules and conventions to which action in a given social order conform (*sic*) we cannot omit reference to the rationality or otherwise of those rules and conventions.' Further, 'the beginning of an explanation of why certain criteria are taken to be rational in some societies is that they *are* rational. And since this has to enter into our explanation we cannot explain social behaviour independently of our own norms of rationality.'

I turn now to criticism of this argument. Consider first MacIntyre's account of changes in an existing 'stock' of available descriptions of actions. How does a candidate for inclusion *qualify* for admission to the stock? Unless there are limits, all MacIntyre's talk about possibilities of description circumscribing possibilities of action becomes nugatory, for there would be nothing to stop anybody inventing some arbitrary verbal expression, applying it to some arbitrary bodily movement, and thus adding that expression to the stock of available descriptions. But of course the new description must be an *intelligible* one. Certainly, its intelligibility cannot be decided by whether or not it belongs to an *existing* stock of descriptions, since this would rule out precisely what is being discussed: the addition of *new* descriptions to the stock. 'What can intelligibly be said' is not equivalent to 'what has been intelligibly said', or it would never be possible to say anything new. *Mutatis mutandis* it would never be possible to *do* anything new. Nevertheless the intelligibility of anything new said or done does depend in a certain way on what already has been said or done and understood. The crux of this problem lies in how we are to understand that 'in a certain way'.

In 'Is Understanding Religion Compatible with Believing?' MacIntyre asserts that the development through criticism of the standards of intelligibility current in a society is ruled out by my earlier account (in *The Idea of a Social Science*) of the origin in social institutions themselves of such standards. I shall not now repeat my earlier argument, but simply point out that I did, in various passages,[27] emphasize the *open* character of the 'rules' which I spoke of in connection with social institutions: i.e. the fact that in changing social situations, reasoned decisions have to be made about what is to count as 'going on in the same way'. MacIntyre's failure to come to terms with this point creates difficulties for him precisely analogous to those which he mistakenly attributes to my account.

It is a corollary of his argument up to this point, as well as being intrinsically evident, that a new description of action must be intelligible to the members of the society in which it is introduced. On my view the point is that what determines this is the further development of rules and principles already implicit in the previous ways of acting and talking. To be emphasized are not the actual members of any 'stock' of descriptions; but the *grammar* which they express. It is through this that we understand their structure and sense, their mutual relations, and the sense of new ways of talking and acting that may be introduced. These new ways of talking and acting may very well at the same time involve modifications in the grammar, but we can only speak thus if the new grammar is (to its users) intelligibly related to the old.

But what of the intelligibility of such changes to observers from another society with a different culture and different standards of intelligibility? MacIntyre urges that such observers must make clear 'what the agent's criterion was and why he made use of this criterion rather than another and why the use of this criterion appears rational to those who invoke it'. Since what is at issue is the precise relation between the concepts of rationality current in these different societies it is obviously of first importance to be clear about *whose* concept of rationality is being alluded to in this quotation. It seems that it must be that which is current in the society in which the criterion is invoked. Something can appear rational to someone only in terms of *his* understanding of what is and is not rational. If *our* concept of rationality is a different one from his, then it makes no sense to say that anything either does or does not appear rational to *him* in *our* sense.

When MacIntyre goes on to say that the observer 'cannot omit reference to the rationality or otherwise of those rules and conventions' followed by the alien agent, whose concept of rationality is now in question: ours or the agent's? Since the observer must be understood now as addressing himself to members of his own society, it seems that the reference must here be to the concept of rationality current in the observer's society. Thus there is a *non sequitur* in the movement from the first to the second of the passages just quoted.

MacIntyre's thought here and in what immediately follows, seems to be this. The explanation of why, in Society *S*, certain actions are taken to be rational, has got to be an explanation for *us*; so it must be in terms of concepts intelligible to us. If then, in the explanation, we say that in fact those criteria *are* rational, we must be using the word '*rational*' in *our* sense. For this explanation would require that we had previously carried out an independent investigation into the actual rationality or otherwise of those criteria, and we could do this only in terms of an understood concept of rationality—*our* understood concept of rationality. The explanation would run: members of Society *S* have seen to be the case something that we know to be the case. If 'what is seen to be the case' is common to us and them, it must be referred to under the same concept for each of us.

But obviously this explanation is not open to us. For we start from the position that standards of rationality in different societies do not always coincide; from the possibility, therefore, that the standards of rationality current in *S* are different from our own. So we cannot assume that it will make sense to speak of members of *S* as discovering something which we have also discovered; such discovery presupposes initial conceptual agreement.

Part of the trouble lies in MacIntyre's use of the expression, 'the rationality of criteria', which he does not explain. In the present context to speak thus is to cloak the real problem, since what we are concerned with are differences in *criteria of rationality*. MacIntyre seems to be saying that certain standards are taken as criteria of rationality because they *are* criteria of rationality. But whose?

There are similar confusions in MacIntyre's other paper: 'Is Understanding Religion Compatible with Believing?' There he argues that when we detect an internal incoherence in the standards of intelligibility current in an alien society and try to show why this does not appear, or is made tolerable to that society's members, 'we have already invoked our standards'. In what sense is this true? Insofar as *we* 'detect' and 'show' something, obviously we do so in a sense intelligible to us; so we are limited by what *counts* (for us) as 'detecting', 'showing' something. Further, it may well be that the interest in showing and detecting such things is peculiar to our society—that we are doing something in which members of the studied society exhibit no interest, because the institutions in which such an interest could develop are lacking. Perhaps too the pursuit of that interest in our society has led to the development of techniques of inquiry and modes of argument which again are not to be found in the life of the studied society. But it cannot be guaranteed in advance that the methods and techniques we have used in the past—e.g., in elucidating the logical structure of arguments in our own language and culture—are going to be equally fruitful in this new context. They will perhaps need to be extended and modified. No doubt, if they are to have a logical relation to our previous forms of investigation, the new techniques will have to be recognizably continuous with previously used ones. But they must also so extend our conception of intelligibility as to make it possible for us to see what intelligibility amounts to in the life of the society we are investigating.

The task MacIntyre says we must undertake is to make intelligible (*a*) (to us) why it is that members of *S* think that certain of their practices are intelligible (*b*) (to them), when in fact they are not. I have introduced differentiating letters into my two uses of 'intelligible', to mark the complexity that MacIntyre's way of stating the position does not bring out: the fact that we are dealing with two different senses of the word 'intelligible'. The relation between these is precisely the question at issue. MacIntyre's task is not like that of making intelligible a natural phenomenon, where we are limited only by what counts as intelligibility for us. We must somehow bring *S*'s conception of intelligibility (*b*) into (intelligible!) relation with our own conception of intelligibility (*a*). That is, we have to create a new unity for the concept of intelligibility, having a certain relation to our old one and perhaps requiring a considerable realignment of our categories. We are not seeking a state in which things will appear to us just as they do to members of *S*, and perhaps such a state is unattainable anyway. But we *are* seeking a way of looking at things which goes beyond our previous way in that it has in some way taken account of and incorporated the other way that members of *S* have of looking at things. Seriously to study another way of life is necessarily to seek to extend our own—not simply to bring the other way within the already existing boundaries of our own, because the point about the latter in their present form, is that they *ex hypothesi* exclude that other.

There is a dimension to the notions of rationality and intelligibility which may make it easier to grasp the possibility of such an extension. I do not think that MacIntyre takes sufficient account of this dimension and, indeed, the way he talks about 'norms of rationality' obscures it. Rationality is not *just* a concept *in* a language like any other; it is this too, for, like any other concept it must be circumscribed by an established use: a use, that is, established in the language. But I think it is not a concept which a language may, as a matter of fact, have and equally well may not have, as is, for instance, the concept of politeness. It is a concept necessary to the existence of any language: to say of a society that it has a language[28] is also to say that it has a concept of rationality. There need not perhaps be any *word* functioning in its language as 'rational' does in ours, but at least there must be features of its members' use of language analogous to those features of *our* use of language which are connected with our use of the word 'rational'. Where there is language it must make a difference what is said and this is only possible where the saying of one thing rules out, on pain of failure to communicate, the saying of something else. So in one sense MacIntyre is right in saying that we have already invoked our concept of rationality in saying of a collection of people that they constitute a society with a language: in the sense, namely, that we imply formal analogies between their behaviour and that behaviour in our society which we refer to in distinguishing between rationality and irrationality. This, however, is so far to say nothing about what in particular constitutes rational behaviour in that society; that would require more particular knowledge about the norms they appeal to in living their lives. In other words, it is not so much a matter of invoking 'our own norms of rationality' as of invoking our notion of rationality in speaking of their behaviour in terms of 'conformity to norms'. But how precisely this notion is to be applied to them will depend on our reading of their conformity to norms—what counts for them as conformity and what does not.

Earlier I criticized MacIntyre's conception of a 'stock of available descriptions'. Similar criticisms apply to his talk about 'our norms of rationality', if these norms are taken as forming some finite set. Certainly we learn to think, speak, and act rationally *through* being trained to adhere to particular norms. But having learned to speak, etc., rationally does not *consist* in having been trained to follow those norms; to suppose that would be to overlook the importance of the phrase 'and so on' in any description of what someone who follows norms does. We must, if you like, be open to new possibilities of what could be invoked and accepted under the rubric of 'rationality'—possibilities which are perhaps suggested and limited by what we have hitherto so accepted, but not uniquely determined thereby.

This point can be applied to the possibilities of our grasping forms of rationality different from ours in an alien culture. First, as I have indicated, these possibilities are limited by certain formal requirements centering round the demand for consistency. But these formal requirements tell us nothing about what in particular is to *count* as consistency, just as the rules of the propositional calculus limit, but do not themselves determine what are to be proper values of p, q, etc. We can only determine this by investigating the wider context of the life in which the activities in question are carried on. This investigation will take us beyond merely specifying the rules governing the carrying out of those activities. For, as MacIntyre quite rightly says, to note that certain rules are followed is so far to say nothing about the *point* of the rules; it is not even to decide whether or not they have a point at all.

MacIntyre's recipe for deciding this is that 'in bringing out this feature of the case one shows also whether the use of this concept is or is not a possible one for people who have the standards of intelligibility in speech and action which we have'.[29] It is important to notice that his argument, contrary to what he supposes, does not in fact show that our *own* standards of rationality occupy a peculiarly central position. The appearance to the contrary is an optical illusion engendered by the fact that MacIntyre's case has been advanced in the English language and in the context of twentieth century European culture. But a formally similar argument could be advanced in *any* language containing concepts playing a similar role in that language to those of 'intelligibility' and 'rationality' in ours. This shows that, so far from overcoming relativism, as he claims, MacIntyre himself falls into an extreme form of it. He disguises this from himself by committing the very error of which, wrongly as I have tried to show, he accuses me: the error of overlooking the fact that 'criteria and concepts have a history'. While he emphasizes this point when he is dealing with the concepts and criteria governing action in particular social contexts, he forgets it when he comes to talk of the *criticism* of such criteria. Do not the criteria appealed to in the criticism of existing institutions equally have a history? And in whose society do they have that history? MacIntyre's implicit answer is that it is in ours; but if we are to speak of difficulties and incoherencies appearing and being detected in the way certain practices have hitherto been carried on in a society, surely this can only be understood in connection with problems arising *in* the carrying on of the activity. Outside that context we could not begin to grasp what was problematical.

Let me return to the Azande and consider something

which MacIntyre says about them, intended to support the position I am criticizing.[30]

> The Azande believe that the performance of certain rites in due form affects their common welfare; this belief cannot in fact be refuted. For they also believe that if the rites are ineffective it is because someone present at them had evil thoughts. Since this is always possible, there is never a year when it is unavoidable for them to admit that the rites were duly performed, but they did not thrive. Now the belief of the Azande is not unfalsifiable in principle (we know perfectly well what would falsify it —the conjunction of the rite, no evil thoughts and disasters). But in fact it cannot be falsified. Does this belief stand in need of rational criticism? And if so by what standards? It seems to me that one could only hold the belief of the Azande rational *in the absence of* any practice of science and technology in which criteria of effectiveness, ineffectiveness and kindred notions had been built up. But to say this is to recognize the appropriateness of scientific criteria of judgment from our standpoint. The Azande do not intend their belief either as a piece of science or as a piece of non-science. They do not possess these categories. It is only *post eventum*, in the light of later and more sophisticated understanding that their belief and concepts can be classified and evaluated at all.

Now in one sense classification and evaluation of Zande beliefs and concepts does require 'a more sophisticated understanding' than is found in Zande culture: for the sort of classification and evaluation that are here in question are sophisticated philosophical activities. But this is not to say that Zande forms of life are to be classified and evaluated in the way MacIntyre asserts: in terms of certain specific forms of life to be found in our culture, according as they do or do not measure up to what is required within these. MacIntyre confuses the sophistication of the interest in classification with the sophistication of the concepts employed in our classificatory work. It is of interest to us to understand how Zande magic is related to science; the concept of such a comparison is a very sophisticated one; but this does not mean that we have to see the unsophisticated Zande practice in the light of more sophisticated practices in our own culture, like science—as perhaps a more primitive form of it. MacIntyre criticizes, justly, Sir James Frazer for having imposed the image of his own culture on more primitive ones; but that is exactly what MacIntyre himself is doing here. It is extremely difficult for a sophisticated member of a sophisticated society to grasp a very simple and primitive form of life: in a way he must jettison his sophistication, a process which is itself perhaps the ultimate in sophistication. Or, rather, the distinction between sophistication and simplicity becomes unhelpful at this point.

It may be true, as MacIntyre says, that the Azande do not have the categories of science and non-science. But Evans-Pritchard's account shows that they do have a fairly clear working distinction between the technical and the magical. It is neither here nor there that individual Azande may sometimes confuse the categories, for such confusions may take place in any culture. A much more important fact to emphasize is that *we* do not initially have a category that looks at all like the Zande category of magic. Since it is we who want to understand the Zande category, it appears that the onus is on us to extend our understanding so as to make room for the Zande category, rather than to insist on seeing it in terms of our own ready-made distinction between science and non-science. Certainly the sort of understanding we seek requires that we see the Zande category in relation to our own already understood categories. But this neither means that it is right to 'evaluate' magic in terms of criteria belonging to those other categories; nor does it give any clue as to *which* of our existing categories of thought will provide the best point of reference from which we can understand the point of the Zande practices.

MacIntyre has no difficulty in showing that *if* the rites which the Azande perform in connection with their harvests are 'classified and evaluated' by reference to the criteria and standards of science or technology, then they are subject to serious criticism. He thinks that the Zande 'belief' is a sort of *hypothesis* like, e.g., an Englishman's belief that all the heavy rain we have been having is due to atomic explosions.[31] MacIntyre believes that he is applying as it were a neutral concept of '*A* affecting *B*', equally applicable to Zande magic and western science. In fact, however, he is applying the concept with which *he* is familiar, one which draws its significance from its use in scientific and technological contexts. There is no reason to suppose that the Zande magical concept of '*A* affecting *B*' has anything like the same significance. On the contrary, since the Azande do, in the course of their practical affairs, apply something very like our technical concept—though perhaps in a more primitive form—and since their attitude to and thought about their magical rites are quite different from those concerning their technological measures, there is every reason to think that their concept of magical 'influence' is quite different. This may be easier to accept if it is remembered that, even in our own culture, the concept of causal influence is by no means monolithic: when we speak, for example, of 'what made Jones get married', we are not saying the same kind of thing as when we speak of 'what made the aeroplane crash'; I do not mean simply that the events of which we speak are different in kind but that the relation between the events is different also. It should not then be difficult to accept that in a society with quite different institutions and ways of life from our own, there may be concepts of 'causal influence' which behave more differently.

But I do not want to say that we are quite powerless to find ways of thinking in our own society that will help us to see the Zande institution in a clearer light. I only think that the direction in which we should look is quite different from what MacIntyre suggests. Clearly the nature of Zande life is such that it is of very great importance to them that their crops should thrive. Clearly too they take all kinds of practical 'technological' steps, within their capabilities, to ensure that they *do* thrive. But that is no reason to see their magical rites as a further and misguided step. A man's sense of the importance of something to him shows itself in all sorts of ways: not merely in precautions to safeguard that thing. He may want to come to terms with its importance to him in quite a different way: to contemplate it, to gain some sense of his life in relation to it. He may wish thereby, in a certain sense, to *free* himself from dependence on it. I do not mean by making sure that it does not let him down, because the point is that, *whatever* he does, he may still be let down. The important thing is that he should understand *that* and come to terms with it. Of course, merely to understand that is not to come to terms with it, though perhaps it is a necessary condition for so doing, for a man may equally well be transfixed and terrified by the contemplation of such a possibility. He must see that he can still go on even if he is let down by what is vitally important to him; and he must so order his life that he still *can* go on in such circumstances. I stress once again that I do not mean this in the sense of becoming technologically independent, because from the present point of view technological independence is yet another form of dependence. Technology destroys some dependencies but always creates new ones, which may be fiercer—because harder to understand—than the old. This should be particularly apparent to *us*.[32]

In Judaeo-Christian cultures the conception of 'If it be Thy Will', as developed in the story of Job, is clearly central to the matter I am discussing. Because this conception is central to Christian prayers of supplication, they may be regarded from one point of view as freeing the believer from dependence on what he is supplicating for.[33] Prayers cannot play this role if they are regarded as a means of influencing the outcome for in that case the one who prays is still dependent on the outcome. He frees himself from this by acknowledging his complete dependence on God; and this is totally unlike any dependence on the outcome precisely because God is eternal and the outcome contingent.

I do not say that Zande magical rites are at all like Christian prayers of supplication in the positive attitude to contingencies which they express. What I do suggest is that they are alike in that they do, or may, express an attitude to contingencies; one, that is, which involves recognition that one's life is subject to contingencies, rather than an attempt to control these. To characterize this attitude more specifically one should note how Zande rites emphasize the importance of certain fundamental features of their life which MacIntyre ignores. MacIntyre concentrates implicitly on the relation of the rites to consumption, but of course they are also fundamental to social relations and this seems to be emphasized in Zande notions of witchcraft. We have a drama of resentments, evil-doing, revenge, expiation, in which there are ways of dealing (symbolically) with misfortunes and their disruptive effect on a man's relations with his fellows, with ways in which life can go on despite such disruptions.

How is my treatment of this example related to the general criticisms I was making of MacIntyre's account of what it is for us to see the *point* of the rules and conventions followed in an alien form of life? MacIntyre speaks as though our own rules and conventions are somehow a paradigm of what it is for rules and conventions to have a point, so that the only problem that arises is in accounting for the point of the rules and conventions in some other society. But in fact, of course, the problem is the same in relation to our own society as it is in relation to any other; no more than anyone else's are *our* rules and conventions immune from the danger of being or becoming pointless. So an account of this matter cannot be given simply in terms of any set of rules and conventions at all: our own or anyone else's; it requires us to consider the relation of a set of rules and conventions to something else. In my discussion of Zande magical rites just now what I tried to relate the magical rites to was a sense of the significance of human life. This notion is, I think, indispensable to any account of what is involved in understanding and learning from an alien culture; I must now try to say more about it.

In a discussion of Wittgenstein's philosophical use of language games[34] Mr Rush Rhees points out that to try to account for the meaningfulness of language solely in terms of isolated language games is to omit the important fact that ways of speaking are not insulated from each other in mutually exclusive systems of rules. What can be said in one context by the use of a certain expression depends for its sense on the uses of that expression in other contexts (different language games). Language games are played by men who have lives to live—lives involving a wide variety of different interests, which have all kinds of different bearings on each other. Because of this, what a man says or does may make a difference not merely to the performance of the activity upon which he is at present engaged, but to his *life* and to the lives of other people. Whether a man sees point in what he is doing will then depend on whether he is able to see any unity in his multifarious interests, activities, and relations with other men; what sort of sense he sees in his life will depend on the nature of this unity. The ability to see this sort of sense in life depends not merely on the individual concerned, though this is not to say it does not depend on him at all; it depends also on the possibilities for making such sense which the culture in which he lives does, or does not, provide.

What we may learn by studying other cultures are not merely possibilities of different ways of doing things, other techniques. More importantly we may learn different possibilities of making sense of human life, different ideas about the possible importance that the carrying out of certain activities may take on for a man, trying to contemplate the sense of his life as a whole. This dimension of the matter is precisely what MacIntyre misses in his treatment of Zande magic: he can see in it only a (misguided) technique for producing consumer goods. But a Zande's crops are not just potential objects of consumption: the life he lives, his relations with his fellows, his chances for acting decently or doing evil, may all spring from his relation to his crops. Magical rites constitute a form of expression in which these possibilities and dangers may be contemplated and reflected on—and perhaps also thereby transformed and deepened. The difficulty we find in understanding this is not merely its remoteness from science, but an aspect of the general

D

difficulty we find, illustrated by MacIntyre's procedure, of thinking about such matters at all except in terms of 'efficiency of production'—production, that is, for consumption. This again is a symptom of what Marx called the 'alienation' characteristic of man in industrial society, though Marx's own confusions about the relations between production and consumption are further symptoms of that same alienation. Our blindness to the point of primitive modes of life is a corollary of the pointlessness of much of our own life.

I have now explicitly linked my discussion of the 'point' of a system of conventions with conceptions of good and evil. My aim is not to engage in moralizing, but to suggest that the concept of *learning from* which is involved in the study of other cultures is closely linked with the concept of *wisdom*. We are confronted not just with different techniques, but with new possibilities of good and evil, in relation to which men may come to terms with life. An investigation into this dimension of a society may indeed require a quite detailed inquiry into alternative techniques (e.g., of production), but an inquiry conducted for the light it throws on those possibilities of good and evil. A very good example of the kind of thing I mean is Simone Weil's analysis of the techniques of modern factory production in *Oppression and Liberty*, which is not a contribution to business management, but part of an inquiry into the peculiar form which the evil of oppression takes in our culture.

In saying this, however, I may seem merely to have lifted to a new level the difficulty raised by MacIntyre of how to relate our own conceptions of rationality to those of other societies. Here the difficulty concerns the relation between our own conceptions of good and evil and those of other societies. A full investigation would thus require a discussion of ethical relativism at this point. I have tried to show some of the limitations of relativism in the next chapter. I shall close the present essay with some remarks which are supplementary to that.

I wish to point out that the very conception of human life

involves certain fundamental notions—which I shall call 'limiting notions'—which have an obvious ethical dimension, and which indeed in a sense determine the 'ethical space', within which the possibilities of good and evil in human life can be exercised. The notions which I shall discuss very briefly here correspond closely to those which Vico made the foundation of his idea of natural law, on which he thought the possibility of understanding human history rested: birth, death, sexual relations. Their significance here is that they are inescapably involved in the life of all known human societies in a way which gives us a clue where to look, if we are puzzled about the point of an alien system of institutions. The specific forms which these concepts take, the particular institutions in which they are expressed, vary very considerably from one society to another; but their central position within a society's institutions is and must be a constant factor. In trying to understand the life of an alien society, then, it will be of the utmost importance to be clear about the way in which these notions enter into it. The actual practice of social anthropologists bears this out, although I do not know how many of them would attach the same kind of importance to them as I do.

I speak of a 'limit' here because these notions, along no doubt with others, give shape to what we understand by 'human life'; and because a concern with questions posed in terms of them seems to me constitutive of what we understand by the 'morality' of a society. In saying this, I am of course disagreeing with those moral philosophers who have made attitudes of approval and disapproval, or something similar, fundamental in ethics, and who have held that the *objects* of such attitudes were conceptually irrelevant to the conception of morality. On that view, there might be a society where the sorts of attitude taken up in *our* society to questions about relations between the sexes were reserved, say, for questions about the length people wear their hair, and vice versa. This seems to me incoherent. In the first place, there would be a confusion in *calling* a concern of that sort a 'moral' concern, however passionately felt. The story of Samson in the Old Testament confirms rather than refutes this point, for the interdict on the cutting of Samson's hair is, of course, connected there with much else: and pre-eminently, it should be noted, with questions about sexual relations. But secondly, if that is thought to be merely verbal quibbling, I will say that it does not seem to me a merely conventional matter that T. S. Eliot's trinity of 'birth, copulation and death' happen to be such deep objects of human concern. I do not mean just that they are made such by fundamental psychological and sociological forces, though that is no doubt true. But I want to say further that the very notion of human life is limited by these conceptions.

Unlike beasts, men do not merely live but also have a conception of life. This is not something that is simply added to their life; rather, it changes the very sense which the word 'life' has, when applied to men. It is no longer equivalent to 'animate existence'. When we are speaking of the life of man, we can ask questions about what is the right way to live, what things are most important in life, whether life has any significance, and if so what.

To have a conception of life is also to have a conception of death. But just as the 'life' that is here in question is not the same as animate existence, so the 'death' that is here in question is not the same as the end of animate existence. My conception of the death of an animal is of an event that will take place in the world; perhaps I shall observe it—and my life will go on. But when I speak of 'my death', I am not speaking of a future event in my life;[35] I am not even speaking of an event in anyone else's life. I am speaking of the cessation of my world. That is also a cessation of my ability to do good or evil. It is not just that *as a matter of fact* I shall no longer be able to do good or evil after I am dead; the point is that my very *concept* of what it is to be able to do good or evil is deeply bound up with my concept of my life as ending in death. If ethics is a concern with the right way to live, then clearly the nature of this concern must be deeply affected by the concept of life as ending in death. One's attitude to one's life is at the same time an attitude to one's death.

This point is very well illustrated in an anthropological datum which MacIntyre confesses himself unable to make any sense of.[36]

> According to Spencer and Gillen some aborigines carry about a stick or stone which is treated *as if* it is or embodies the soul of the individual who carries it. If the stick or stone is lost, the individual anoints himself as the dead are anointed. Does the concept of 'carrying one's soul about with one' make sense? Of course we can re-describe what the aborigines are doing and transform it into sense, and perhaps Spencer and Gillen (and Durkheim who follows them) misdescribe what occurs. But if their reports are not erroneous, we confront a blank wall here, so far as meaning is concerned, although it is easy to give the rules for the use of the concept.

MacIntyre does not say why he regards the concept of carrying one's soul about with one in a stick 'thoroughly incoherent'. He is presumably influenced by the fact that it would be hard to make sense of an action like this if performed by a twentieth-century Englishman or American; and by the fact that the soul is not a material object like a piece of paper and cannot, therefore, be carried about in a stick as a piece of paper might be. But it does not seem to me so hard to see sense in the practice, even from the little we are told about it here. Consider that a lover in our society may carry about a picture or lock of hair of the beloved; that this may symbolize for him his relation to the beloved and may, indeed, change the relation in all sorts of ways: for example, strengthening it or perverting it.[37] Suppose that when the lover loses the locket he feels guilty and asks his beloved for her forgiveness: there might be a parallel here to the aboriginal's practice of anointing himself when he 'loses his soul'. And is there necessarily anything irrational about either of these practices? Why should the lover not regard his carelessness in losing the locket as a sort of betrayal of the beloved? Remember how husbands and wives may feel about the loss of a wedding ring. The aborigine is clearly expressing a concern with his life as a whole in this practice; the anointing shows the close connection between such a concern and contemplation of death. Perhaps it is precisely this practice which makes such a concern possible for him, as religious sacraments make certain sorts of concern possible. The point is that a concern with one's life as a whole, involving as it does the limiting conception of one's death, if it is to be expressed *within* a person's life, can necessarily only be expressed quasi-sacramentally. The form of the concern shows itself in the form of the sacrament.

The sense in which I spoke also of sex as a 'limiting concept' again has to do with the concept of a human life. The life of a man is a man's life and the life of a woman is a woman's life: the masculinity or the femininity are not just *components* in the life, they are its *mode*. Adapting Wittgenstein's remark about death, I might say that my masculinity is not an experience in the world, but my way of experiencing the world. Now the concepts of masculinity and femininity obviously require each other. A man is a man in relation to women; and a woman is a woman in relation to men.[38] Thus the form taken by a man's relation to women is of quite fundamental importance for the significance he can attach to his own life. The vulgar identification of morality with sexual morality certainly *is* vulgar; but it is a vulgarization of an important truth.

The limiting character of the concept of birth is obviously related to the points I have sketched regarding death and sex. On the one hand, my birth is no more an event in my life than is my death; and through my birth ethical limits are set for my life quite independently of my will: I am, from the outset, in specific relations to other people, from which obligations spring which cannot but be ethically fundamental.[39] On the other hand, the concept of birth is fundamentally linked to that of relations between the sexes. This remains true, however much or little may be known in a society about the contribution of males and females to procreation; for it remains true that man is born of woman, not of man. This, then, adds a new dimension to the ethical institutions in which relations between the sexes are expressed.

I have tried to do no more, in these last brief remarks, than to focus attention in a certain direction. I have wanted to indicate that forms of these limiting concepts will necessarily be an important feature of any human society and that conceptions of good and evil in human life will necessarily be connected with such concepts. In any attempt to understand the life of another society, therefore, an investigation of the forms taken by such concepts—their role in the life of the society—must always take a central place and provide a basis on which understanding may be built.

Now since the world of nations has been made by men, let us see in what institutions men agree and always have agreed. For these institutions will be able to give us the universal and eternal principles (such as every science must have) on which all nations were founded and still preserve themselves.

We observe that all nations, barbarous as well as civilized, though separately founded because remote from each other in time and space, keep these three human customs: all have some religion, all contract solemn marriages, all bury their dead. And in no nation, however savage and crude, are any human actions performed with more elaborate ceremonies and more sacred solemnity than the rites of religion, marriage and burial. For by the axiom that 'uniform ideas, born among peoples unknown to each other, must have a common ground of truth', it must have been dictated to all nations that from these institutions humanity began among them all, and therefore they must be most devoutly guarded by them all, so that the world should not again become a bestial wilderness. For this reason we have taken these three eternal and universal customs as the first principles of this Science.[40]

NOTES

[1] London and New York, 1958.
[2] Oxford, 1937.

[3] At this point the anthropologist is very likely to start speaking of the 'social function' of the institution under examination. There are many important questions that should be raised about functional explanations and their relations to the issues discussed in this essay; but these questions cannot be pursued further here.

[4] E. E. Evans-Pritchard, 'Lévy-Bruhl's Theory of Primitive Mentality', *Bulletin of the Faculty of Arts* (University of Egypt, 1934).

[5] 'Science and Sentiment', ibid., 1935.

[6] Indeed, one way of expressing the point of the story of Job is to say that in it Job is shown as going astray by being induced to make the reality and goodness of God contingent on what happens.

[7] R. G. Collingwood, *Principles of Art* (Oxford: Galaxy Books, 1958), p. 67.

[8] *Witchcraft, Oracles and Magic among the Azande*, p. 64.

[9] Op. cit., p. 12.

[10] The italics are mine throughout this quotation.

[11] For further criticism of Pareto see Peter Winch, *The Idea of a Social Science*, pp. 95–111.

[12] Evans-Pritchard's italics.

[13] Op. cit., p. 72.

[14] Ibid., p. 319.

[15] Wittgenstein, *Tractatus Logico-Philosophicus*, paras. 5.6–5.61.

[16] Evans-Pritchard, op. cit., p. 194.

[17] I shall discuss this point in a more general way in Part 2 of this essay.

[18] Ibid., p. 24.

[19] Ibid., p. 25.

[20] L. Wittgenstein, *Remarks on the Foundations of Mathematics*, Part II, § 77. Wittgenstein's whole discussion of 'contradiction' in mathematics is directly relevant to the point I am discussing.

[21] Notice that I have *not* said that Azande conceptions of witchcraft have nothing to do with understanding the world at all. The point is that a different form of the concept of understanding is involved here.

[22] And now also in *Faith and the Philosophers*, edited by John Hick (London: Macmillan, 1964).

[23] Edited by Peter Laslett and W. G. Runciman (Oxford: Basil Blackwell, 1962).

[24] Ibid., p. 58.

[25] Ibid., p. 60.

[26] Ibid., p. 61.

[27] Pp. 57-65, 91-4, 121-3.

[28] I shall not discuss here what justifies us in saying *this* in the first place.

[29] 'Is Understanding Religion Compatible with Believing?'

[30] Ibid.

[31] In connection with what follows compare Wittgenstein's 'Remarks on Frazer's *Golden Bough*', translated in *The Human World*, No. 3, May 1971;

and also various scattered remarks on folk-lore in *The Notebooks* of Simone Weil (London, 1963).

[32] The point is beautifully developed by Simone Weil in her essay on 'The Analysis of Oppression' in *Oppression and Liberty* (London: Routledge & Kegan Paul, 1958).

[33] See D. Z. Phillips, *The Concept of Prayer* (London: Routledge & Kegan Paul and New York: Schocken, 1965).

[34] Rush Rhees, 'Wittgenstein's Builders', *Proceedings of the Aristotelian Society*, 1960, Vol. 20, pp. 171-86.

[35] Cf. Wittgenstein, *Tractatus Logico-Philosophicus*, 6.431-6.4311.

[36] 'Is Understanding Religion Compatible with Believing?'

[37] Compare the role played by Clavdia Chauchat's X-ray photographs in Hans Castorp's affair with her in Thomas Mann's *The Magic Mountain*.

[38] These relations, however, are not simple converses. See Georg Simmel 'Das Relative und das Absolute im Geschlechter-Problem' in *Philosophische Kultur* (Leipzig, 1911).

[39] For this reason, among others, I think A. I. Melden is wrong to say that parent-child obligations and rights have nothing directly to do with physical genealogy. Cf. Melden, *Rights and Right Conduct* (Oxford, 1959).

[40] Giambattista Vico, *The New Science*, §§ 332-3.

3

Nature and Convention

There is a celebrated discussion of the distinction between the natural and the conventional in Aristotle's *Nicomachean Ethics* Book V, Chapter VII, from which I quote:

> There are two forms of justice, the natural and the conventional. It is natural when it has the same validity everywhere and is unaffected by any view we may take of the justice of it. It is conventional when there is no original reason why it should take one form rather than another and the rule it imposes is reached by agreement after which it holds good ... Some philosophers are of opinion that justice is conventional in all its branches, arguing that a law of nature admits no variation and operates in exactly the same way everywhere—thus fire *burns* here and in Persia—while rules of justice keep changing before our eyes. It is not obvious what rules of justice are natural and what are legal and conventional, in cases where variation is possible. Yet it remains true that there is such a thing as natural, as well as conventional justice.

Many philosophers in our time would dispute the last statement of Aristotle's I have quoted, being of the opinion that justice is conventional in all its branches. Karl Popper is perhaps the leading exponent of this view,[1] holding that all norms of human behaviour are logically akin to decisions and that there is such a 'dualism of facts and decisions' that any talk of 'natural' morality or law must involve a confusion between two logically quite distinct modes of utterance: laws of nature of the sort established and used in the sciences; and prescriptive norms which are decided upon and adhered to or enforced in the regulation of human behaviour in society. Fire burns here and in Persia, while rules of justice keep changing before our eyes.

I intend to dispute this view. First, I shall try to show, negatively, that Popper fails to establish his desired dualism; later I shall argue, more positively, that there are certain aspects of morality which make it necessary to say that it is not entirely based on convention but that, on the contrary, it is presupposed by any possible conventions. Such a view need not imply, as Popper thinks it must, the nonsensical idea that norms can be laid down 'in accordance with natural laws' in the scientific sense.

2

Like the Sophistic thinkers to whom Aristotle was referring, Popper lays great stress on the alleged fact that whereas norms of behaviour are variable and alterable, laws of nature are not. But his discussion suffers from his tendency to run together that point with the quite different one that it makes sense to speak of men breaking and contravening the norms current in their society, but no sense at all to speak of scientific laws of nature being contravened by the things the behaviour of which the laws are used to describe or explain. It belongs to the grammar of the word 'norm' that it is intelligible to say that a man may choose not to adhere to any given norm; but this does not entail that it is always intelligible to speak of the possibility of *altering* any given norm. Often of course it is: as with norms governing rates of income tax; but that this must always be true remains to be shown. There is, it is true, an important logical relation between the possibility of saying that a norm of behaviour holds good in a society and the fact that people in that society do in fact adhere to the norm more often than they break it, or at least that they tend to manifest some sort of hostile reaction to breaches of it, by way, for instance, of condemnation or remorse. But in order to use this relation to prove that all norms are necessarily alterable in principle, one would have also to show in addition that in respect of *any* given norm, it must always be possible to imagine people in a society *not* adhering to it more often than they break it, or *not* tending to manifest disapprobatory attitudes to breaches of it. I shall try to show subsequently in this essay that the latter condition is not fulfilled for some fundamental cases; not because people's adherence to such a norm is guaranteed by any scientific law of nature but because the idea of their non-adherence is made unintelligible by certain features of the concept of the social life of human beings.

However, it is certainly true that a great many very important norms of human behaviour are variable and changeable as between one society or historical period and another. But do they differ from scientific laws of nature in this respect? Science develops and modern physics, for example, cannot be expressed in a set of propositions that would have been uttered by Aristotle, or even Newton, any more than modern morality can be expressed in a series of propositions that would have been uttered by Abraham. Of course, the logic of scientific development is not the same as that of moral change; but then I am not arguing that there is no logical difference between science and morality, only that this difference cannot be elucidated in terms of Popper's concept of alterability.

Popper would perhaps say that when different laws of nature come to be accepted in science, this is because those accepted previously have been shown to be false, insufficiently precise, or too narrow in scope; that this has been shown by a more searching investigation of the facts, whereas human norms do not change as a result—at least not as a direct result—of any 'investigation of the facts', but rather as a result of human decisions. But the role ascribed here to 'the unchanging facts and regularities' in science has not been made sufficiently clear. What *is* true is the following. Modern scientific theories could be used to describe and explain natural phenomena occurring in the time of Abraham as well as they can be used for phenomena occurring now; but modern *moral* concepts could not be used to describe and explain the actions of Abraham and his contemporaries. The relation between moral ideas and human behaviour is different from that between scientific ideas and the behaviour of natural phenomena.

Nevertheless, we cannot say without qualification that modern scientific theories are about the same sets of facts as the theories of earlier stages of scientific development were about. I do not mean simply that new and more precise observations have been made, which have had to be taken into account by the new theories; scientific *concepts* have changed too, and with them scientists' views on what is to count as a relevant fact. 'Time' in relativity theory does not mean what it did in classical mechanics. Of course, the two concepts are related in a way which could be brought out by describing the historical development of physics between then and now. But we shall obscure the nature of this development if we think of it in terms of the building of new and better theories to explain one and the same set of facts; not because the facts themselves change independently, but because scientists' criteria of relevance change. And this does not mean that earlier scientists had a *wrong* idea of what the facts were; they had the idea appropriate to the investigation *they* were conducting.

If it is true that men's moral standards change as a result of human decisions, this is equally true of men's scientific ideas. The relevant decisions here are to adopt this rather than that line of enquiry, to develop particular techniques of investigation, and so on. Scientific concepts and theories can only be understood in the context of the ways in which scientific investigation is carried on, and, *a fortiori*, changes in the one can only be understood in the context of changes in the other.

If you think of some of the things which enrich the present time: atonality in music, or the structure of the genetic material which gives to all living things the quality of life, or such a notion as parity, which has been prominent in discoveries in basic physics, these are not things which were quite so simply given and there to be found, simply, by anyone. It required a tradition, a culture, a background, even to come to these things, even to define them, even to know the means by which they can be found. *It depends on where you are, what you are, how you talk.*[2]

The barrier that stands in the way of a layman who wants to understand something in modern physics is a cultural barrier. 'The deep things in physics, and probably in mathematics too, are not things you can tell about unless you are talking to someone who has lived a long time acquiring the tradition.'[3] Something formally analogous to this is also true of our difficulty in understanding the *moral* ideas and practices of a historically or culturally remote society. Consider, for instance, the practice of child sacrifice in pre-Abrahamic Hebrew society. This is a practice which, in terms of our own way of living and the moral ideas that go along with it, is just unintelligible. To try to understand it is to try to understand something of what life and thought must have been like in that society. What I want to emphasize here is that the main problem about this is one of *understanding* what was involved; not just one of taking up an attitude, for without understanding we should not know what we were taking up an attitude *to*. And it would be no more open to anyone to propose that this practice should be adopted in our own society than it is open to anyone to propose the rejection of the Second Law of Thermodynamics in physics. My point is not just that no one would listen to such a proposal but that no one would understand what was being proposed. What made child-sacrifice what it was, was the role it played in the life of the society in which it was practised; there is a *logical* absurdity in supposing that the very same practice could be instituted in our own quite different society.

What this indicates is that *decision* is not the fundamental concept in morality. For a decision can only be made within the context of a meaningful way of life and a moral decision can only be made within the context of a morality. A morality cannot be *based* on decisions. What decisions are and what are not possible will depend on the morality within which the issues arise; and not *any* issue can arise in a given morality.

Popper's account does not really make room for the question whether a decision is intelligible or not. This is important since it is only when questions of intelligibility can be raised that the concept of a decision can have application.

What makes a decision intelligible is its relation to the facts of the situation in which it is made; and this relation is a logical one. Popper seems to deny this with his Humean doctrine that 'decisions can never be derived from facts (or statements of facts), although they pertain to facts.'[4] Now it is true that in any situation where I can be said to have made a decision it must be conceivable that I might have decided differently; but this does not mean that a different decision would have been necessarily intelligible. Suppose that two men, *A* and *B*, are arguing about a proposed relaxation of the divorce laws. *A* convinces *B* that the divorce laws as they exist generate much human misery and that the proposed relaxation would not bring with it any deleterious after-effects, such as a weakening in public respect for the institution of marriage. Suppose then that *B*, having accepted all this and without raising any counter-considerations of his own, then says that he has decided to oppose any relaxation in the law. Of course, we can imagine *B* acting like this; but I suggest we should find what he was doing unintelligible. And if he were *always* to act like this, we should say he was incapable of rational decision. It is true that the relation between factual premisses and decision in this example is very much unlike the relation between a scientific theory and the experimental evidence cited in its support by a scientist. But this difference provides no support for Popper's dualism. There are very many, and very diverse, kinds of relation between factual premiss and factual

conclusion which are quite unlike anything to be found in
theoretical science: for instance, the relation between the
evidence an historian appeals to and his interpretation of the
events he is relating. And again there are very many different
ways in which decisions can be supported by facts; consider,
for instance, the differences between the appropriate ways
of supporting decisions in morality, politics, business. Rather
than a dualism, we have here a highly variegated and over-
lapping pluralism of different kinds of factual statement and
different kinds of decision. The dualistic view obscures the
fact that what counts as a relevant fact in a given mode of
life is logically related to the kind of decision which is appropriate in that mode of life. One could not make clear what is
meant by a 'business fact' without taking into account the
kind of decision which has to be taken in the running of a
business.

It is important to emphasize in this connection that
making a statement is just as much a human action as is
taking a decision. If a conclusion follows logically from a set
of premisses this does not mean that we can be confident that
anyone who accepts the premisses will also accept the conclusion. For men often act irrationally, *both* in the way they
argue *and* in the way they act and decide. The notion of
logic is the notion of what is and what is not intelligible in
human behaviour and it can be applied to anything men do.
If it is abstracted from the ways in which men live it loses its
significance *as* logic even as applied to relations between
statements, for a statement is essentially something which
men may make in the course of their lives.

'Facts are *there*, whereas decisions have to be *made*.' This
is the kind of view suggested by Popper's discussion. And
there is a sense in which this is true: when it is a question of
investigating a particular set of facts, we have to find out
what they are; this is not a matter for decision. But Popper
is discussing the general concept of a fact and its relation to
the concept of a decision, and the matter cannot be left
there. We may be able to say that particular facts are given,
but that is not to say that the concept of factuality is given;

it arises out of the way men live. We have to consider the conditions which make it possible for us to have a concept of 'the facts', which involves taking into account the modes of human life together with the kinds of decisions involved in them, in which the concept of 'the facts' plays a part and from which it receives its sense.

> Knowledge itself cannot be described independently of volition; the ascription of sensible knowledge and of volition go together . . . The identification served by colour-names is in fact not primarily that of colours, but of objects by means of colours; and thus too the prime mark of colour discrimination is doing things with objects—fetching them, placing them—according to their colours. Thus the ascription of sensible discrimination and that of volition are inseparable; one cannot describe a creature as having the power of sensation without also describing it as doing things in accordance with perceived sensible differences.[5]

There are in human life many different kinds of 'doing things with objects', as many ways in which facts may be important to men—in science, morality, business, law, politics, etc.—and as many different kinds of fact and ways in which facts may be related to decisions.

3

However, to abandon the dualism of facts and decisions is not in itself to refute the idea that norms of behaviour are conventional in character. For even if we admit that standards of what is acceptable in social behaviour colour all our thinking, even our conceptions of what are to count as the facts, still, such standards are not fixed and established for all time. Modes of social activity vary and differ greatly from time to time and from place to place, and so do men's associated conceptions of what is permissible and what is not. So it may seem a completely contingent, purely historical or sociological, matter *what* norms of behaviour are adhered to in any particular society.

E

I shall not deny that there is an irreducible historical contingency in the norms that a society adheres to; neither shall I claim that what is thus contingent is any the less morally important for a member of the society. But I do wish to argue against the idea that there need be no fixed points in all this change and variety, that there are no norms of human behaviour which could not be different from what they are in fact, and that everything in human morality is therefore ultimately conventional in character.

To this end I shall examine a conception which plays a leading role in A. I. Melden's monograph, *Rights and Right Conduct*, the conception of a 'moral community'. Melden argues, with great force, that moral conceptions only have sense within the life of such a community and that a fruitful moral philosophy is only possible if such conceptions are placed in the mode of life which gives them their meaning. Now this philosophical procedure is of course familiar from other branches of philosophical enquiry: in the philosophy of science, for instance, one cannot get far without relating the realm of scientific discourse that one is concerned to elucidate to the context of the investigatory procedures established in the scientific community within which it is spoken. Nevertheless, the notion of a 'moral community' is in some fundamental respects quite unlike that of a 'scientific community'. I shall argue that although there may be and are human societies which are not, and do not contain, scientific communities, there could not be a human society which was not also, in some sense, a moral community. In trying to show this, I shall also try to indicate more specifically certain moral conceptions which, in one form or another, must be recognized in any human society.

Notice first that morality cannot be called, in the same sense as can science, a 'form of activity'; it is not something one can choose to engage in or not at will. It would hardly make sense, for instance, for someone to say he had spent six weeks working hard at morality (unless this meant something like moral *philosophy*), though it would be perfectly in order for him to say he had spent the time working hard at science.

A connected point is that whereas a man can become involved with scientific problems only by choosing to concern himself with science, he does not become involved in moral problems by choosing to concern himself with morality. (It is also significant that in the previous sentence 'involved *in*' seems more appropriate to the case of moral problems than the 'involved *with*' I used of scientific problems.) Moral issues may force themselves on you whether you want to be concerned with them or not. If you are morally obtuse, or corrupt, you may fail or refuse to see the moral issues with which your situation faces you; but that will not mean that your situation does not in fact face you with them. Moreover, you will render yourself liable to a moral judgment in not facing up to them. You cannot put yourself outside the sphere of moral discourse by saying it does not interest you. But a man who refuses to concern himself with scientific issues does not thereby expose himself to *scientific* judgment; if somebody like Sir Charles Snow tells him he ought thus to concern himself, that will be a *moral* judgment.

This suggests that moral conceptions arise out of any common life between men and do not presuppose any *particular* forms of activity in which men may engage together. I shall now examine some features of this notion of a 'common life' which are particularly important here.

It belongs to our notion of a social community that such a community should contain a shared language and that specifically human intelligence should be exercised in the life of its members. This has always been recognized as important by social philosophers, but everything turns on precisely *how* it is thought to be relevant. Hobbes, for example, tries to use this feature of human life to prove precisely the opposite of the position I wish to maintain: to prove, namely, that the natural state of men living together is the *bellum omnium contra omnes*. His conception of the 'state of nature' follows directly from his individualistic conception of human language and intelligence.[6]

It is true that certain living creatures, as bees, and ants,

> live sociably one with another, which are therefore by
> Aristotle numbered amongst political creatures; and yet
> they have no other direction, than their particular
> judgments and appetites; nor speech, whereby one of
> them can signify to another, what he thinks expedient
> for the common benefit: and therefore some man may
> perhaps desire to know, why mankind cannot do the same.

The points Hobbes makes in reply to this objection all rest
on the fact that man has language and the sort of prudential
intelligence that his philosophy envisages as providing the
basis for language.[7] 'Competition for honour and dignity', a
man's 'joy in comparing himself with other men', his belief
that he is better able to administer the common business
than another, 'that art of words, by which some men represent to others, that which is good, in the likeness of evil;
and evil, in the likeness of good', the ability to 'distinguish
between *injury* and *damage*'. 'Lastly, the agreement of these
creatures is natural; that of man, is by covenant only, which
is artificial: and therefore it is no wonder if there be something else required, besides covenant, to make their agreement constant and lasting.'

The last point is crucial, because it is on Hobbes's conception of the relation between rationality and agreement
and the related conception of agreement as covenant that
everything turns. Briefly, Hobbes holds that covenant is the
only form of agreement possible between human beings; it is
made possible by rationality, which in its turn is what rules
out the possibility of any other kind of 'natural' agreement.
Thus everything comes back to his analysis of rationality and
his belief that it can be elucidated in purely individual terms,
without presupposing any sort of developed social life and
institutions. It is this point which bears the weight of Vico's
attack on Hobbes.

I shall not here restate the case for saying that human
rationality is essentially social in character which on another
occasion I based on Wittgenstein's treatment of the concept
of *following a rule*.[8] Instead, I want to carry the argument a
stage further by suggesting that the social conditions of

language and rationality must also carry with them certain fundamental *moral* conceptions.

To this end I shall offer some reflections on what Wittgenstein says about the kind of *agreement* that must exist between users of a common language. I am thinking here not so much of the agreement in using words in the same way which plays such an important part in his account of linguistic rules, as of the different though related conception of the 'agreement in *judgments*', which he argues is a condition of the possibility of anyone's ever *saying* something.[9]

242. If language is to be a means of communication there must be agreement not only in definitions but also (queer as this may seem) in judgements. This seems to abolish logic, but does not do so.—It is one thing to describe methods of measurement, and another to obtain and state results of measurement. But what we call 'measuring' is partly determined by a certain constancy in results of measurement.

241. 'So you are saying that human agreement decides what is true and false?'—It is what human beings *say* that is true and false; and they agree in the language they use. That is not agreement in opinions but in form of life.

The 'agreement' that is referred to here is very complex, as can be seen by noticing the various ways in which it might *not* be achieved. This might, for instance, be due to the erratic behaviour of the things we wanted to use as measuring rods; or to the failure of people to react in the appropriate way to teaching, as the chimpanzee in the Kellogg experiment failed, beyond a certain point, to do. Might it also be because nobody, or hardly anybody, could ever be relied on to *speak truthfully*? We can hardly put it in this way, since a distinction between 'telling the truth' and 'not telling the truth' presupposes a going system of communication. But one can say that the notion of a society in which there is a language but in which truth-telling is not regarded as the norm is a self-contradictory one. The conception of a distinction between true and false statements (and therefore the conception of statements *simpliciter*) could not *precede* a general adherence to the norm of truth-telling. The relation between these is totally unlike that, say, between a conception of the distinction between the left hand and the right hand side of the road and an adherence to the norm of driving on the left hand side; for here we could first contemplate the two alternatives and *then* decide which one to adopt. But adherence to the norm of truthfulness *goes along with* the distinction between true and false statements; without the one there could not be the other. I am not here speaking of what a given individual may do, but of what must be the case generally in a society. An individual who can talk can of course deliberate on a given occasion whether to tell the truth or not. But he will already have learned what telling the truth *is*; and what I wish to argue is both that learning this is part of the process of learning to speak and also that learning this involves at the same time learning that speaking truthfully is the norm and speaking untruthfully a deviation. What kinds of 'norm' and 'deviation' I shall consider more closely shortly.

Let us suppose, *per absurdum*, that the 'other alternative' were adopted: that what we now call 'true' statements were always uttered in place of what we now call 'false' statements, and vice versa. All that would happen would be that statements would come to be taken in the opposite sense from that which they now carry. That is, those utterances which, as things are, express true (false) statements would then express false (true) statements. So the supposition that telling lies could be the norm and telling the truth a deviation from it is self-contradictory. And again, if *per absurdum* the incidence of 'true' and 'false' statements were statistically random, there could be no distinction between truth and falsity at all, therefore no communication. For to communicate it must be possible for people's utterances to be taken in certain specific ways by other people.

It would, then, be nonsense to call the norm of truth-telling a 'social convention', if by that were meant that there might be a human society in which it were not generally adhered to. Of course, the existence of this norm is possible only in a society in which there are also certain (linguistic and other) conventions, but that is quite different from saying that it is itself conventional. Rather, general adherence to such a norm is a feature of any society in which there are conventions, that is, any society *tout court*.

4

Somebody who assented to much of what has gone before might still hesitate to accept my statement that the existence of a norm of truth-telling is a *moral* condition of language. It might be supposed that before we can say that truthfulness is regarded in a given society as a moral virtue, and not merely that people as a matter of fact make true statements more often than they make false ones, something more has to be added that is only contingently, and not logically, connected with the conditions for the existence of a society with a common language as such: perhaps something like a specifically moral approbation of those who adhere to the norm and disapprobation of those who contravene it. I shall try to meet some forms of this objection shortly.[10] But first I should like to point out that even if the objection be conceded, what I have said so far, if sound, would still be enough to refute the view that there could be a society in which telling the truth were generally regarded as a moral *vice*. For this would surely entail that it was something that people tried to avoid doing as a general rule; which would be absurd.

I shall also point out that what I have said does not commit the obvious mistake of equating cases of truthfulness with cases in which merely true statements are made; I do not exemplify the virtue of truthfulness every time I say something true. What I *have* said is that some concern with the virtue of truthfulness is a necessary background condition in any society in which it is to be possible for anyone to make true statements.

Now it might be said that in attaching moral significance

to truth-telling as I have discussed it, I have confused two quite distinct senses of words like 'right': namely as meaning (*a*) *morally* right and (*b*) *correctly* used. For someone who uses language incorrectly is not thereby a moral delinquent; and all that is needed for the existence of language is agreement on its correct use. But while the first half of this last statement is true, the second half is false. To lie is not to use language incorrectly. One has to use language correctly (at least within certain limits of grammatical error) in order to make a statement at all, whether a truthful one or a lying one. Again, someone who believes another's lie, has not failed to understand what the speaker has *said*; for only if he has understood this is he in a position to believe the lie. But there is something about the situation that he has failed to understand; and this we might express by saying he has failed to understand the *speaker*, in the sense that he has failed to understand what the speaker has *done*, or where the speaker stands. And this understanding of the role played by the speaker of an utterance is an essential part of language. Communicating is not *just* understanding and using *words*.

Failure to make this distinction mars the presentation of a case with similar import advocated by Michael Polanyi,[11] who rightly lays great emphasis on the notions of 'commitment' and 'trust' as essential to the understanding of what language is. The trouble lies in his talk about 'commitment' 'heuristic passions', 'fiduciary acts' as 'tacit *components*' in acts of assertion, often as if they were a sort of *feelings*. 'Unless an assertion of fact is accompanied by some heuristic or persuasive feeling, it is a mere form of words, saying nothing.'[12] This leads him to 'the paradox of self-set standards; if the criteria of reasonableness, to which I subject my beliefs, are ultimately upheld by my confidence in them, the whole process of justifying these beliefs may appear but a futile authorisation of my own authority'.[13] Polanyi embraces this paradox with the words 'Yet so be it', and never really succeeds in making it look less paradoxical.

Yet the paradox could have been avoided if the vital distinction had been observed between 'what a statement means' and 'what a person means in making the statement'. Polanyi says:[14] 'It is not words that have meaning, but the speaker or listener who means something by them.' To this the proper answer is: words may have a meaning and so, in a different though related sense, may a speaker mean something by the words he uses. But this latter kind of meaning would be impossible if the words used did not already mean something in the first sense—something which the speaker did not himself *make* them mean. Humpty-Dumptyism is an absurdity. Of course words may be defined arbitrarily for a special purpose, but only in terms of other words with an established common meaning or of commonly understood techniques such as ostensive definition. Nobody can make his words mean something simply by willing that they should, still less by having a feeling when he utters them.

Because of his confusion over this Polanyi misconstrues the significance of the lie.[15]

> Every conceivable assertion of fact can be made in good faith or as a lie. The statement remains the same in both cases, but its tacit components are different. A truthful statement commits the speaker to a belief in what he has asserted: he embarks in it on an open sea of limitless implications. An untruthful statement withholds this belief, launching a leaking vessel for others to board and sink in it.

I call this a misconstruction, because the liar is no less *committed* to a belief in what he says than is he who speaks truthfully. One is committed by one's words and deeds and, given these, one cannot in addition *will* that one shall or shall not be committed in certain ways. The point about the liar is that he is letting down those with whom he *has* committed himself.

The notion of commitment marks the distinction and the connection between the following two concepts: *what words mean* and *what people mean by words*. People can only say something and mean it if they use words that mean something; and it belongs to the kind of meaning that words have that they can be used by people in statements that they (the people) mean. But this is only possible in a society where people are so related that for one person to say something is for him to commit himself with others; and an important part of such a relation is that there should be a common respect for truthfulness.

Consider now another objection.[16] To say that something is regarded as a moral virtue in a society is to say that people regard non-compliance with it with a special sort of disapproval. But could there not be a society in which nobody ever in fact failed to comply with the 'norms'? Where the possibility of doing this never occurred to anyone? Here there would be no concept of a breach of the norms and correspondingly there could be no recognizably moral attitude either to 'breaches of' or 'adherences to' the norms. In fact there would be no norms, as we understand them. People would just naturally be truthful, kind to their friends and neighbours, etc.: a society like that of Swift's Houyhnhnms.

I shall argue that this apparent description of a possible society is not in fact as intelligible as it may appear. Consider first the case of 'natural kindness', which was the one particularly urged by Wisdom. Such a people would have no conception of unkindness; but in this case to say that they 'act kindly' cannot mean quite the same as it means when applied to the behaviour of somebody in our own society. For us this is a description which presupposes the possibility of acting *un*kindly. Now Wisdom might say: 'Very well. We should not call such behaviour "kind", because this is a *moral* term and moral virtues do require the possibility of choice between alternatives which is lacking in my postulated society. But my point was that there could be a society like that, i.e., a society lacking what we should call "moral values".'

This argument is hard to answer so far as the example of kindness is concerned. But consider now the much more fundamental case of truthfulness.[17] Swift's Houyhnhnm argues thus:

That the use of speech was to make us understand one another and to receive information of facts; now if any-one said the thing which was not, those ends were de-feated, because I cannot properly be said to understand him, and I am so far from receiving information that he leaves me worse than in ignorance, for I am led to believe a thing black when it is white, or short when it is long.

A confusion very like Polanyi's is committed here. It is true in a sense that if someone gets me to believe his lie 'I cannot properly be said to understand *him*', for I understand him to mean what he says when he does not. But it does not follow that I do not understand *what he says*; for unless I do I shall not fail to *mis*understand *him* in the way I do. Further-more, this latter failure of understanding must be possible if anything is to take place that we can call 'communication'; for a speaker must be able to mean what he says and a hearer to understand him as meaning what he says. And this can only be so where the speaker may *not* mean what he says, since meaning something is not an event that can just *happen*; and where it makes sense for the hearer to ask whether the speaker means what he says or not. None of these questions could arise in Wisdom's 'society'; hence one could not speak of any 'communication' between its members; hence it is not really a possible *society*.

It may now be said that even if all this is true, it still does not follow that truthfulness must have any *moral* signifi-cance.[18] Certainly, the maintenance of established (linguistic and other) standards involves an agreement in reactions, including an agreement in reactions to deviations from the standards. But does this mean there must be an agreement in *moral* reactions? Consider a gambling game between card-sharpers, mutually recognized as such.[19] There clearly must be rules which the players are expected to adhere to; but in what sense of 'expected to'? Might not Hobbes's description apply here: 'only that to be every man's, that he can get: and for so long, as he can keep it'? These players might *expect* their opponents to break the rules if they think they can get away with it, and not think any the worse of them for that, but simply try to ensure that they cannot by the threat of their guns on the table.

Clearly such a situation is possible; but it does not follow that it is a possible microcosm of a whole society. That would mean that a man's expectation that others will, in general, tell the truth would have to be of a similar kind, as would his own attitude to the alternatives of speaking truthfully and lying. Speaking could only be regarded as a means of attaining some advantage by manipulating the reactions of other people in a desired way: the view of language as rhetoric put to Socrates by his Sophistic opponents in Plato's *Gorgias*. Of course an individual can, at least sometimes, regard his utterances in that way, but not all, or even most, uses of language in a society could be generally so regarded. For one can only use words to manipulate the reactions of other men in so far as those others at least think they *understand* what one is saying. So the concept of understanding is presupposed by the possibility of such manipulation of reactions and cannot be elucidated in terms of it.

Richard Rovere writes of that arch-manipulator of reactions, Senator Joe McCarthy:[20]

> He never really took himself seriously. He was the leader of a fanatical movement, and he gave his name to a fanatical doctrine, but he was no kind of fanatic himself . . . This most successful and menacing of all our apostles of hatred was himself incapable of true rancour, spite, and animosity as a eunuch is incapable of marriage. . . . Basically, of course, he was a great sophisticate in human relationships, as every demagogue must be. He knew a great deal about people's fears and anxieties, and he was a superb juggler of them. But he was himself numb to the sensations he produced in others. He could not comprehend true outrage, true indignation, true anything.

McCarthy's operations presupposed the existence of men who *were* true fanatics, who *could* experience true outrage and indignation, and so on. Similarly McCarthy's use of the 'paraphernalia of rationality'—stuffed brief-case, footnotes, etc.—in order to impress people presupposed the existence of the real thing: something that could not be accounted for in terms of its usefulness in getting people to do and believe certain desired things, but which implies that certain values are respected for their own sakes.

Wittgenstein writes:[21]

> A rule *qua* rule is detached, it stands as it were alone in its glory; although what gives it importance is the facts of daily experience.
>
> What I have to do is as it were to describe the office of a king; in doing which I must never fall into the error of explaining the kingly dignity by the king's usefulness, but I must leave neither his usefulness nor his dignity out of account.

Because there is rational discourse and understanding men can often induce others to act as they want. But the nature of rational discourse and understanding cannot be accounted for in terms of this fact.

5

I have said that there could not be a human society in which truthfulness were not in general regarded as a virtue. This does not mean that no one can ever be justified in lying. But it does imply that a lie always needs special justification if it is not to be condemned. What is regarded as such a justification will depend on the particular institutions of the society in question.

I am not committed to saying that truthfulness must have precisely the *same* moral significance in any human society. Its peculiar role in *our* lives, for instance, has to do with the importance for us of commerce, with its necessity for reliance on contractual fulfilment and accurate specification of goods; and again with the importance for us of scientific research with its concomitant need for trustworthiness in the reports of experiments and integrity in argument. To say that the virtue of truthfulness must play some part in the life of any society is not to describe the peculiar part it plays in the life of a particular society.

There is a more general concept for which my argument could be adapted: that of *integrity*, which is to human institutions generally what truthfulness is to the institution of language. There are important formal analogies between language and other social institutions; for to act in the context of a social institution is always to commit oneself in some way for the future: a notion for which the notion of being committed by what one *says* provides an important parallel. But the concept of integrity is inseparable from that of commitment. To lack integrity is to act with the appearance of fulfilling a certain role but without the intention of shouldering the responsibilities to which the role commits one. If that, *per absurdum*, were to become the rule, the whole concept of a social role would thereby collapse.

Of course, the particular form which integrity will take, what will count as 'integrity' and 'lack of integrity', will depend on the particular institutions within the context of which the question arises. And it is not necessary that the concept of integrity should always be singled out and made a matter of special explicit emphasis, as it is for instance in the climate of culture we call 'Romanticism'.[22] But a people can show a regard for particular manifestations of integrity without necessarily building a whole ethos round the concept.

What I am saying about the relation between the general idea of these virtues and their particular social manifestations is expressed in the following remark of Vico's, with whose conception of the 'natural law of the peoples' my thesis has certain similarities:[23]

> There must in the nature of human things be a mental language common to all nations, which uniformly grasps the substance of things feasible in human social life, and expresses it with as many diverse modifications as these same things may have diverse aspects. A proof of this is afforded by proverbs and maxims of vulgar wisdom, in which substantially the same meanings find as many diverse expressions as there are nations ancient and modern.

Vico could say this while being more alive than most to the

extraordinary variety in the qualities of life and thought to be found at different periods of human history.

In some respects integrity is to human institutions generally what fair play is to games. What constitutes fair play in a particular instance must be specified in relation to the particular rules of the game in question. It is a foul to handle the ball in Association Football but not in Rugby; and of course handling the ball does not enter at all into what is meant by cheating at patience. We might, it is true, teach someone the meaning of 'fair play' by introducing him to a number of different examples like this. But his grasp of the concept would not be shown by his ability to remember and recognize just these examples, but by his ability to use the concept in connection with *other* games which did not enter into his training in the concept. The sense of the notion of fair play has to do with its importance for the general idea of a game rather than with its particular manifestations in the rules of any particular game. Similarly, the sense of the concept of integrity has to do with its importance for the general idea of a social institution.

I have not of course contended that one is under an obligation to admire every single manifestation of integrity; that would be to mistake my logico-philosophical thesis for a quite absurd moral doctrine. The concentration camp commandant towards the end of Irwin Shaw's *The Young Lions* exhibited integrity of a peculiarly revolting sort from the point of view of Western liberal morality. He was morally revolting because of the unspeakable role he was playing; to say that he was playing it with integrity is, for most of us, an additional count against him, not a point in his favour. But the propensity of people to act like that was nonetheless an essential factor in the continued existence of such institutions. There could not be a convention to the effect that such attitudes should not, *in general*, be adopted.

NOTES

[1] See *The Open Society and Its Enemies* (London: Routledge & Kegan Paul), 3rd edition, Vol. I, Chapter 5.

[2] Robert Oppenheimer: 'Tradition and Discovery', *American Council of Learned Societies Newsletter*, October 1959, Vol. X, No. 8, p. 5. The italics are mine.

[3] Ibid., p. 13.

[4] Loc. cit., p. 62.

[5] G. E. M. Anscombe: *Intention*, p. 67.

[6] *Leviathan*, Part II, Chapter 17.

[7] Ibid., Part I, Chapter 4.

[8] See *The Idea of a Social Science* (London: Routledge & Kegan Paul, 1958).

[9] *Philosophical Investigations*, p. 88ᵉ. I have transposed the order of these two sections in order to make the train of thought, out of context, more intelligible.

[10] In what follows I am particularly indebted to criticisms made of an earlier draft of this paper at meetings of the Cambridge Moral Sciences Club and the University College of Swansea Philosophical Society.

[11] In his *Personal Knowledge* (London: Routledge & Kegan Paul, 1962), especially Sections II and III.

[12] Ibid., p. 254.

[13] Ibid., p. 256.

[14] Ibid., p. 252.

[15] Ibid., p. 253.

[16] Made in discussion by Professor John Wisdom.

[17] Of course these cases are connected, as Aristotle makes clear in Book VIII of the *Nicomachean Ethics*, where he speaks of 'friendship' as one of the most fundamental of social virtues. But he strains this notion, especially when he speaks of 'the friendship because of advantage' which is 'the connecting link of shopkeepers', and 'legal friendship', where 'the friendly element is the delay in requiring the discharge' of a contractual obligation. But he is certainly talking of something important which is overlooked by writers like Hobbes.

[18] The following line of argument was suggested in discussion by Rush Rhees, though I do not think he regards it as capable of being pressed to its apparent conclusion.

[19] Rhees's example.

[20] In *Senator Joe McCarthy* (New York: Harcourt Brace Jovanovich, 1959). My quotation is from an excerpt in the *Observer* of 10 January 1960.

[21] *Remarks on the Foundations of Mathematics*, V-3, p. 160ᵉ.

[22] This was pointed out to me by Sir Isaiah Berlin.

[23] *The New Science*, para. 161.

4

Human Nature

The concept of human nature usually enters discussions of the nature and implications of the social sciences in connection with one or another form of 'relativism'. Confronted with the enormous and apparently conflicting variety of phenomena of human life at different places and times, we are inclined to ask whether there is not something which holds these phenomena together and unifies them. Stated thus baldly this question is no doubt so vague as to approach meaninglessness; it will have to be posed in different forms—and probably answered differently—according to the particular phenomena of human life which we happen to have in mind. In this essay I shall concentrate my attention on some questions about the relevance of sociological investigations to our understanding of ethics and about the treatment of ethics in such investigations. I shall be particularly interested in the way in which the concept of human nature enters into such discussions; and I shall devote a good deal of attention to Professor Alasdair MacIntyre's recent *A Short History of Ethics*.[1] It is a large merit of this book that it explicitly and invigoratingly relates the manner of its historical exposition to a distinctive philosophico-sociological standpoint concerning the nature of morality. I call this a 'merit' and want to stand by that characterization even though I think that there are important confusions enshrined in MacIntyre's approach. A large part of the task which I want to set myself in this essay is to make clear the nature and importance of these confusions.

The concept of human nature has been thought important in at least three different, though related, ways by those who have considered morality from a sociological standpoint: in connection with questions about the *identification* of those features of a society's life which are to be subsumed under the concept of morality; in connection with the *explanation* of the features thus classified; and in connection with attempts at the *justification* of particular moral choices. Though these types of question run into each other and cannot always be held apart, it will be convenient for me to develop my argument by considering each type of question in turn. I start with questions about identification.

The phenomena of human life do not reach the sociological investigator in a pre-packaged state, labelled 'economic', 'religious', 'aesthetic', 'ethical', and the like. He has to decide, often with considerable difficulty, what he is going to count as belonging to one or the other of such categories. Sometimes he will feel that the facts he is confronted with do not fit without distortion into any of the categories he is already familiar with and that he must invent new ones. Problems of this sort most obviously arise in cases where the investigator—if, for instance, he is a social anthropologist—is studying a society or a culture which looks very different from that within which he has learnt to apply such categories hitherto (probably the one he grew up in). But not only there. It requires little sophistication to be struck by the problematic application of such categories nearer home too. Rush Rhees gives us a striking example of this.[2] He refers to a reported interview between a local committee of a 'Moral Welfare Council' and an unmarried expectant mother, in which the line of the committee's chairman was: 'Do you know you can be locked up if you go on like this? Do you want to be locked up?', etc. Rhees contrasts the 'moral' outlook expressed here with what he himself feels inclined to say: that 'the activities of those moral enthusiasts are foul and filthy'. For my purposes (as for Rhees's in the essay cited) the point of the contrast is not to raise the question which of these outlooks is the 'morally right' one, which if either of the two we ought to endorse; it is rather to point out difficulties in saying that *both* these outlooks either are or are not forms of 'moral' outlook. Rhees comments:

> Suppose I *dispute* the remark that 'their activities are foul and filthy' is a moral judgement—what would be said to show that it *is*? I think the differences are just as important as the similarities. And if you offered reasons for saying that both are forms of moral judgement, I think there are reasons just as strong for saying they are not.

Rhees does not particularize the differences he has in mind. But I take it that one important difference would be that the committee chairman would take herself to be committed to doing something about, intervening to remove, the evils (as she regards them) confronting her. Rhees on the other hand might well, I imagine, disown any commitment to do anything about the council's activities beyond saying what he thinks of them—or even just thinking it.

However that may be, there is undoubtedly a difficulty here about what cases we are going to call cases of a 'moral outlook' and about what is involved in so calling them. One very common approach to such difficulties—exemplified, in some of the writings of Mrs Philippa Foot—is to try to locate the moral in certain alleged features of human nature, to say what human needs morality answers to and to refer to such needs as criteria for what can be accepted as a moral concern and what cannot. These needs are used to give content to a notion of 'human good and harm', and the claim is that all genuine moral judgments involve a reference, though sometimes more explicitly than at other times, to such a notion. But the undoubted attractiveness of such a move is considerably lessened if we notice what has been suggested by some critics of the 'neo-naturalist' movement, that the identification of these human needs—at least in many important cases—may itself be a matter for dispute of a kind which it is hard not to characterize as a moral dispute. One of the interesting features of Alasdair MacIntyre's *Short History* is that it attempts to reconcile this sort of appeal to human needs in determining what belongs to the moral with a recognition of the extent to which what we are prepared to recognize as being human needs varies *pari passu* with the moral outlook we are prepared to embrace. I think Mac-Intyre's attempt fails; and indeed I think the failure inevitable. I will now try to develop my reasons for this by discussing what MacIntyre writes about the 'explanation' of the existence of such a feature as morality in the social life of human beings.

One context in which MacIntyre develops this theme is an important criticism which he makes of Professor R. M. Hare's account of moral discourse. Hare makes a distinction between the language in which we express our personal likes and dislikes and our private feelings about people and actions, our individual choices and the commands and injunctions which we may at times issue, and the language in which we express our moral evaluations. MacIntyre accepts this general distinction but complains that Hare's account still leaves us with a question to which it is unable to provide an answer, namely 'why there should exist any specifically moral language over and above the ordinary language of feelings, liking, choice and imperatives.'[3] He himself offers an answer to his question which, taken by itself, is puzzling:[4]

> My attitudes and my imperatives have authority for me just because they are mine. But when I invoke words such as *ought* and *good* I at least seek to appeal to a standard which has other and more authority. If I use these words to you, I seek to appeal to you in the name of those standards and not in my own name.

To understand the force of what MacIntyre is saying here, we must bring more explicitly into the light his conception of a human nature which is not an invariable datum but which changes in response to new social and historical conditions. It is a pervasive theme of his book that moral concepts can be made sense of only in their particular historical setting, that they change as forms of social life change and are indeed 'embodied in and . . . partially con-

stitutive of forms of social life'.[5] He concludes from this that
moral concepts may be expected to play different roles in
different social settings and accordingly that, when we find
moral philosophers giving different accounts of 'morality' it
is dangerous for us to assume that they are talking about the
same subject-matter. Here we see how the difficulties concerning the identification of the social phenomena we are
going to count as 'moral', which I raised earlier, merge with
the problems about the 'explanation' of such phenomena,
which MacIntyre claims that Hare is unable to deal
with.

The difficulties which MacIntyre feels over Hare's account
can now be expressed as follows. Hare's formalistic account
of moral language seems to leave him with a problem about
the source of the specific content of people's moral evaluations. He tries to overcome this (in *Freedom and Reason*) by
taking an agent's own interests, desires and inclinations as a
datum and then transmuting them into genuine moral
judgments by means of the mechanism of universalization.
But, leaving aside other difficulties about this transmutation,
MacIntyre asks why one agent's moral evaluations, the content of which springs from a consideration of his own
interests and inclinations, should carry any authority at all
for another agent who perhaps has different inclinations
and interests. Will it not be simply a lucky chance if two
agents manage to arrive at even roughly the same evaluations
in this way? Moreover, even if they do manage to agree, will
not each man's evaluations have authority for him only in so
far as they are backed by his own interests and inclinations?
MacIntyre's move at this point is to shift the centre of
gravity from the purely personal concerns of any individual
agent to the institutions and values generally accepted in the
society to which he and those with whom he is in communication equally belong. In that society 'there is a *recognised* list of
virtues, an *established* set of moral rules, an *institutionalised*
connection between obedience and rules, the practice of
virtues, and the attainment of ends'.[6] Thus, when I express
a moral judgment to someone else, I appeal to an authority

which is not *my* authority and one which I can expect him to recognize as well as myself.

Now MacIntyre's account does so far seem to me to be superior to Hare's in its suggestion about where we should locate the source of the particular contents of people's moral judgments at particular times and places: namely in a historical tradition at a particular stage of its development. The point perhaps comes into clearer focus if we compare Hare with Kant in this connection. Kant's attempt, in the *Tugendlehre*, to derive particular duties from his account of the general form of morality, runs into very similar difficulties. And since our views about many practices have changed a good deal since Kant's day, it may be easier for us to see, in his case, to what a great extent his claims about specific duties are drawn from ideas which happened to be current in the life of his time—contrary, of course, to what he himself claimed for them.

However, MacIntyre seems to claim more for his criticism of Hare than what I have just tried to bring out. He suggests that his account, unlike Hare's, offers us an *explanation* 'why there should exist any specifically evaluative language'. I do not think this claim can be sustained; and I think that MacIntyre only makes it because he has not fully seen the implications of what he has said about the concept of human nature. What MacIntyre in fact offers us is a reminder, valuable enough in itself, that an evaluative use of language *does* exist within the context of such and such social institutions and practices. To speak of a 'recognized' list of virtues and an 'established' set of moral rules is simply to *assert* that the standards I appeal to in making moral evaluations also carry authority for other people. This is so; but it has certainly not been 'explained'. And it is hard to see how, once human nature is no longer thought of as something at least relatively permanent and unchanging, it possibly can provide any explanation of morality of the sort MacIntyre seems to be seeking. If you take the view that it belongs to the nature of human beings to have more or less fixed needs and wants, you may seem able to 'explain' particular moral codes as different ways in which those needs may be ministered to in different social contexts. But once you allow the conception of human needs to float freely, like a currency with no fixed parity, alongside the changing moral codes, then those needs will as much (or as little) require explanation as the codes themselves.

I have, though, still not said enough about the kind of connection MacIntyre thinks exists between adherence to a morality and the 'attainment of ends'. This matter can be best discussed if I turn now to the third sort of question about morality which I distinguished at the beginning of this lecture: about the *justification* of moral choices.

Talk about different moralities or diversity of standards often causes uneasiness; and not least among those whom Lord Devlin likes to call 'rationalist philosophers'. It may be the case, they want to object, that people's moral beliefs are diverse, but the important question for a philosopher is which, if any, of those beliefs are right. Now the conception of a human nature involving certain needs and wants has very often been brought into play to answer questions of this sort too. Thus, it has been thought, you determine what are to count as 'moral' beliefs by asking whether the beliefs in question have to do with what is thought to satisfy human needs; you explain the existence of such beliefs by pointing out the urgency for human beings to satisfy those needs; and you distinguish correct from incorrect moral judgments by asking whether they are right in their implications about what will satisfy the most important human needs.

It is in his treatment of this last sort of view that the incoherences in the way MacIntyre thinks of human nature become most obvious. I shall now try to expound briefly what I take his view to be, then criticize it and finally conclude with some general reflections on what I take to be matters of very great philosophical importance which are connected with the difficulties in MacIntyre's position.

MacIntyre takes the goal of a 'theory of morals' to be to make clear the 'kind of backing [which] is logically appropriate to moral rules',[7] and thinks that this 'backing' will have to be accounted for in terms of a 'theory of human nature'. But since he wants to insist that moralities are diverse not merely in respect of their content but even in respect of the logical form of their judgments, he holds that their respective systems of 'rules' will require backing in terms of different conceptions of human nature. And when he speaks of different conceptions of human nature here, I think he means not merely different views about the specific needs human beings have, but also different views about the sense in which human beings can be said to have needs at all, about the extent to which there is anything constant about those needs, and about the *kind* of importance in human life which those needs have. If, then, a man has to choose (as far as his own life is concerned) between alternative moral systems, he will need at the same time and by the same token to decide between rival conceptions of human nature. For a reasoned choice between different moralities requires a vocabulary in which the reasoning may be expressed; this vocabulary is provided by a man's 'social past', i.e. by the way in which moral conceptions have grown up and developed in the context of historically conditioned 'forms of social and moral practice'. Each such form of practice 'carries with it its own picture of human nature. The choice of a form of life and the choice of a view of human nature go together.'[8] Thus the conception of human nature provides us with no 'neutral standard' by reference to which such choices may be guided. And in line with this conclusion MacIntyre maintains (on p. 148) that it is 'arbitrary and illegitimate' in examining the logical structure of different moralities to specify as *the* logical form of moral argument that form which is characteristic of argument within any one of them.

If this were all MacIntyre wanted to say I should not find much cause to quarrel, beyond expressing a doubt about whether in that case the discussion were really helped by introducing the conception of human nature into it. But it turns out that this is not by any means all that MacIntyre wants to say. He follows his argument for the illegitimacy of saying that any particular form constitutes *the* logical form of moral argument with a discussion designed to show the 'superiority' of the Aristotelian view of human nature and of its relation to morality in comparison with, e.g., those to be found in Christianity, the Sophists and Hobbes. And a question which cries out to be asked at this point is whether we are to take this view as an expression of MacIntyre's own 'choice'—a choice of which it would be improper to say that it is *logically* in any better shape than would be a contrary choice—or whether, rather, he is making a logical comment about what can be said in general about the nature of such choices. This latter interpretation would be hard to reconcile with those assertions of MacIntyre's to which I have already referred; nevertheless I think it is clear from the larger context of his argument in the book as a whole that this must be the interpretation intended.

For MacIntyre the virtue of the Aristotelian view is two-fold. On the one hand it does not take human needs and desires as a fixed datum, but rather as a subject for criticism and for modification by such criticism. On the other hand—more to our immediate point—it does squarely link up duties with specific social roles and with the social rewards and satisfactions provided for one who fulfils those roles worthily within the life of his society. One of the main over-all contentions of MacIntyre's book is that the notion of a moral duty is originally at home, and is only fully intelligible, in the context of a society offering its members more or less clearly defined roles together with definite satisfactions ensuing on their proper fulfilment. Thus the Kantian categorical imperative is interpreted as the product of a society in which this sort of connection has broken down: the word 'ought' is still used but lacks the social background which alone would make it intelligible—a background, namely, in which a man can have a rational expectation that if he does his duty he will be rewarded with social satisfactions of a sort he can understand and aim at. In this connection MacIntyre refers[9] to Kant's view—put forward in a theological context —that 'it would be intolerable if in fact duty were not in the

end crowned with happiness'. He comments that the in-
determinacy of the notion of happiness when it is separated
from any 'socially established ends' turns this view into 'a
tacit admission that without some such notion, not morality
itself, but the Kantian interpretation of it scarcely makes
sense'.

But the qualification in that last clause is really something
of an evasion. For MacIntyre does want to say that Kant's
interpretation is applicable to a way in which people really
had come to use the word 'ought' in the society to which
Kant was implicitly referring. So he must, apparently, think
that the morality expressed in this use of the word itself
'scarcely makes sense'. This interpretation is borne out by his
treatment of our contemporary situation and of the relevance of Hare's theory of morals to it. Hare, so MacIntyre in
effect argues (e.g. on p. 266), is spokesman for that large
section of contemporary mankind who adhere to no tradi-
tional morality and to whom 'those who speak from within
[such a morality] appear merely to be uttering imperatives
which express their own liking and their private choices'.[10]
I take it that the reason why it appears like this to such
people is that this is in fact what they themselves are doing
when they use moral language. And it seems clear that
MacIntyre regards this use as one which does not make much
sense as anything distinct from an expression of personal likes
and dislikes. It appears, for instance, from what I said earlier
in the essay about his treatment of Hare, that he would
regard such a use of language as in no way appealing to any
authoritative standard in a way which would make it
rational for one man to be convinced by another that he
should *change* his 'moral' views.

Thus the prescriptivist account of moral language, on
MacIntyre's view, is not a misdescription but a quite
accurate representation of how a great many people do use
moral language: in a way, namely, that MacIntyre regards as
not making much sense. What makes this use senseless, he
thinks, is the absence of any social link between definite roles
and definite ends, the attainment of which carries a rational

expectation of some satisfaction for the agent. It looks as though MacIntyre were considerably less liberal than once appeared concerning what can and what cannot be accepted in morality. He is willing to accept variations in the social goods and personal satisfactions with which the fulfilment of duties is linked; but he is not willing to accept duties not linked with *any* such goods or satisfactions. And this, I must reiterate, not as a matter of his own moral standpoint, but as a logical point about what can be understood as being a moral standpoint which can be made sense of at all.

A question we should ask at this point is what authority we should regard this general requirement of MacIntyre's as having for us. How does he *know* that the expression of a 'duty' outside such a context is somehow incomplete and incoherent? A remark of his own, at the beginning of his book, is germane here. Historical study of ethical concepts, he says, may 'break down . . . our too narrow views of what can and cannot be thought, said, and done . . . in face of the record of what has been thought, said and done'.[11] However, it is not through mere carelessness that he has got himself into this, as it seems to me, embarrassing position; rather it is due to a very fundamental philosophical difficulty which confronts us all and about which I must now try to say something.

'The record of what has been thought, said and done' cannot be taken as meaning just the record of any old thing which anybody has ever felt like saying, thinking or doing. For people sometimes talk nonsense and behave in ways which make no sense. As philosophers one of our primary concerns is precisely to distinguish sense from nonsense. Here we have to ask what this involves and how we are to tell when we have done it successfully. One of the chief uses to which the concept of human nature has been put by philosophers is in an attempt to answer this question. They have thought that it is by their relation, or lack of it, to human nature that we decide what ways of thinking and acting make sense and what do not. What is most interesting about MacIntyre's book is that it shows some recognition of the

constricting effect of this way of thinking on our interpretation of human life and thought without, however, coming
to the realization that the whole matter is being represented
here in a topsy-turvy way. Putting the matter briefly, and
therefore over-crudely, what I want to say is this: what we
can ascribe to human nature does not determine what we can
and what we cannot make sense of; rather, what we can and
and what we cannot make sense of determines what we can
ascribe to human nature. It is indeed precisely for this
reason that the concept of human nature is not the concept
of something fixed and given; i.e. the reason for this is a
philosophical, not a sociological, one.

A child is born within, and grows up into the life of, a
particular human society. He learns to speak and to engage
in various kinds of activity in relation to other people. In the
course of these activities he encounters problems of extremely
diverse kinds, problems which change in character as he
matures, and problems that bring him into new kinds of
relations with other people. Along with this development
there comes a growth in his understanding of what constitute
problems and difficulties for them. This growing understanding manifests itself in the way he comes to treat people
in the course of his daily life, which will include a development in his ideas of what is permissible in his treatment of
them and what is ruled out. This growth in his understanding of other people through his dealings with them is at
the same time a growth in his understanding of himself,
which is in its turn a development of the kind of person he is.
The way a person develops in these dimensions will be influenced by the kinds of people, the kinds of situation and the
kinds of problems which he finds himself confronted with in
the course of his life. But of course it is also true that his
growth will depend on what he himself brings to the situations he faces. Our problem is to understand the relation
between these two 'factors'.

But there is something misleading in this way of formulating the issue. A man is not 'confronted' with situations and
problems as he is 'confronted' with a brick wall. A brick wall

confronts a man whether he recognizes it or not; but the same is not unqualifiedly true of the other case.[12] A passage from R. G. Collingwood's *Autobiography*[13] will help to bring out what I mean.

> My father had plenty of books and allowed me to read in them as I pleased. Among others, he had kept the books of classical scholarship, ancient history, and philosophy which he had used at Oxford. As a rule I left these alone; but one day when I was eight years old curiosity moved me to take down a little black book lettered on its spine 'Kant's Theory of Ethics'. It was Abbott's translation of the *Grundlegung zur Metaphysik der Sitten*; and as I began reading it, my small form wedged between the bookcase and the table, I was attacked by a strange succession of emotions. First came an intense excitement. I felt that things of the highest importance were being said about matters of the utmost urgency: things which at all costs I must understand. Then, with a wave of indignation, came the discovery that I could not understand them. Disgraceful to confess, here was a book whose words were English and whose sentences were grammatical, but whose meaning baffled me. Then, third and last, came the strangest emotion of all. I felt that the contents of this book, although I could not understand it, were somehow my business: a matter personal to myself, or rather to some future self of my own. It was not like the common boyish intention to 'be an engine driver when I grow up', for there was no desire in it; I did not, in any natural sense of the word, 'want' to master the Kantian ethics when I should be old enough; but I felt as if a veil had been lifted and my destiny revealed.

Our first reaction to this passage is likely to be that the young Collingwood must have been a very remarkable little boy. This reaction expresses our perception that for most people of that age—indeed of any age—coming across Kant's *Grundlegung* would not pose any problem at all, but merely an occasion to put the book down as quickly as possible and look for something more entertaining. A vocation needs someone with ears to hear as well as a call. But of course a call is necessary too and we should ask what are the conditions necessary for this. In Collingwood's case it was necessary that there should have existed a tradition of thought in which there were certain live problems, questions which had not been answered. Someone who feels moved to ask himself such questions, who, speaking more generally, finds that his situation confronts him with problems, discovers something about himself by that very fact—as the young Collingwood discovered something about himself in dimly feeling the force of the questions Kant was asking. But we could not say *what* a man discovers about himself in such a situation without referring to the nature of the problems he finds himself faced with; for it is in his response to those problems that he makes the discovery. And we understand what those problems are only in the context of the traditions of thought and activity out of which they arise. The fact that some will see problems where others will not may tempt us to say that the capacity for understanding must be 'in' someone from the start. But while it is not exactly wrong to say this, it may make us overlook the fact that the *possibility* of such capacities, as we might say 'the space within which such capacities can exist', comes from outside. The question whether or not a given individual has a certain capacity—e.g. to understand higher mathematics— can only be asked within the context of the problems of higher mathematics. We may be able to ask of someone from a culture with no mathematical traditions whether he is the sort of person who would have been able to become a mathematician—though it is a pretty tenuous sort of question— but we, who ask the question, necessarily do have some relation to such traditions; in the absence of such traditions such a question could not be asked at all.

There are two objections to this way of looking at the matter which come together in the appeal to 'human nature'. In the first place it may be said that while what I have called 'the space' within which human capacities of various kinds can exist comes from outside the nature of any given individual, it is still conditioned by human nature in that the systems of ideas and practices within which individual capacities may be conceived and may develop are systems of *human* ideas and practices and are therefore limited by what human beings can attach sense to. The second objection reinforces the first. I, as one individual, find other human beings making various claims to be able to do and think certain things which I have to assess: that is, I have to decide whether or not those claims are intelligible. It is no good saying that the intelligibility of the claims depends on whether there is a space within which they can be fitted, because the question of their intelligibility precisely *is* a question about the existence of such a space.

This point is quite valid as an objection to the idea that the concept of 'the space within which human capacities exist' provides a *criterion* for distinguishing sense from nonsense. But then I have introduced the concept precisely in the context of an argument for saying that there is *no* such general criterion. And in fact the objection is just as fatal to the idea that 'human nature' provides such a criterion. MacIntyre's arguments for the relativity of the conception of human nature to particular historical traditions and periods really show this. He tries to avoid the full consequences of his own argument by saying in effect that while men's particular needs vary from one form of society to another, and while the form of a society's morality is at the same time a determinant of the needs of that society's members, still what is not variable is that an intelligible morality must provide for the satisfaction of its practitioners' needs if they do what is morally required of them. Like most philosophical positions, this one *can* be held as a last bastion as long as one is prepared to drain it of content. One can, for example, say that in so far as a man does feel that something is required of him, he feels a need to do what is required of him and this need is satisfied when he does it. But this is pretty obviously no more than a juggling act with the words 'need' and 'satisfaction'; it tells us nothing whatever about the form of a moral requirement and places no limits on what can be made sense of. For a philosopher will still have to ask about the conditions under which he can accept, or must reject, a man's claim to see that something is required of him. What, then, can we say about this crucial question?

It is very common in philosophical discussion to find that a way of speaking and thinking which seems perfectly intelligible and acceptable to oneself is met with incomprehension by other people; and of course vice versa. In such circumstances one is bound to ask whether what one wants to say really does make sense or not. Discussion with other people will often be very important in one's attempt to settle this question—it was, after all, the incredulous, uncomprehending reactions of others which prompted the doubt in the first place (though this need not always be so). Discussion will take the form of raising difficulties and trying to see one's way around them. Sometimes one will think one has dealt with the difficulties satisfactorily; sometimes that the view under criticism meets with difficulties so insurmountable as to be really incomprehensible. But if one recognized the possibility of being mistaken in one's initial belief that one had understood what was being said, or that one had shown it to be unintelligible, one can equally, after discussion, recognize that one may have over- or underestimated the difficulties which have emerged in its course. But that does *not* mean that one's views are subject to the test of some ultimate criterion, the criterion of what does and what does not belong to human nature. It means only that new difficulties, and perhaps new ways of meeting the difficulties, are always lurking below the horizon and that discussion continues. Sometimes, if one is lucky, the discussion clarifies or extends one's conception of what is possible for human beings. But it is no use saying that this is contingent on what *is* or *is not* possible for human beings; for our only way of arriving at a view about that is by continuing to try to deal with the difficulties that arise in the course of discussion.

NOTES

[1] Alasdair MacIntyre, *A Short History of Ethics* (New York: Macmillan, 1966).

[2] *Without Answers* (London: Routledge & Kegan Paul, 1969), pp. 97-8.

[3] Op. cit., p. 264.

[4] Ibid., p. 265.

[5] Ibid., p. 7.

[6] Ibid., p. 265; my italics.

[7] Ibid., p. 148.

[8] Ibid., p. 268.

[9] Ibid., p. 196.

[10] Ibid., p. 266.

[11] Ibid., p. 4.

[12] Cf. 'Moral Integrity', Chapter 9, p. 171 ff.

[13] R. G. Collingwood, *An Autobiography* (Oxford University Press, 1939), pp. 3-4.

5

Man and Society in Hobbes and Rousseau

Both Hobbes and Rousseau believed that a life suitable to human needs is possible—given the world as we find it—only in the context of the state; and that the state can exist only where there is sovereign authority of a sort which is as absolute as it is possible to conceive. What is more, they agree that a society in which such absolute sovereign authority is exercised will not be maintained in the natural course of events: human effort and artifice is necessary. In particular, men must be *taught* to understand those conditions of human life which necessitate its acceptance. Thus the whole of Hobbes's *Behemoth* is an exposure, illustrated by the follies of the men of the Long Parliament, the Presbyterians, The Sectarians, the King's advisers, etc., of what Hobbes claims inevitably happens if men are ignorant of the principles of the true science of politics (as expounded in *Leviathan*).[1]

> You may perhaps think a man has need of nothing else to know the duty he owes his governor, and what right he has to order him, but a good natural wit; but it is otherwise. For it is a science, and built upon sure and clear principles, and to be learned by deep and careful study, or from masters that have deeply studied it. And who was there in the Parliament or in the nation, that could find out those evident principles, and derive from them the necessary rules of justice, and the necessary connexion of justice and peace?

Compare this with Rousseau in *A Discourse on Political Economy*:

> I conclude this part of public economy where I ought to have begun it. There can be no patriotism without liberty, no liberty without virtue, no virtue without citizens; create citizens, and you have everything you need; without them, you will have nothing but debased slaves, from the rulers of the State downwards. To form citizens is not the work of a day; and in order to have men it is necessary to educate them when they are children.

Of course Rousseau differs from Hobbes more strikingly than he resembles him in what he says about the relation between education and politics. For one thing, the content and general tendency of the education Rousseau recommends is the very reverse of what Hobbes would have approved. But there is another, equally important, difference. Whereas Hobbes thinks in terms of inculcating his citizens with a theory, a 'science', Rousseau is concerned with a whole course of training, from childhood up. The theory of *The Social Contract* is indeed taught to Émile at the culmination of his education; but it is clear that Rousseau would have thought this futile if the ground had not been carefully prepared first.

This difference in understanding of the sense in which education is related to politics is a manifestation of a very deep division between the philosophies of Hobbes and Rousseau. The 'science' which Hobbes would have his citizens taught is based on a theory about what human nature *is*. This theory in its turn is based on an elaborate monistic, materialist metaphysics, which claims to show that everything that can be intelligibly said must be reducible to a statement about the motion of a material substance. This metaphysical underpinning serves to emphasize that men must be just accepted for what they necessarily are and that any account of the possible social relations between men must take this basic human nature as a datum. The science of politics in fact consists of a demonstration of the possible relations between beings of this sort: either a *bellum omnium contra omnes* or a commonwealth consisting of subjects owing allegiance to an absolute sovereign.

In his *New Science* Giambattista Vico's most serious criticism of Hobbes is that the men who could conclude Hobbes's covenant and thereby set up a sovereign would have already to be philosophers: and my quotation from *Behemoth* does indeed suggest that this must be so. What Vico in effect urges is that men who could understand the reasons for covenanting away their freedom to a sovereign are conceivable only as the products of a very considerable and extremely sophisticated social development.

In his brief, but very interesting, discussion of the origin of language in *A Discourse on the Origin of Inequality* Rousseau makes a closely related point. He there emphasizes what is lacking from Hobbes's account of language, the enormous complexities of grammar which have to be presupposed if we are to understand the apparently simple relation between name and object (which forms the basis of Hobbes's account). Rousseau concludes that 'if men need speech to learn to think, they must have stood in much greater need of the art of thinking, to be able to invent that of speaking'.[2] Hobbes of course had tried to credit his individual man with the power of thought prior to the power of speech; but this is not Rousseau's point. 'Man hardly thinks at all by nature. Thinking is an art which, like any other, has to be learnt, and with even greater difficulty.'[3] And he objects to Condillac, as he might to Hobbes, 'that he assumes what I question, viz. that a kind of society must already have existed among the first inventors of language.'[4] On Rousseau's view, questions about the development of language and of human society go together.

If thinking has to be learnt, *how* a man comes to think will depend on the conditions under which this learning has taken place, i.e. on the nature of his education. The concept of human nature plays as large a role in Rousseau's account of politics and its relation to education as it does in Hobbes's but it is a quite different role. Where Hobbes thinks that the citizen must be taught what man's nature unchangeably *is*, Rousseau's view is that a man's nature is *created* by his education. This does not mean, however, that there are no principles on which such an education can be based. A man must be taught what his true needs are and the conditions under which they can be fulfilled. It is true that men's needs are not immutable, but are modified by their changing social environment,[5] but still, children are born into a specific social environment and we can understand their needs by reference to that environment. But social life does not merely create perfectly genuine needs, it also generates forces tending to obscure from men what their needs really are and to deceive them into thinking they have other needs which are not in fact genuine. It is for this very reason that education is necessary.

A large part of Rousseau's *Émile* analyses these obscurantist forces in social life, summed up under the general heading of 'opinion'. The analysis is closely bound up with epistemological ideas adumbrated in the *Profession de foi du vicaire savoyard* and elsewhere in *Émile*, about which something must now be said. Rousseau distinguishes between sensation and judgment. In sensation a man is passively affected by things outside himself; for this reason it involves no explicit self-consciousness, as Rousseau argues in a way reminiscent of Hume: 'For, being affected continuously by sensations, how can I know if the sentiment of *myself* is something beyond these same sensations and if it can exist independently of them?'[6] Judgment on the other hand is an activity, consisting in the comparison of sensations and the perception of relations between them. It is by way of such perception of relations that a child forms ideas of objects and becomes capable of entertaining thoughts which he can recognize as true or false. 'On my view the distinctive faculty of an active or intelligent being is the ability to give a sense to the word *is*.'[7] Rousseau argues that it is an essential concomitant of the capacity to judge that its possessor should come to make a distinction between himself, who judges, and the world concerning which he judges.[8]

> Give what name you like to that power of my mind
> which brings my sensations together and compares them:
> call it attention, meditation, reflection, or what you will;
> it remains true that it is in me and not in things, that I
> alone exercise it, although I do so only on the occasion
> of the impression which objects make on me. I cannot
> control whether I sense or do not sense, but I can control
> whether I examine more or less attentively what I
> sense.

Truth is to be found in the relations which actually do sub-
sist between objects and is to be arrived at by attention to
those independently existing relations; error, on the other
hand is the product of the judger's own activity. Hence 'the
less I put of myself into the judgments I make, the surer I
am of approaching the truth'. But this elimination of the
self from judgment is difficult; for judgment consists in the
perception of relations and one possible *relatum* which is
always present—one moreover in which I have a very special
interest—is myself. So the very structure of judgment provides me with the temptation to evaluate and understand
things according to their relations to *me* rather than according to their relations to *each other*. Moreover, I do not live
alone in the world but am surrounded by other men who are
equally attached to those judgments of which they themselves are the source. My consciousness of myself involves the
consciousness that I am an object for the consciousness of
other men and from this arises the possibility, indeed the
probability, of vanity or *amour propre*. Hence the tyranny of
opinion: in its extreme form this consists in judging according
to the relations between myself and other men rather than
according to the relations between the ostensible objects of
my judgment. I say what gratifies other men's expectations
of me rather than what I have good reason to believe true.
This tyranny is increased by the mechanism of social development analysed in the *Discourse on Inequality*, by which the
increasing division of labour increases inequalities in wealth
and prestige. The power of the wealthy and prestigious to
harm me is added to my natural desire to be thought well of

and I come to say, and perhaps even to believe, what the powerful want me to say and believe.

My judgment concerning my own needs and interests is just as susceptible to clouding by these forces as is my judgment concerning anything else, perhaps more so. Rousseau distinguishes between *amour propre* which involves a necessary relation to others in the sense just adumbrated, and self-love, consisting in a concern for my own true interests, which he regards as perfectly natural and unexceptionable. Self-love favours a clear judgment concerning what my true interests are and such a judgment requires a clear understanding of my place in the world and of my position *vis-à-vis* other men. But this understanding can only be achieved as long as I am interested in what is truly the case rather than in the figure which I shall cut in men's eyes—my own included—in professing certain beliefs.

If a man's presence in the world is for Rousseau fundamentally that of an intelligence who judges the relations between things, what is it for Hobbes? The answer is that, like everything else in the world, a man is a body that moves in certain ways, distinguished from other bodies only by the characteristic mode of his motion. Sensations are internal bodily motions produced by the impact of external bodies. These internal motions linger and reverberate in the form of images which come to be strung together into a '*consequence*, or train of thoughts'.[9] Thus there is no fundamental distinction of kind to be made, as in Rousseau, between sensation and judgment. And it is worth remarking that, at this early stage, Hobbes has failed to see the importance of grammar in making the distinction between senseless strings of images and structured thoughts, a distinction which Rousseau is enabled to make by his insistence that sensations become ideas, capable of forming part of a judgment, only in so far as they are seen as having a determinate relation to each other.

In addition to this capacity to be affected in characteristic ways by the impact of external bodies, a man's body itself moves spontaneously towards, or away from, certain external bodies: motions which Hobbes labels 'desire' and 'aversion'. These desires and aversions tend to affect the trains of thoughts which the impact of external bodies has set up in us.[10]

> For the impression made by such things as we desire or fear, is strong, and permanent, or, if it ceases for a time, of quick return: so strong it is sometimes, as to hinder and break our sleep. From desire, ariseth the thought of some means we have seen produce the like of that which we aim at; and from the thought of that, the thought of means to that mean; and so continually, till we come to some beginning within our own power.

Practical reason—deliberation—consists in the succession to and fro of such desires and aversions, along with their accompanying trains of thoughts; and the will is nothing more than the last member of such a series.

It is a consequence of Hobbes's general metaphysico-epistemological position that men's actions—i.e. the movements of their bodies—cannot be said to be 'guided' by judgments of good and evil. On the contrary, the concepts of good and evil are epiphenomenally related to those movements.[11]

> But whatsoever is the object of any man's appetite or desire, that is it which he for his part calleth *good*: and the object of his hate and aversion, *evil*; and of his contempt, *vile* and *inconsiderable*. For these words of good, evil, and contemptible, are ever used with relation to the person that useth them: there being nothing simply and absolutely so; nor any common rule of good and evil, to be taken from the nature of the objects themselves . . .

Indeed, it is misleading to speak of 'judgment' in this connection at all: good and evil are simply 'sensed'. '*Pleasure* therefore, or *delight*, is the appearance, or sense of good; and *molestation*, or *displeasure*, the appearance, or sense of evil.'[12]

In all this, then, there is no question of any sort of 'grammar', springing from the nature of the life a man leads with other men, according to which he can formulate the difficulties which arise in the course of such a life and attempt to overcome those difficulties. In saying this I want to point a contrast with Rousseau's procedure in *Émile* of developing his pupil's capacity to judge of good and evil by bringing him into relations with other men in a way which brings certain practical moral problems into focus. I have in mind, for instance, the instruction in the notion of property embodied in the clash between Émile and the gardener in Book II; and the lesson in the evils of vanity conveyed by the fairground incident in Book III. The point of these lessons, in terms of Rousseau's account of judgment, is to place Émile in a position from which he can see his actions for what they are, in their relation to the impact they have on other people's lives, and so encourage him not merely to respond immediately to his own desires and aversions.

Because Hobbes does not recognize the possibility of such a point of view he must hold that the world simply confronts an individual as something which acts upon him and is acted upon by him; not as an intelligible realm immersion in which can stimulate the growth of the understanding. For Hobbes all practical questions arising from my relation to the world— including the world of other men—have the form: what are the obstacles to my desires and how can I remove the obstacles and avail myself of instruments to my advantage?

> The power *of a man*, to take it universally, is his present means, to obtain some future apparent good . . .[13]

So one of the most important aspects of a man's ability to satisfy his wants will be his understanding of the causal processes in the world around him and the extent to which he can intervene in the operation of those processes and divert them towards the satisfaction of his wants. Correspondingly, since one of the most important features of a man's environment is the existence of other men, the principles on which these other men will tend to act are among the most important causal processes which he will do well to understand. He will try to achieve this understanding both by careful observation of the ways in which other men behave and attention to the motives which seem to make them behave thus; and also by attention to the principles on which he himself acts, which he will then extrapolate to explain the action of others. Like everything else in the world other men are, for this Hobbist individual, obstacles or instruments in relation to his desires and aversions; he will understand that he himself is equally such an instrument or obstacle in the eyes of other men; so he will realize that an important means of influencing their actions in his own interest will be the use of his own instrumental or counter-instrumental status for them as a bargaining counter. 'Also, what quality soever maketh a man beloved, or feared of many; or the reputation of such quality, is power; because it is a means to have the assistance, and service of many.'[14] It is this feature of human relationships which makes the covenant possible.

Here the fundamental difference in Rousseau's account of a man's relation to other men, as compared with that of Hobbes, is most apparent. Whereas for Hobbes it is important to know what other men's beliefs are, simply because we can thereby predict how they are likely to behave, Rousseau says roundly: 'To know what they think is an evil, if one does not know whether what they think is true or false'.[15] The evil against which Rousseau warns here is precisely that of acting so as to flatter the beliefs and expectations of other men without considering whether those beliefs and expectations are justified. He insists that any power which depends, by way of what is in fact a Hobbist mechanism, on the support of other men is illusory:[16]

> Domination is itself servile when it depends on opinion; for it depends on the prejudices of those whom you govern by prejudice. In order to make them behave according to your wishes, you have to behave according to their wishes.
>
> As soon as you have to see with others' eyes, you have to will with their wills.

His point is that such a posture is incompatible with a

genuinely independent and critical point of view in that it smothers any possible consideration of what is really the best way to live under consideration of what one can get away with in a world full of watchful eyes.

Now, of course the whole purpose of Hobbes's argument is to remove the possibility of such an independent critical standpoint. For Hobbes, Rousseau's enquiry into the truth or falsity of men's judgments—when these are judgments involving the concepts of good and evil—is an enquiry into a non-question. And Hobbes does in fact move straight from the contention that there is no 'common rule of good and evil, to be taken from the nature of the objects themselves' to the conclusion that the only alternatives are an anarchy of conflicting individual judgments or a commonwealth under an 'arbitrator or judge, whom men disagreeing shall by consent set up, and make his sentence the rule thereof'. If there is to be any sort of coherent social life, that is, all claims to independent criticism of policy proposals affecting the life of that society must be given up to an all-powerful sovereign. Rousseau could hardly have found a better advocate for his own views about the true nature of power; though he would have added that the so-called 'power' of Hobbes's sovereign is really a form of servility.

The disagreement between Hobbes and Rousseau turns on whether it does indeed make sense to raise the kind of question Rousseau wants to raise. Hobbes's way of attacking the political point of view upheld by Rousseau is to argue that it rests on the attempt to raise questions which are only pseudo-questions. That is why the issue is a philosophical one. It depends on what account we can give of judgment and, more particularly, what account we can give of judgments concerning good and evil. Obviously I cannot consider that question further here. What I shall do instead is to pursue the development of Hobbes's and Rousseau's arguments further, into the realm of the more strictly political, and indicate, with the help of Rousseau, how Hobbes's philosophy of human nature leads to incoherences in his political philosophy.

The central question of political philosophy concerns the nature of the authority of the state. The concept of such authority generates characteristically philosophical puzzlement because it seems to involve a paradox: on the one hand it seems to involve a power to override the will of the individual citizen, while on the other hand its existence seems in a certain sense to depend on the wills of the individuals who are subject to it, in that they can decide whether or not to acknowledge it as *legitimate*. Where there is not (at least some measure of) such acknowledgment, such recognition of legitimacy, one feels hesitant in saying that one is dealing with an instance of 'political' authority at all. This paradox concerns both Hobbes and Rousseau, though they cope with it very differently. To understand what they say, therefore, we must be clear about the accounts they give of the relation between power and will in a political context.

Rousseau expresses the paradox thus in Book I, Chapter III of *The Social Contract*:

> The strongest is never strong enough to be always the master, unless he transforms strength into right, and obedience into duty. Hence the right of the strongest, which, though seemingly meant ironically, is really established in principle. But will no one ever explain this expression for us? Strength is physical power; I do not see what morality can ever result from its effects. To yield to force is an act of necessity, not of will; at the most it is an act of prudence. In what sense can this be a duty?

No doubt questions of quite different sorts are raised in this passage. There is for instance a 'sociological' question about the conditions under which someone can maintain his power over a society. There is the question what sort of state we ought to recognize as legitimate. But there is also—and this is what I want to concentrate on here—the question *what it is* to recognize a state as legitimate. Concerning this question Rousseau is saying that any acceptable answer to it must allow such recognition to be 'an act of will', rather than an act of either necessity or of prudence. Let us now ask where Hobbes's account of the authority of the sovereign stands in relation to this requirement.

In Part II, Chapter 25 of *Leviathan* Hobbes devotes some care to distinguishing clearly between what he calls 'command' and 'counsel' as a vital part of his attempt to explain what sovereignty is and to locate it unambiguously in one will. This is partly because he needs to distinguish between acts of the sovereign and acts of the sovereign's ministers, who both advise him and execute his will. But it is also important for his account of the relation between sovereign and subject. For the sovereign owes his position to the wills of his subjects and he will continue to remain in that position only for as long as he more or less fulfils the expectations (the maintenance of security which his subjects had in placing him there.)[17]

> COMMAND is, where a man saith, *do this*, or *do not this*, without expecting other reason than the will of him that says it. From this it followeth manifestly, that he that commandeth, pretendeth thereby his own benefit: for the reason of his command is his own will only and the proper object of every man's will, is some good to himself.
> COUNSEL, is where a man saith, *do*, or *do not this*, and deduceth his reasons from the benefit that arriveth by it to him to whom he saith it. From this it is evident, that he that giveth counsel, pretendeth only, whatsoever he intendeth, the good of him, to whom he giveth it.

Now if 'the proper object of every man's will is some good to himself', then the proper object of the will of one who obeys a command (as well as that of the one who issues it) must be some good to himself. But in that case, a man who gives a command 'without expecting other reason' than his own will to be the reason why the one commanded does what he is told must surely be deluded. For the man commanded, like everyone else, will act only if he sees, or thinks he sees, some good for himself in so doing. So the reason why he does what X tells him to do is not simply that X has told him to do it, but rather that he expects some good (or the avoidance of some evil) to himself in doing what X tells him to do. 'The bonds of words are too weak to bridle men's ambition, avarice, anger, and other passions.' Well, if this is true of the expression of a man's will in a covenant, it is equally true of the expression of a man's will in a command: and in that case there is the added difficulty that the command expresses the will of *another* man. The expression of the commander's will is, for the one commanded, just words: words which have no reality sufficient to move *his* will unless he can find some ulterior reason why he should take notice of them. Rousseau's words seem to characterize the situation exactly: 'at the most it is an act of prudence'.

The general difficulty here is that of seeing what room there can be for the notion of the subject's *will* in the political relation, as is essential if we are to be able to talk about 'legitimacy', 'duty' and 'right' in this connection. Hobbes wishes to be able to talk like this but makes it more than ordinarily difficult for himself to do so by espousing the doctrine (which is bound up, in its turn, with much else in his philosophy) that the object of a man's will must always be some good to himself. But it is a difficult enough notion to elucidate without this complication. How can obedience to the will of a political authority ever be more than an act of 'prudence' or 'necessity'? If it is necessity, my will does not come into the matter at all and there can be no question of my recognizing the authority's legitimacy. If it is prudence, then indeed my act can be said to spring from my will; but in this case the existence of the authority is for me no more than an external fact of my environment which I have to take account of—and I shall only continue to act according to its dictates as long as it seems worth my while to do so. This once again seems to leave out any recognition of legitimacy and duty. But how can I follow the will of someone else in any other sense than these? Only, it seems, if it is somehow possible for me to recognize that will as *my* will; and in fact both Hobbes and Rousseau, in very different ways, try to establish this possibility.

Rousseau raises a closely related issue in his argument to establish that sovereignty cannot be delegated.[18]

> I maintain, therefore, that sovereignty, being no more than the exercise of the general will, can never be alienated, and that the sovereign, who is a collective being only, can be represented by no one but himself. Power can be transmitted, but not will.
>
> If, therefore, the People undertake simply and solely to obey, they, by that very act, dissolve the social bond and so lose their character as a People. Once the Master appears upon the scene, the sovereign vanishes, and the body politic suffers destruction.

This is worth comparing with the point Hobbes was making in his distinction between command and counsel. 'Power can be transmitted, but not will.' A ruler may delegate his power to a minister, in the sense that the operations necessary to carrying out a measure, even the actual decision to carry it out, are taken entirely by the minister. But in so far as the minister's actions and decisions are taken to be legitimate exercises of state authority, they are taken to be expressions not of his will, but of the will of the state (of the sovereign). If we try to think of *that* as delegated, we entirely lose the conception of measures as carrying the sovereign authority.

Hobbes had seen this point as a corner-stone of his doctrine of the relation between sovereign and subject. Yet Rousseau seems to advance the very same point in refutation of the Hobbist doctrine. Who is in the right here?

Rousseau's claim is that the notion of an undertaking 'simply and solely to obey' is anyway an incoherent one; but that even if we could make sense of it in general, it could only yield a relation antithetical to the political relation. For my acquiescence in an edict of the state must be on the grounds that it is the exercise of a power which I recognize as legitimate; that is, I accept what is decreed simply because it is the state (recognized by me as legitimate) which has decreed it. Now the difficulty is to understand the force of the word 'because' in that last sentence. Rousseau's objection to Hobbes is that an undertaking simply and solely to obey leaves no free space in which I can continue to exercise my judgment that a given decree really is the exercise of a legitimate state authority. Hobbes had wanted questions about legitimacy to be settled once and for all in the original covenant: the sovereign has to be sole judge of legitimacy—otherwise he is not sovereign. Rousseau, while agreeing with this last point, argues, in effect against Hobbes, that this is only intelligible as long as we think of the citizen himself as in some sense the *continuing* source of the state's legitimacy, i.e. as long as we think of sovereignty as vested in the citizen.

Let us look a little more closely at Hobbes's account of sovereignty in the light of Rousseau's remark that 'power can be transmitted, but not will'. Hobbes thinks of the covenant on which sovereignty is based in terms of a 'renunciation of rights' on the part of those who are to be subjects. Now we might expect that the renunciation of a right could be understood as something like a transmission of will; and Hobbes does seem to treat it like this in one context, viz. his discussion 'Of Persons, Authors, and Things Personated'.[19]

> A PERSON, is he *whose words or actions are considered, either as his own, or as representing the words or actions of another man, or of any other thing, to whom they are attributed, whether truly or by fiction.* When they are considered as his own, then is he called a *natural person*: and when they are considered as representing the words and actions of another, then is he a *feigned* or *artificial person*.

The covenant plainly creates such an 'artificial' or 'feigned' person whose acts are 'considered' to be the acts of the person represented. But it is of the highest importance that we should not forget that this is '*by fiction*': which is as much as to say that 'will' cannot *really* be transmitted.

What Hobbes does think is really transmitted to the sovereign in the covenant is power. For the 'right of nature' is 'the liberty each man hath, to use his own power, as he will himself, for the preservation of his own nature'; and this liberty consists simply in 'the absence of external impedi-

ments'.[20] To 'renounce' a right, of which transferring a right
(e.g. to the sovereign) is a special case, is 'to divest himself of
the *liberty*, of hindering another of the benefit of his own
right to the same . . . So that the effect which redoundeth to
one man, by another man's defect of right, is but so much
diminution of impediments to his own right original'.

On the other hand it is really essential to Hobbes that he
should be able to speak of the relation of subject to sovereign
in the legalistic way apparently provided by his account of
'representation'. It is essential, e.g., to his attempt to account
for the sense in which a body politic forms a unity and thus
to his attempt to provide criteria for determining over whom
precisely sovereignty is being exercised. But it is important
in a wider context too. All political philosophers have
perceived that there is a sense in which the legitimacy of a
regime depends on its relation to the special character of a
particular society. Hobbes's account of this seems to be
unequivocal:[21]

> A multitude of men, are made *one* person, when they are
> by one man, or one person, represented; so that it be
> done with the consent of every one of that multitude in
> particular. For it is the *unity* of the representer, not the
> *unity* of the represented, that maketh the person *one*.
> And it is the representer, that beareth the person, and
> but one person: and *unity* cannot otherwise be understood
> in multitude.

Now some of his most important contentions hang on this
point: for instance the impossibility of supposing there to be
any covenant between sovereign and subject. In the first
place there can be no covenant between a sovereign and a
society as a whole, because no unitary society exists in the
absence of a sovereign. And a covenant between sovereign
and each subject individually will not work. 'Sovereign and
subject' are categories created by the covenant; a series of
unrelated individual covenants between one individual and
a multitude of other individuals would not make that one
individual sovereign, since sovereignty is essentially exercised

H

over a body politic and there is no body politic where there is no unitary will. In other words the covenants which establish a sovereign must be mutually related. Of course the peculiar form which Hobbes gives his covenant is part of an attempt to solve this difficulty:

> as if every man should say to every man, *I authorize and give up my right of governing myself, to this man, or this assembly of men, on this condition, that thou give up thy right to him, and authorize all his actions in like manner.*

The importance of this formulation is that it seems to provide, simultaneously, universal mutuality and also a focus. This is clear from the way Hobbes uses it to define a 'commonwealth' as

> *one person, of whose acts a great multitude, by mutual covenants one with another, have made themselves every one the author, to the end he may use the strength and means of them all, as he shall think expedient, for their peace and common defence.*

But the difficulty is to see how there can be such mutuality as Hobbes conceives the 'each one' in the state of nature. How then can there be a passage from 'each one' to 'them all'?

Here we are close to familiar difficulties concerning the compatibility of what Hobbes says about the state of nature with what he says about the covenant. I will resist the temptation to embark on a general discussion of the difficulties here and simply emphasize an aspect of Hobbes's argument which is particularly relevant to the main issues I have raised in this essay. What I have just been noticing is the split in Hobbes's argument between a legalistic way of speaking (in what he says about 'authorization', 'transference of rights' and 'representation') and what we might call a 'sociological' way of speaking. I mean by this latter expression to refer to his talk about the 'sword', with which military metaphor he refers to social forces which *compel* people to act in a way which will maintain the cohesion of a political unit. What he does not sufficiently recognize is that the concepts of 'feigning' and 'fiction' (or, as we might say, 'deeming') which are indispensable to his account of representation are at home only within the confines of a settled legal system whereas it is essential to his purposes to be able to use them in his analysis of the conditions which make such a settled legal system possible.

The same fusion of two different types of question appears in Hobbes's refusal to recognize any distinction between questions of legality and questions of justice. Now the central contention in what Rousseau says about the relation between citizen and sovereignty is that this relation is unintelligible except in terms of a notion of justice which cannot be reduced to concepts of legality. The distinction is made clearly by Simone Weil in a Rousseauesque essay on the legitimacy of the French government in the period immediately preceding and during the 1939 War:[22]

> After 1937, the government did not merely *de facto* abandon the forms of legality—that would not matter much, for the British government did the same, and yet there never was a British Prime Minister who was more legitimate than Winston Churchill—but the feeling for legitimacy was gradually extinguished. Practically no Frenchman approved of Daladier's usurpations. Practically no Frenchman became indignant about them. It is the feeling for legitimacy which makes one indignant about usurpations.

This extra-legal conception of justice is used by Rousseau in his account of the way in which he conceives the citizen to be the continuing source of a regime's legitimacy. Hobbes had contended that talk about legitimacy can only be made sense of within the framework provided by the dictates of the sovereign will. He regarded it as a corollary that, once the sovereign has been established, no further question can be raised about his legitimacy. Here we have to ask how we can talk about the 'establishment' of a sovereign unless the act of establishment is the establishment of a rule which commits people to a certain course of conduct in the future.[23] The notion of the sovereign's *power* is insufficient to allow us to talk in this way since what is in question is precisely the warrant we have for talking of a continuing sovereign whom we can regard as *entitled* to exercise that power. Rousseau avoids this difficulty by adding to the Hobbist contention (which he accepts) that the notion of the sovereign will is required if talk about legitimacy is to be intelligible, the further contention that talk about the sovereign will (the general will as distinct from the will of all) is only intelligible where the citizens have what Simone Weil calls 'the feeling for legitimacy'.

This is as much as to say that the relation between citizen and sovereign cannot be understood simply in *quantitative* terms (Hobbes's 'strengths united') but requires a certain *quality* of life shared by the citizens. What it requires is a life in which the citizens can exercise judgment and in which they do apply that judgment to questions about the justice of social arrangements. It is at this point that the various strands in Rousseau's thought, which I tried to distinguish earlier in this essay, come together. As he emphasizes in both the *Discourse on Inequality* and *Émile*, men are born and grow up in societies which are all riddled with injustices of various sorts. This must be taken as a datum in any discussion of the possibility of political arrangements which will embody conceptions of justice, permit of liberty in the relations between citizens and state, and thereby allow us to think of the state as legitimate. That is to say, we cannot make sense of an immediate Hobbist transition from a state of nature in which considerations of justice make no sense at all to a civil society in which all justice is embodied in a concrete set of factual political arrangements. Conceptions of justice are only developed through discussions of injustices. Men capable of becoming citizens must then receive an education which enables them to understand what those injustices are, an education which consists not merely in inculcating a 'science' of what human relationships necessarily are, but rather in creating human beings of a sort who will be capable of discerning qualitative distinctions between different types of human relationship and who will therefore be capable of entering into such relationships.

NOTES

1 *Behemoth*, Dialogue IV.

2 *A Discourse on the Origin of Inequality*

3 *Émile*, Book V.

4 *A Discourse on the Origin of Inequality*.

5 Cf. *Émile*, Book III. 'Now, men's needs change according to their environment. There is a big difference between natural men living in the state of nature and natural man living in the social state.'

6 *Émile*, Book IV.

7 Ibid.

8 Ibid.

9 *Leviathan*, Part I, Chapter 3.

10 Ibid.

11 Ibid., Part I, Chapter 6.

12 Ibid.

13 Ibid., Part I, Chapter 10.

14 Ibid.

15 *Émile*, Book III.

16 Ibid., Book I.

17 As Rousseau says: 'Pour les conduire comme il te plaît, il faut te conduire comme il leur plaît' (*Émile*, Book I).

18 *The Social Contract*, Book II, Chapter I.

19 *Leviathan*, Part I, Chapter 16.

20 Ibid., Part I, Chapter 14.

21 *Leviathan*, Part I, Chapter 16.

22 'La légitimité du gouvernement provisoire' in *Écrits de Londres* (Paris: Gallimard, 1957).

23 H. L. A. Hart, *The Concept of Law* (Oxford: Clarendon Press, 1961), Chapter IV.

6

Wittgenstein's Treatment of the Will

This is an exegetical paper. Wittgenstein said in the 'Preface' to the *Philosophical Investigations* that his 'new thoughts' 'could be seen in the right light only by contrast with and against the background of my old way of thinking'. It has been argued that we are not bound to accept this. And of course Wittgenstein could have been wrong about it—it could be that the thought of the *Philosophical Investigations* is obscured when seen against the background of the *Tractatus*.

However, I do not believe that this is so: and I am going to try here to see what the *Tractatus* background *is* as far as concerns the *Investigations* treatment of the will. I believe this can be illuminating—both as concerns our understanding of Wittgenstein's thought and as concerns our understanding of all sorts of questions in philosophy.

In the *Tractatus* the discussion of the will begins at 6.373:

The world is independent of my will.

This discussion comes immediately after a prolonged treatment of the nature of causality and of 'laws of nature' in science. It turns into some reflections on ethics and value, which in their turn are linked with the final remarks on 'das Mystische'. What Wittgenstein says about the will in the *Tractatus* is the tip of an iceberg, some of the underside of which is revealed in various entries in the *Notebooks, 1914-16*. These entries reveal the enormous difficulties which the

110

concept of the will gave Wittgenstein. They also reveal something else and very curious. In a long entry dated 4 November 1916, Wittgenstein clearly achieves a major breakthrough. He suddenly introduces some ideas which are entirely new as compared with his previous entries on the subject and sketches an account which (as Miss Anscombe remarks in her *An Introduction to Wittgenstein's Tractatus*) appears to contain many of the essentials of the views developed in the *Philosophical Investigations*. Yet none of these new ideas appears in the *Tractatus*. Now two questions which I find interesting and which I want to raise in this essay are:

(1) What is the relation between this new approach and the earlier one?

(2) Why is it not introduced into the *Tractatus* treatment of the will?

I believe that some quite large issues concerning Wittgenstein's philosophy as a whole are bound up with the answers to these questions. But I have quite a long way to go before I can elucidate this.

Let me start by drawing attention to certain apparent contradictions between different things Wittgenstein says about the will in the *Tractatus*. I believe that many of these really are contradictions, but that the difficulties which give rise to them lie beneath the surface and that the contradictions themselves are not quite what they appear to be at first sight.

5.631 There is no such thing as the subject that thinks or entertains ideas.

If I wrote a book called *The World as I found it*, I should have to include a report on my body, and should have to say which parts were subordinate to my will, which were not, etc., this being a method of isolating the subject, or rather of showing that in an important sense there is no subject for it alone could *not* be mentioned in that book.

Now there are already internal difficulties involved in understanding this passage. How is one to combine the view that my book, *The World as I found it*, will have to distinguish between different kinds of event in the world according as their occurrence is or is not dependent on my will, with the view that I, the subject—that is, surely, the *willing* subject— can*not* receive any mention? How then, one asks, is the distinction in question between different kinds of event to be expressed? It looks as though whatever would show that 'in an important sense there is no subject' would *also* show that the distinction referred to is an illusory one.

It might be argued that this difficulty merely rests on a mistaken interpretation: that of identifying the 'subject' here alluded to with the *willing* subject. For in the *Notebooks* (p. 80) Wittgenstein distinguishes between the willing subject and the thinking subject, as follows: 'The thinking subject is surely merely illusion. But the willing subject exists.' Now it is not easy to reconcile this with the view that, in distinguishing between those parts of my body which are, and those which are not, subject to my will, I am 'isolating the subject' *and showing that it does not exist*. Moreover, at other points in the *Notebooks*, Wittgenstein shows himself to be attracted by the idea that thinking itself is an activity of the will and that it is impossible to conceive of a being capable of Idea, but not Will—in which case I suppose that the distinction between the real willing subject and the illusory thinking subject would have to go by the board. Interestingly he also wonders in the *Notebooks* (p. 77) whether this idea of thinking as an activity of the will is not precisely the mistake which is getting him into difficulties. But this is an issue I must shelve till later.

Tractatus 5.631 does seem to say unequivocally that there *is* a distinction between parts of my body which are, and parts which are not, 'subordinate to my will'. Indeed, how could this be denied? I can raise my arm at will, but not change the functioning of my liver—at least not directly, though I can of course do other things, like eating certain kinds and quantities of food, which will result in a change in the functioning of my liver. Any philosophy which ignores these obvious facts would seem to have little prospect of carrying conviction.

But in closely adjacent passages of the *Tractatus* Wittgenstein says other things which are hard to reconcile with this admission.

6.373 The world is independent of my will.

And again:

> 5.1362 The freedom of the will consists in the impossibility of knowing actions that still lie in the future. We could know them only if causality were an *inner* necessity like that of logical inference.—The connection between knowledge and what is known is that of logical necessity.

I shall consider this passage more closely in a moment. But it seems clear that in both passages Wittgenstein wants to place human actions on the same level as all other events. And indeed, it is clear that he thought it essential to do this, as appears in an extremely revealing passage in the *Notebooks* (p. 88), which will be very important to what I want to say later:

> The consideration of willing makes it look as if one part of the world were closer to me than another (which would be intolerable).

> But, of course, it is undeniable that in a popular sense there are things that I do, and other things not done by me.

> In this way then the will would not confront the world as its equivalent, which must be impossible.

Now the following points emerge from this passage at the present stage. First, that there are general philosophical considerations which make Wittgenstein reject what a consideration of the 'popular sense' in which I am said to do some things and not others *seems* to imply. Second, there *is some* sense to the popular way of speaking, which remains to be accounted for. Third, when this has been done, there will nevertheless remain something to be said about the will which goes beyond this 'popular sense'.

It will be best to postpone fuller examination of the first point—the general philosophical considerations which lie behind the difficulty—until I am in a position to consider the relevance of this topic to the general relations between the philosophy of the *Tractatus* and the philosophy of the *Philosophical Investigations*. But something must now be said about the second two points; and this means that a hitherto unmentioned, but vital, distinction of Wittgenstein's must now be introduced. In the *Tractatus* (6.423) he distinguishes between 'the will as a phenomenon' (which he says 'is of interest only to psychology') and 'the will in so far as it is the subject of ethical attributes' (of which, he says, 'it is impossible to speak'). Now the notion of 'the will as a phenomenon' belongs to Wittgenstein's account of acting in the popular sense, of the difference between those parts of my body which are 'subordinate to my will' and those which are not. It is apparent, e.g. from *Tractatus* 5.136 to 5.1362, that Wittgenstein wants to elucidate this distinction in terms of causality. Exposition of this point is made difficult by the fact that he claims that prediction justified by reference to causal relations can *never* amount to knowledge, on the grounds that belief in 'the causal nexus' is in general 'a superstition', so that 'we *cannot* infer the events of the future from those of the present' since 'there is no causal nexus to justify such an inference'. But I do not think that this doctrine needs to be engaged at the present point. When Wittgenstein says that the freedom of the will consists in 'the impossibility of knowing actions that still lie in the future', his point is that our predictions of our own future actions have no different basis from our predictions about anything else. The relation between the will *qua* phenomenon and the phenomenon of the willed action is like the relation between any other pair of phenomena which stand as cause to effect. This is supported by a remark in the

Notebooks (p. 77), made at a time when Wittgenstein still conflated willing with wanting (which he later came to think of as radically distinct): 'it is a fact of logic that wanting does not stand in any logical connection with its own fulfilment'. That is, whether or not what is wanted actually happens depends on conditions other than the condition merely of being wanted. So (construing willing as a form of wanting) I have to discover by experience what events are causally connected with my willing and what are not. I cannot will that anything should be connected with my will; and in *this* sense 'the world is independent of my will'. This is amplified in the *Tractatus*, 6.374:

> Even if all we wish for were to happen, still this would only be a favour granted by fate, so to speak: for there is no *logical* connection between the will and the world, which would guarantee it, and the supposed physical connection itself is surely not something that we could will.

But, for just the same reasons, my will *qua* phenomenon is *itself* dependent on conditions outside my control: on other phenomena. Wittgenstein makes this point in the *Philosophical Investigations* (I, § 611) where, obviously restating his *Tractatus* view for criticism, he says:

> 'Willing too is merely an experience', one would like to say (the 'will' too only 'idea'). It comes when it comes, and I cannot bring it about.

If the world is independent of my will, this does not mean that I am independent of the world. On the contrary, so far as I am to be considered simply in terms of the phenomenal will, I am entirely dependent on the world.

> I cannot bend the happenings of the world to my will: I am completely powerless. (*Notebooks*, p. 73)

> The world is *given* me, i.e. my will enters into the world completely from outside as into something that is already there ... That is why we have the feeling of being

dependent on an alien will. *However this may be,* at any rate we *are* in a certain sense dependent, and what we are dependent on we can call God. In this sense God would simply be fate, or, what is the same thing: the world,—which is independent of our will. (*Notebooks,* p. 74)

So it is an illusion to suppose that I can exert my will—my phenomenal will—and so make myself even relatively independent of the course of events. Now strictly this is all there is to say; for all that is left for us in any attempt to show that there is any sense in which we are *in*dependent of the world is the 'will as the subject of ethical attributes' and of this, Wittgenstein has said, 'nothing can be said'. The reason why nothing can be said of the will as the subject of ethical attributes—which I will sometimes call the 'transcendental will', both because it is shorter and also to note the Kantian analogies to what is going on here—are closely connected with the reasons why the notion of the phenomenal will cannot do what is needed and, through them, with the general philosophy of language from which all these difficulties stem. The transcendental will cannot involve us in any relation with particular phenomena—otherwise it itself at once becomes a phenomenon—and so, if it *does* bring us into any relation with the world, it can only be the world as a whole; and about *this* 'nothing can be said'.

> If the good or bad exercise of the will does alter the world, it can alter only the limits of the world, not the facts—not what can be expressed by means of language.

> In short the effect must be that it becomes an altogether different world. It must, so to speak, wax and wane as a whole. The world of the happy man is a different one from that of the unhappy man. (*Tractatus,* 6.43)

Now, whatever exactly this means, it is obviously connected with Wittgenstein's view of ethics as 'transcendental', which is hinted at in the *Tractatus* and the *Notebooks* and developed more fully later in the *Lecture on*

Ethics. This view of ethics is also of course connected with his doctrine that the existence of the will *qua* phenomenon does *not* really mean that anything in the world is under my control—his doctrine that the 'willed' movements of my body have exactly the same status as all other happenings. He says (*Notebooks*, p. 84):

> A stone, the body of a beast, the body of a man, my body, all stand on the same level.

> That is why what happens, whether it comes from a stone or from my body is neither good nor bad.

But as far as concerns the transcendental will, the position seems to be this: values are not to be found in the world; they constitute its limits; they are, we might perhaps say, a feature of how I regard the world; and this notion ot 'how I regard the world' involves the notion of an exercise of the will—in the transcendental sense. What I now want to ask is: what sense are we to make of *this* notion of an 'exercise of the will' and how is it related to the notion of the will *qua* phenomenon? (The question is, of course, closely analogous to that with which Kant was concerned in his account of freedom as attaching to the noumenal rather than to the phenomenal self and his attempt to show that one and the same action could consistently be regarded as both free *and* determined.)

In the *Notebooks* Wittgenstein seems to me to suggest two accounts of what might be involved in such an act of will which are quite different and which answer to contrary pulls in his thought. The first account is in some ways strongly reminiscent of Spinoza. It comes at page 81 of the *Notebooks*:

> Suppose that a man could not exercise his will, but had to suffer all the misery of this world, then what could make him happy?

> How can a man be happy at all since he cannot ward off the misery of this world?

> Through the life of knowledge.

Good conscience is the happiness that the life of knowledge preserves.

The life of knowledge is the life that is happy in spite of
the misery of the world.

The only life that is happy is the life that can renounce
the amenities of the world.

To it the amenities of the world are so many graces of
fate.

When Wittgenstein says, at the beginning of this passage,
'Suppose that a man could not exercise his will', he is clearly
speaking of the will *qua* phenomenon. He is asking us to
suppose a man whose experience does not include the
'phenomenon of willing' which the experience of the rest of
us is supposed to contain. But, of course, it is clear from
Wittgenstein's discussion of the phenomenal will, that
whether a man has such an experience or not makes no difference to his power to escape the misery of the world. We
are *all* 'powerless'. The supposition here is a rhetorical
device to ensure that we do not succumb to the illusion of
having some power over the course of events.

But Wittgenstein still asks of such a man how he *can* be
happy—as if there is some choice that is open to him. I think
we must clearly regard this choice as an exercise of the
ethical (transcendental) will, which is *not* a phenomenon.
And this exercise consists in taking up a certain attitude to
the world. Later, on page 87 of the *Notebooks*, Wittgenstein
explicitly talks of the will as 'an attitude of the subject to the
world'. The attitude of a happy man will be one based on the
recognition that the appearance of power created by the
existence of the will *qua* phenomenon is an illusion. It seems
to me that it must come very close to that 'patience' which
Kierkegaard describes in *Purity of Heart* as the state of mind
of a man who 'wills the Good', a notion which I discuss in
'Can a Good Man be Harmed?'[1]

The point to emphasize about *this* account of the ethical

will is that it is in terms not of a man's deciding to do this rather than that, but in terms of what one might call the 'spirit in which' he does, or suffers anything at all. The emphasis is on what has sometimes been called the 'inwardness' of the agent rather than on his external acts. It might look, then, as if one could speak of an exercise of the ethical will without running into the difficulties involved in attaching any sense to the idea that human action is the exercise by human beings of power over events: the difficulties, that is, stemming from Wittgenstein's attempt to treat this idea in terms of the concept of the will *qua* phenomenon.

Attractive as it would be for this to be the case, however, it is unfortunately *not* entirely the case. For though the distinction between the man who (to use Kierkegaard's language) 'wills the good' and other 'double-minded men' is not as such a distinction between men who do *these* actions and men who do *those*, it is nevertheless the case that such a man *will* sometimes act differently from other men. Or, if this were to be denied, we should still be left with the problem of giving an account of the difference in attitude between a good and a double-minded man and this would surely involve some reference—as it does in Kierkegaard—to differences in the ways one and the same action may be performed by different men. And such differences, being as 'phenomenal' as differences between actions themselves, do not escape the difficulties arising from the account of action in terms of the phenomenal will.[2] In other words, it looks as though the ethical will must be related to the phenomenal will after all; and some account of this relation is required.

This problem crops up in the *Notebooks* in the following way. On page 75 he writes:

In order to live happily I must be in agreement with the world. And that is what 'being happy' *means*.

I am then, so to speak, in agreement with that alien will on which I appear dependent. That is to say: 'I am doing the will of God'.

Fear in face of death is the best sign of a false, i.e. a bad, life.

Now 'being in agreement with the world' is a matter of one's attitude to the world, rather than of the particular things one does in the world *as such*. Nevertheless, there is an internal connection between the possibility of such an attitude and the particular things one does and has done. This appears from the continuation of the entry I started to quote.

> When my conscience upsets my equilibrium, then I am not in agreement with Something. But what is this? Is it *the world*?

> Certainly it is correct to say: Conscience is the voice of God.

> For example: it makes me unhappy to think that I have offended such and such a man. Is that my conscience?

> Can one say: 'Act according to your conscience whatever it may be'?

> Live happily!

If one *can* say, 'Act according to your conscience', and if this is connected with the ethical will in terms of which the worlds of the happy man and of the unhappy man are described, then it seems that *a* condition of having the attitude of a happy man is deciding to do certain things rather than others: and, failing an alternative account of action, *this* seems to reintroduce the will *qua* phenomenon.

Wittgenstein faces this problem directly on pages 76–7 of the *Notebooks*.

> What really is the situation of the human will? I will call 'will' first and foremost the bearer of good and evil.

> Let us imagine a man who could use none of his limbs and hence could, in the ordinary sense, not exercise his

will. He could, however, think and *want* and communicate his thoughts to someone else. Could therefore do good or evil through the other man. Then it is clear that ethics would have a validity for him, too, and that he in the *ethical sense* is the bearer of a *will*.

Now is there a difference in principle between this will and that which sets the human body in motion?

Or is the mistake here this: even *wanting* (thinking) is an activity of the will? (And in this sense, indeed, a man *without* will would not be alive.)

But can we conceive a being that isn't capable of Will at all, but only of Idea (of seeing for example)? In some sense this seems impossible. But if it were possible then there could also be a world without ethics.

What Wittgenstein is presumably trying to do with this example is to think of a situation in which a man could be said to have an ethical will, without having a will in the ordinary sense. It is noteworthy, though, that in the example too there is reference to *doing* good and evil: hence, presumably, doing one thing rather than another. And it seems that the notion of the will 'in the ordinary sense' is involved after all: in the decision of the man, for instance, to communicate or not to communicate, his thoughts to another. What sort of 'communication' is in question is not explained. If it is by *talking*, then this seems to involve at least some movement of the body. But even if it is conceived as a sort of immediate thought-transference—telepathy—it seems to me that nothing in principle is changed. For it is clearly being regarded as possible for the man to choose between thus transferring and not transferring his thoughts. And the outcome of this decision is being held to affect what *happens*.

On the evidence of the *Notebooks* it seems to me that this is the extreme limit to which Wittgenstein was able to take the problem, as conceived from within the *Tractatus* position. And obviously it leaves things in a bit of a mess. Now towards the end of the *Notebooks* (pp. 86–8) there

I

occurs a long entry (dated 4 November 1916), which clearly represents a major breakthrough. In it a conception of the will is developed which contains many of the essentials of the sort of view Wittgenstein puts forward in the *Philosophical Investigations*, §§ 611 ff. Here Wittgenstein raises the question: what is the 'foothold for the will in the world'. He rejects the idea (involved in his previous talk about the will 'as a phenomenon') that this foothold consists in any 'feelings by which I ascertain that an act of the will takes place', since these do not have 'any particular characteristic which distinguishes them from other ideas' (cf. the discussion of kinaesthetic sensations in relation to the will in the *Philosophical Investigations*, II, viii). He abandons the idea that the will is the cause of the action and replaces it with the idea that it is 'the action itself'; and, as a corollary, he for the first time makes a clear distinction between *willing* and *wishing*.

> Does not the willed movement of the body happen just like any unwilled movement in the world, but that it is accompanied by the will?
>
> Yet it is not accompanied just by a *wish*! But by will. We feel, so to speak, responsible for the movement.
>
> Wishing is not acting. But willing is acting.
>
> The fact that I will an action consists in my performing the action, not in my doing something else which causes the action.
>
> The wish precedes the event, the will accompanies it.
>
> Suppose that a process were to accompany my wish. Should I have willed the process?
>
> Would not this accompanying appear accidental in contrast to the compelled accompanying of the will?

Wittgenstein also seems flatly to contradict the view which appears in the *Tractatus* that I cannot know my own future actions. He says:

Then is the situation that I merely accompany my actions with my will?

But in that case how can I predict—as in some sense I surely can—that I shall raise my arm in five minutes' time? That I shall will this?

Now it is at first sight extremely puzzling that none of these ideas appears in the *Tractatus*, and I want to raise the question why this is so. The answer, I think, lies in the fact that this new account is quite flatly and fundamentally at variance with the whole conception of the relation between language, thought and the world, which the *Tractatus* expresses. And that Wittgenstein was well aware of this is shown by the remarks which I alluded to earlier and left unexplained:

> For the consideration of willing makes it look as if one part of the world were closer to me than another (which would be intolerable).

> But, of course, it is undeniable that in a popular sense there are things that I do, and other things not done by me.

> In this way then the will would not confront the world as its equivalent, which must be impossible. (*Notebooks*, p. 88)

Why are these things 'intolerable' or 'impossible'?

The reason is surely this. In the *Tractatus* my relation to the world is mediated through, and only through, the proposition. The proposition is a picture of a state of affairs and the relation between a proposition and a state of affairs is always of the same sort. I discover whether a proposition is true by comparing it with a state of affairs—by seeing whether things are in reality as the proposition says they are. But the consideration of willing seems to imply that I can be related to reality in quite a different way: that I can formulate a proposition and then not discover whether it is true by comparing it with the facts, but *make* it true by tinkering with the facts. The point is the one that Miss G. E. M. Anscombe and A. J. Kenny have both talked about in terms of 'practical knowledge', distinguished from theoretical knowledge, according as, given a discrepancy between proposition and fact, what is wrong is located in the fact or in the proposition. Kenny compares, e.g. one and the same plan considered first as appearing in a guide book (theoretical knowledge) and second as appearing as an architect's blueprint (practical knowledge).[3] But to allow anything like this is to allow a role for the proposition totally different from anything that could be accommodated within the general *Tractatus* position. Or, to put the same point differently, it presupposes quite a different conception of 'the world'.

I want now to raise the question: what, with regard to the will, is the nature of the change from the *Tractatus* to the *Philosophical Investigations* account of the way language enters into the relation of men to the world? Two points have emerged concerning the treatment of the will in the *Tractatus* which are important here: (1) will 'in the ordinary sense', 'as a phenomenon', i.e. as involving the idea that there are some happenings in the world which I can control and some which I cannot control, is for the *Tractatus* an anomaly to be explained away; (2) nevertheless, Wittgenstein was strongly inclined to say that the idea of a being capable of Idea but not of Will was an impossibility. Whether 'will' in this context is to be taken 'in the ordinary sense' or 'as the subject of ethical attributes' is not absolutely clear, though some of the passages from the *Notebooks* that I have discussed suggest the latter. I think the point really is that the thinking through of this idea is impossible if the will is thought of in terms of this distinction. The reason for (2) is not made entirely clear; but it seems to rest on the idea that thinking itself is somehow an exercise of the will. Connected with this may be the idea that the correlations between names and objects necessary for language, as conceived in the *Tractatus*, involve an exercise of will. This consideration also counts in favour of saying that it is not the *phenomenal* will that can be in question here, since these correlations are at the *limits* of the world and are not facts *in* the world.

Now, one way of seeing the big difference between the *Tractatus* and the *Philosophical Investigations* is this: in the latter, correlations between words and objects no longer have to be conceived as lying at the limits of the world in any sense which would prevent us from saying anything specific about them. Instead, 'forms of life' are treated as what is 'given' (rather than the 'objects' themselves and their correlations with names). It is argued, indeed, that it is only in the context of forms of life that we can make any sense of the idea of there being objects of a particular category, and *in* making sense of such an idea, we *also* grasp the sort of 'correlation' with a 'name' that goes along with the idea of such an object. But forms of life are, or involve, human activities, things that men do; or better, they provide a context within which we can make sense of the idea of men doing things, in that they enable us to speak of standards and criteria by reference to which human choices are made and understood: by reference to which, that is, we can see what it is for a man to have an alternative before him and to do one thing rather than another. So we can say that the human will is placed much more firmly and explicitly at the centre of the whole account of the relation between thought and the world than it was in the *Tractatus*: the 'human will', that is, in the sense in which it is involved in the 'popular' idea of a human action. It is now no longer a question of building up the concept of human action from the more primitive concept of the will (something which the *Tractatus* attempted and failed to do); rather, the concept of a human action is taken as what is primitive and the notion of the will is explained in terms of it.

In so far as, in making use of the concept of forms of life, we are concerned with actual things that people do and refrain from doing, we are concerned with what the *Tractatus* concept of the will as a phenomenon was introduced to account for. But the new centre of gravity makes it impossible to draw the sort of distinction between the will as a phenomenon and the will as the subject of ethical attributes which was characteristic of the earlier position. For it is now no longer possible for Wittgenstein to speak as he had done about the world as 'the totality of facts' and of the 'limits' to that totality. The argument of the *Philosophical Investigations* shows that it is only from within a given form of life that we can make the distinction between what is and what is not a phenomenon. The role which the concept of an action plays in our various forms of life does *not* allow for the concept of willing as a phenomenon. But to say 'willing is not a phenomenon' is not to say that willing lies outside the realm of phenomena, at its limits, for there *is no* 'realm of phenomena'; and so, in rejecting the notion of the will *qua* phenomenon, we are not forced back on to the notion of the transcendental will as the subject of ethical attributes. If the ethical dimension of human life does involve a conception of the will which differs from that involved in the ordinary concept of acting, then this too will have to be accounted for by reference to the particular features of certain forms of life, language games, and not by reference to any all-embracing distinction between what lies in the world and what lies at its limits. It may indeed be the case that certain language games (e.g. certain religious language games) do make *a* distinction between the world and what lies beyond the world, but, if so, that distinction will have to be understood as it is in fact made in such language games not as a distinction which underlies the whole possibility of language. Regrettably though, this line of thought is not followed up in the *Philosophical Investigations*, and the range of questions which exercised Wittgenstein in the *Notebooks*, which I have alluded to in this essay, is not given any further treatment. I think it is quite certain, though, that many of these questions remain and are not automatically dissolved along with the dissolution of the distinction between the will *qua* phenomenon and the will as the subject of ethical attributes as it had been made earlier.

Let me amplify the point I made a little way back about the way in which, in the *Philosophical Investigations*, the human will is given a central place in the discussion of the nature of language and its relation to reality, instead of being regarded, as it seems to be in the *Tractatus*, as an anomaly which has to be dealt with after the main outlines of the picture have been drawn. There is a very strong analogy between the *Investigations* account of intentional action on the one hand and of following a rule on the other: the latter notion, of course, being a dominant component in the conception of a form of life and in the account of language. This analogy is noticed by Wittgenstein himself:

> The grammar of the expression 'I was then going to say . . .' is related to that of the expression 'I could have gone on'. In the one case I remember an intention, in the other I remember having understood. (*Philosophical Investigations*, I, § 660)

And in the cases both of intending and of following a rule Wittgenstein insists on a point which he had equally insistently denied in the *Tractatus*—that when it is a question of my own actions I can *know* what is going to happen (what I am going to do) in a sense which does not imply that my knowledge is based on inductive evidence (or indeed on any evidence at all).

A point I feel inclined to make in this connection—one that Wittgenstein himself does not, I believe, make and which might be regarded as contrary to the spirit of the way he does speak in the *Philosophical Investigations*—is this: whereas in the *Tractatus*, the idea that I can know my own future actions in a way in which I cannot know of other events in the future is regarded as anomalous; the *only* way in which I can make predictions (not amounting to knowledge in any case) is by inductive methods; in the *Investigations* such knowledge is in a way *more* fundamental than inductive knowledge. For the possibility of inductive knowledge itself depends on the existence of forms of life in the context of which certain kinds of investigation are carried on and certain kinds of inference made—and those involve the idea (or something like the idea) of acting in accordance with established rules and standards; and the elucidation of what is involved in acting in accordance with such rules and standards *always* involves the conception 'now I can go on', i.e. the conception of *knowing* what my actions in certain future circumstances will be, in a way which is not itself based on inductive evidence.

However, talk about one thing being 'more fundamental' than another is dangerous and, in general, it is quite contrary to the spirit of the *Investigations* to attempt to find any one conception in terms of which everything else has to be understood. Certainly, from Wittgenstein's new point of view there is no difficulty in the idea that 'one part of the world should be closer to me than another'; he insists, indeed (II, x), that 'My own relation to my words is wholly different from other people's'—and it is a corollary, I think, that my relation to my own actions is wholly different from my relation to anything else. This 'different relation' will have to be explained in terms of different language games, or forms of life; and this is what Wittgenstein does (cf. I, §§ 630–1).

Here, the relation between the will and action is no longer seen as the relation between a mental process and a bodily movement. Instead, the concept of an action, in its context in certain sorts of language game, is taken as primary and then Wittgenstein asks what role the notion of the will, in relation to that of an action, plays in that language game.

> 'Willing, if it is not to be a sort of wishing, must be the action itself. It cannot be allowed to stop anywhere short of the action.' If it is the action, then it is so in the ordinary sense of the word; so it is speaking, writing, walking, lifting a thing, imagining something. But it is also trying, making an effort,—to speak, to write, to lift a thing, to imagine something, etc. (*Philosophical Investigations*, I, § 615)

It is because, besides doing a thing, our talk about action also includes reference to trying, choosing, deciding, intending, etc., to do a thing, that it is possible to drive a wedge between acting and willing. Or, more generally, this possibility arises because the concept of acting requires that agents should have a concept of what they are doing, that there should be such a thing as talking about and discussing one's actions. But the possibility of such a wedge in some cases does *not* mean that it can *always* be driven. There are cases, many and standard cases, where no distinction at all can be drawn between willing and acting.

When I raise my arm I do not usually try to raise it.

'At all costs I will get to that house.'—But if there is no difficulty about it—*can* I try at all costs to get to the house? (Ibid., I, §§ 622–3)

The fact that we have both these sorts of case (where doing is and where it is not distinct from 'willing') reinforces certain more general tendencies in our language, and the result is the idea, which we have seen to give so much trouble in the *Tractatus*, of the will as both in and not in the world.

Doing itself seems not to have any volume of experience. It seems like an extensionless point, the point of a needle. This point seems to be the real agent. And the phenomenal happenings only to be consequences of this acting. 'I *do* . . .' seems to have a definite sense, separate from all experience. (Ibid., I, § 620)

But of course this seeming is a transcendental illusion.*

NOTES

[1] See Chapter 10.

[2] It ought to be said, perhaps, that this remark of mine is more in the spirit of the *Philosophical Investigations* than of the *Tractatus*. I think that, on the *Tractatus* view, it would be misconceived to suppose such an account possible: this is one aspect of the view that one 'cannot speak' of the ethical will. But of course one has got to try to speak of it if one is to make any sense of the notion, and the *Notebooks* provide the spectacle of Wittgenstein trying to speak in a way which his presuppositions rule out as impossible.

[3] A. J. Kenny, 'Practical Inference', in *Analysis*, January 1966. Cf. G. E. M. Anscombe, *Intention*.

* This essay is a great deal better than it otherwise would have been owing to comments made by Miss H. Ishiguro on an earlier draft.

7
Trying

In his paper 'Trying and Attempting'[1] Professor Peter Heath develops an account of the concept of trying which owes much to remarks made about the relation between trying and acting by Wittgenstein in *Philosophical Investigations*. I have already discussed these remarks in 'Wittgenstein's Treatment of the Will'.[2] Heath articulates his view in some detail but summarizes his most important contentions as follows:[3]

> to talk of trying is not to describe anything, but is merely a way of setting actions in a certain context, or construing them in a certain light. The context in question is that of success or failure, and more especially the risks, obstacles or difficulties, real or apprehended, that are faced or overcome by the agent, or by which he is defeated, and which may mitigate or excuse his failure, or enhance the merit of his success.

> Hence trying is not something the agent does within himself. It is a characterisation of his doings, or lack of them, in relation to their assumed goals. As such, it may be given ahead of action, or simultaneously with it, or after the event. And by either the agent himself or someone else.

In introducing his analysis Heath alludes to the view, associated especially with H. A. Prichard,[4] that it is never our duty to do anything, but only to try to do it, since, as Heath puts it, ''tis not in mortals to command success'. The main body of Heath's paper is not concerned with this issue in moral philosophy and he remarks that he does not himself intend to question the Prichardian view. I do not think this should be taken to mean that he *endorses* that view, since the kind of account of trying which he goes on to develop seems to me quite clearly to undermine one of the main foundations people like Prichard have stood on in maintaining it. So while there may of course be features of the concept of trying—analysed on Heathian lines—which would still help to justify such a view, that is a question which must await examination.

It is important to notice that the concept of trying operates in a moral dimension. I do not mean by this the obvious falsity that questions about what someone has tried to do and the relation between that and what he has actually done or not done are always moral issues. I do mean, though, that it is very fundamental to the notion of trying we have that it enters very centrally into many moral issues and that this fact deeply affects what we understand trying to be. That is, we cannot *first* get clear about what trying is (as an exercise, perhaps in 'the philosophy of mind') and then go on to consider as a further interesting, but only contingently connected matter, how the notion of trying enters into our thought about moral matters. Rather, understanding how the notion of trying enters into our thought about moral matters must itself be a very important part of our attempt to understand what trying is. I think that this view is really supported by some things in Heath's paper: especially what he has said about the notion of attempt in legal contexts.[5] It is clear that in such contexts the difficulties about what constitutes an attempt are part and parcel of difficulties about the nature of an agent's legal responsibility for an attempted, as distinct from a realized, crime and would cease to be real difficulties if not seen against the background of such issues. *Mutatis mutandis* it seems to me that something similar must be true of the relation between the common-sense notion of trying and issues concerning an agent's moral responsibility.

Heath gives examples of cases in which it would not make sense to speak of someone as trying to do something. As he says: 'If the performance is simple, easy, direct and costs the agent no trouble, then—as Wittgenstein pointed out—it is just idle to talk of him as trying, or having tried, to do it.' But now it is certainly true, as Heath would no doubt agree, that in such cases an agent can perfectly well be spoken of as having a duty to do something. Suppose this something is paying a bill, and suppose that there are no obstacles of any sort in the way of his paying it: he has the money in his pocket, is not committed in any way to using it for something else, his creditor is there in front of him demanding payment, they are both in full possession of their relevant faculties, and so on. Here is a case, I think, where it would make no sense to speak of the debtor as 'trying' to pay his bill. So what he has a duty to do, presumably, is quite simply to pay his bill. If it makes no sense to speak of him as 'trying to pay his bill' in such circumstances, then equally it makes no sense to speak of him as 'having a duty to try to pay his bill'.

Recognizing this point seems to me in no way to contravene the principle that ' ''Tis not in mortals to command success', for in my example it would make just as little sense to speak of the agent as 'succeeding in paying his bill' as it would to speak of him as 'trying to pay his bill'. I am not claiming that intelligible applications of the words 'try' and 'succeed' are always ruled out by precisely identical considerations—and this is not a question which I mean to discuss. But it does at least seem clear that there are very many cases in which the ruling out of the one word carries with it the ruling out of the other. And this in itself is enough to show that the fact, if it is one, that ' ''Tis not in mortals to command success' in no way supports the doctrine that one can never have a duty to do something. Not all cases of doing something are cases of succeeding in doing something.

I said earlier that the kind of account which Heath develops of trying undermines one of the main foundations of the moral view I have been discussing. Let me say a little more about this. That foundation is described by Heath as follows: 'Trying constitutes the active but immobile phase before change, if any, takes place. Prichard's methods of jumping a ditch appear to be of this order. First you try and then you do it, or else you don't. And your trying is the cause of what you did.' We have to add something to this in order to bring out the full reasons Prichard had for taking the views about duty which he did in 'Duty and Ignorance of Fact'. To say that trying is the cause of what you did is to say that what you did was produced by your trying *given certain further conditions*. My italicized addition is of course of the utmost importance within the structure of a Prichardian position. In the ditch-jumping example, for instance, the further conditions will include things like the width of the ditch, the condition of the ground, the gravitational pull of the earth, atmospheric conditions, the state of my muscles and of my nervous system and so on. And what impressed Prichard was that in all cases of action there will necessarily be many such conditions which I am not able to control at the moment of doing the action which is in question. But it can only be my duty to do what it is in my power to do; and as far as actions are concerned, since their performance depends on factors which it is not within my present power to modify, the argument seems to show that it is not in my power to act (in the ordinary sense), but only to do something which is one of the necessary conditions of my acting. It can hardly be necessary for me to criticize this argument in detail here and I will content myself with saying that its fallaciousness rests, on the one hand, on misunderstandings concerning the proper application of notions like 'in my power' and, on the other hand, the false idea that 'setting myself to' (which for present purposes, with Heath, I treat as roughly synonymous for Prichard with 'trying') is something which is 'in my power' in a metaphysically radical sense in which other things are not: that is, that it is something the doing of which does not itself depend on the existence of conditions. In calling this latter a false idea I am of course being dogmatic: its discussion would involve many considerations concerning notions like 'conditions' and 'dependent', which have many different uses the relations between which would have to be properly understood for a full assessment of Prichard's position. I do not intend to discuss these considerations here.

A way of putting the Prichardian position which is not, I believe, Prichard's would be to say that what an agent actually *does* is never what he is commonly said to do but rather what Prichard calls 'setting oneself to do'. Doing has got to be wholly 'active' (cf. Heath's phrase 'the active but immobile phase before change') and anything the occurrence of which depends on factors which are not an expression of the agent's activity, is to that very extent, not wholly active. When Wittgenstein spoke of the temptation to think of doing as seeming 'not to have any volume of experience' and to be like 'an extensionless point'[6] he was describing a temptation deriving from considerations like these. Wittgenstein's move at this point was to insist on coming back to the ways in which we *do* apply the concept of 'doing'.[7]

> 'Willing, if it is not to be a sort of wishing, must be the action itself. It cannot be allowed to stop anywhere short of the action.' If it is the action, then it is so in the ordinary sense of the word; so it is speaking, writing, walking, lifting a thing, imagining something. But it is also trying, attempting, making an effort,—to speak, to write, to lift a thing, to imagine something, *etc.*

The move Heath makes is essentially the same; and it seems to me entirely the right move to make. But once we have made this move we shall of course have to say different things about duty (and about many other moral concepts which apply to actions and people, like responsibility for instance). As long as we think that what we really do is 'try' or 'set ourselves to', then, on the view that our duty is always to do (or refrain from doing) something and that this is what we are responsible for when done, then of course it must follow for us that all we have a duty to do and all we are responsible for is our trying to do something. But once the Wittgenstein/

Heath move has been made, we are brought back to saying that our duty is to do things in the ordinary sense and that those actions in the ordinary sense are what we are responsible for.

In my last remarks I have of course enlarged the area of moral issues under discussion by adding the notion of 'what one is responsible for' to the notion of 'what one has a duty to do'. In what follows I shall be rather more interested in the latter notion (and others related to it) than in the former. And I shall not concern myself with the interesting questions in Hart and Honoré's *Causation in the Law*[8] about the extent to which we can speak of an agent's responsibility for the 'consequences' of his act as well as for his act itself. I shall confine myself to the notion of an agent's responsibility for what he has *done*. Now, as I have already remarked, on views of the Prichardian type the only thing an agent has actually in the strictest sense done is to have set himself, or tried, to do something. And, as Heath has remarked, this involves looking on an agent's trying as a sort of cause of what he does (in the ordinary sense); though we should perhaps remember that Prichard was worried about saying that the relation between setting oneself to do something (viz., an action) and that action was a causal one and was more inclined to say that the strictly causal relation held between the setting oneself to and the ensuing bodily movement (event). It is the working through of what gave rise to these worries, I think, which has led subsequent writers to shift attention back to action in the ordinary sense and to try to understand trying in terms of that, rather than vice versa.

This causal conception of trying links up with complexities in the notion of responsibility. Sometimes when we speak of *A*'s being responsible for event *E*, we have in mind that *A* is the cause of (or a principal causal factor in the production of) *E*. And here *A* may or may not be a human agent. A protracted succession of freezing and thawing can be responsible for the break-up of a road surface for example; and John can be responsible for the smashing of a valuable vase in the sense that it was he who bumped into it and sent it crashing into the ground. Such questions are different from (although of course not unrelated to) questions about blameworthiness, which may also be expressed in terms of the word 'responsibility'. We may speak colloquially of the freezing and thawing being 'to blame' for the break-up of the road, but this does not mean that we regard the freezing and thawing as 'blameworthy', as deserving condemnation, in the way in which we may sometimes regard a human being as blameworthy. And even if we have established that John was responsible for (= was the immediate cause of) the smashing of the vase, this still leaves open any question about his responsibility (= blameworthiness) for that disaster. It may be, for example, that his impact with the vase was due to his tripping and falling through no fault of his own.

When actions are thought of in the Prichardian way, however, these two aspects of the notion of responsibility are brought together in a much more immediate way. The agent's trying is what he actually *does* and is the cause of the movements of his body (where such do in fact ensue), which in turn may be the cause of other physical occurrences, such as the smashing of a vase. So we may say, on this view, that the agent's trying is what is responsible (in the causal sense) for these subsequent happenings. Or we may say, making what seems a very natural transition, that it is the agent, in trying, who is responsible for these subsequent happenings. But as, on the Prichardian view, the trying is the only thing which the agent in the strictest sense *does* (which springs entirely from him as a moral being), then it is his trying for which he is responsible (in the other aspect of this word's use): that is, it is his trying to which moral blame is to be attached, where this question arises at all. It seems to be a further consequence of this way of thinking that any decision about an agent's moral blame will depend *entirely* on what he tried to do, regardless of what (in the ordinary sense) he actually did. From the point of view of moral responsibility (= blameworthiness) someone who tries to commit a murder and fails is in exactly the same position as one who actually commits the murder. In what follows I want to consider how far this is an acceptable position in itself and how far it is accepted simply as the consequence of an argument based on misunderstanding of the relation between trying and acting.

Now first of all there are qualifications to be made to the way I have stated the consequences of the Prichardian position. A Prichardian is not of course committed to deny-ing that there are no significant moral differences between the position of one who has tried to do something and failed and that of one who has succeeded. The successful murderer for example may be thought of as having acquired obligations to make what reparation he can to the murdered man's widow and fatherless children; whereas, since the unsuccess-ful murderer is not confronted with a widow and orphans, the same obligations cannot attach to him. Conversely, the unsuccessful murderer may be thought of as having acquired obligations to his intended victim, which could not attach to the successful murderer who is no longer confronted with a living intended victim. Apart from the question of doing justice to the Prichardian these considerations do point to a very important fact which has not emerged in what I have already said: namely, the complexity in the kinds of moral judgment that may be occasioned by somebody's action and the impossibility of discussing this whole issue simply in terms of the concept of 'blameworthiness'. There are also concealed complexities in the notion of blameworthiness itself which are germane to our subject.

At this point I find it impossible to take the subject further without raising issues of a more overtly metaphysical nature. Let me ask what is implied about the relation of a man to the world by a Prichardian type view of the relation between the will and action (in the ordinary sense). What seems to be implied is a very radical dualism. A man, considered as a moral being, is an active centre of consciousness. As such, he is not really *in* the world at all: the world, that is, in which actions in the ordinary sense and their consequences occur. This is something which he contemplates and, in a way which on this whole view must remain essentially mysterious, may sometimes causally affect. The mysteriousness of this causal

K

relation is brought out in Wittgenstein's difficulties with the concept of will in the *Tractatus* and *Notebooks, 1914–16*, difficulties which I discussed more fully in 'Wittgenstein's Treatment of the Will'. Thus, Wittgenstein argued with himself, anything which brings about changes in the world must itself be in the world and, if we speak of the will in this connection, it must be a *phenomenon* of which we speak. But if the occurrence of a volition is a phenomenon then it occurs subject to the same sort of conditions (conditions in the world) as does any other phenomenon. But as the 'willing subject' is *not* 'in the world', then *it* cannot be the cause of this (or any other) phenomenon. 'I am completely power-less'.⁹ So if the willing subject is to be spoken of as in any way ethically responsible, this must be in respect of a 'will' in quite a different sense: 'the will as the subject of ethical attributes', which has no special relation to anything in particular that happens in the world but only a relation to 'the world as a whole'. On the other hand, as I argued in 'Wittgenstein's Treatment of the Will', Wittgenstein was unable to give any account of how ethical attributes could attach to the will in this sense without supposing (what he thought he had shown to be impossible) that the willing subject could make a difference to what happens in the world.

Now Prichard did not see all these difficulties in quite the way Wittgenstein did. He was, for example, committed to the view that the will was a causal agency and one attribut-able to a centre of consciousness. The problems he himself raised about what exactly 'setting oneself to' could be said to cause (an action or an event) did indeed point towards the kind of incoherence which Wittgenstein was conscious of finding himself in, but Prichard did not develop the problems in this way. Nevertheless Prichard was still left with con-sequences which he *did* bring out, consequences, namely, concerning what exactly an agent could be held morally res-ponsible for. Because Prichard allowed for a causal relation between trying and phenomenal changes, he could attribute to the agent a special responsibility for those changes in the world which the agent's trying is a causal factor in bringing about, though *only* to the extent that it is *a* causal factor: it would never for him be the *sole* causal factor. To the extent that the agent's trying is such a causal factor in changes, those changes can be taken by Prichard as having a special relevance for the agent in his future deliberations about what he should (set himself to) do. But the *locus* of the responsibility for his original action is his trying and *that* is unaffected by whether or not his trying was crowned with success (which depended on other factors outside the agent's control). That is to say that, for Prichard, while success or failure may make a difference to an agent's future duties it makes no difference at all to his moral status in relation to his original act. His original act, strictly considered, was simply his trying and *that* is what moral assessment must concern itself with. So there can be no moral difference (except in relation to future duties) between someone who has successfully committed a murder and someone who has tried to commit a murder and failed. The question I now want to raise is to what extent this is a consequence which is acceptable in itself.

In discussing this question I shall operate with two simple distinctions: (1) the distinction between what can be said about the act and what can be said about the agent (a distinction implied, for instance, in the saying: 'Condemn the sin but not the sinner'); (2) the distinction between what belongs to a first-person and what to a third-person way of thinking. There *are* these distinctions, though their application in particular cases is by no means a simple matter.

I shall start by considering some of the things which can be said, from a moral point of view, about an act, say of murder. We can describe such an act as 'horrible', or 'terrible'. We can use such words of course also of events which are not acts, earthquakes involving human deaths for instance. But the horror we can feel towards a murder is not the same as the horror we can feel towards death caused by an earthquake. I do not say it is greater or less: it is different. This of course is connected with the fact that we can apply words like 'wicked' in the one case but not in the other. More interestingly perhaps, when we say 'That was a terrible thing to have done', the basis of our judgment need not be our sense of the ghastliness of the situation produced by what has been done. For one thing, no ghastly situation need have been produced by what has been done. For example a man may betray a friend to his friend's enemies and the enemies may then be prevented by further circumstances from harming the betrayed one. That does not alter the fact that the betrayal was a terrible thing to have done. And notice that we are still speaking of what was *done* and not merely of what was attempted. The man actually did betray his friend. In the case of the earthquake, however, I think that our sense of its horror is dependent on the ghastliness of the situation produced. An earthquake in an uninhabited region, which does no damage, may be awe-inspiring, but it is not horrible. And if someone objects that I am cheating by including a human death in the description 'murder' and not in the description 'earthquake', well, my reply is that this is perhaps another way of making the same point as my own. The *internal* connection between there having been a human death and the description of the act as one of 'murder' is a feature of the fact that murder *is* a human act; and this feature is connected with the peculiar sort of horror which may be felt towards such an act.

I have so far been implicitly considering this case from the point of view of judgments made by a third-party spectator. Let me now ask what differences there are between such judgments and those which could be made by the agent (the murderer) himself. The considerations advanced in my previous paragraph of course show that it would be wrong to say that the murder is just an event for the spectator and that the difference therefore lies just in the fact that the agent is considering what happened as an act. The difference lies in the fact that it is his *own* act that the murderer is considering. A man's relation to his own acts is quite different from his relation to the acts of other people. The nature of this difference will, I hope, partly emerge in some of the things I want to say later in the essay. At this stage it will suffice to give an illustration. In a very thought-provoking article about drinking and driving,[10] Molly Parkin quotes the words of a man who once while drunk knocked down and killed a youth with his car. 'He has changed dramatically', she comments and quotes him as saying: 'It's as if I'd been involved in one of the major mysteries of Life, as to Who gives it, and Who takes it away. To end another human being's life is a shocking thing. The most profoundly disturbing experience that can happen to anyone'.[11] Of course, it can also be shocking and disturbing to observe the ending of another human being's life; but again, the shock and the disturbance would be a different kind of thing from what Molly Parkin's friend was talking about.

Let us now consider what may be said of a case of someone's *trying* (and failing) to commit an act of murder. Of course, as Heath makes clear, failure is not a necessary condition of someone's trying to do something, but I concentrate on this case simply to focus attention on what may be said of the trying as such, as distinct from what may be said of the accomplished action (which may or may not have involved trying). Further, though some of the actions actually performed by the agent in the course of his attempt may themselves be horrible (such as knocking someone else on the head in the course of the attempt to reach the victim), this must be discounted here. I am interested only in what may be said of the trying *qua* trying. With this qualification made, then, it is clear that we can still say that trying to murder a man is a terrible, horrible, wicked thing; and it is also clear that these epithets apply to it derivatively: that is, because *what* is attempted—the murder—can be so described. The question I now have to ask is of course the central question: do these, and other, moral epithets apply to the trying in the same way, or to the same degree, as they apply to the doing. I find this a profoundly difficult question to answer. If one is asked outright, in the abstract: Is a man who has attempted murder as morally blameworthy as one who has committed murder? there is certainly a strong inclination to answer yes. But this inclination must be looked on with reserve. As

Wittgenstein said in another connection, it is so far only part of the raw material of philosophy. One aspect of the inclination which should arouse our suspicions is that it is an inclination to answer 'Yes, he *must* be'. That is, it is an inclination deriving from preconceptions we have about what the relation between trying and acting is; and I think they are preconceptions of a Prichardian sort. The fact that we may have abandoned these preconceptions explicitly does not prevent their still being at work in what we feel like saying about connected matters, before we have reflected on the implications for those matters of abandoning the preconceptions. All this of course is not so far to say that the answer we are perhaps inclined to give is not the right answer; it is to raise a question about whether it is the right answer or not which must be settled independently of any connection with the rejected preconceptions. Another complicating factor here is the blanket-like character of the expression 'morally blameworthy', coupled with the mauling this expression has undergone at the hands of generations of moral philosophers. So let us ask some more concrete questions about the kinds of reaction we could make sense of someone's having to a case of attempted murder as distinct from a case of actual murder.

As before, I will start with the act itself and with what a third party may say about it. Here we are at once faced with the difficulty of what we are to say 'the act itself' was. Of course, the trying to commit murder did involve actual deeds, but, as I have said, I am discounting any features these may have considered in themselves in abstraction, that is, from their constituting an attempt to murder somebody. We may of course say that trying to murder a man was something terrible, horrible, wicked; but the possibility of saying this derives from what we can say about the character of the act itself of murdering somebody. The wickedness is, as it were, reflected on to the attempt from what it was an attempt to *do*. And apart from that reflection, there may have been nothing horrible or wicked about what was actually done in the course of the attempt. This argument does not of course show that one cannot, or should not, say that the attempt was horrible and wicked, but it does perhaps show something. In the case of an attempt, there is more difficulty, in third party judgments, in distinguishing between judgments about the act and judgments about the agent. We may perhaps be inclined to say that moral judgments about attempts are, as it were, refracted on to the agent more immediately than is the case with judgments about acts, because until they reach the agent, there is nothing on which they can get a grip. There is also the possibility that a reflected wickedness will not have quite the same character as an unreflected wickedness. But I am very unsure about all this.

Let us consider some words of Christ:

'Hear me, all of you, and understand: there is nothing outside a man which by going into him can defile him; but the things which come out of him are what defile him.'

And he said: 'What comes out of a man is what defiles a man. For from within, out of the heart of a man, come evil thoughts, fornication, theft, murder, adultery, coveting, wickedness, deceit, licentiousness, envy, slander, pride, foolishness. All those things come from within, and they defile a man.' (Mark 7:14)

The emphasis here is, of course, on the coming from within, from the heart; and it might then seem possible to argue from this that Christ is saying that there is no moral difference between doing something evil and merely trying to do it. This line of argument may seem to be reinforced by Matt. 4: 27: 'You have heard that it was said, "You shall not commit adultery". But I say to you that every one who looks at a woman lustfully has already committed adultery with her in his heart.' However, I think that to argue thus would be a mistake. I take it that a large part of the force of the Matthew quotation is that of another of Christ's sayings: 'Judge not and you will not be judged' (Luke 6:37). That is, it is a warning against Pharisaism and a reminder of what we all have it in us to do, but for the grace of God. Moreover, Christ does not say, absurdly, that 'committing adultery in one's heart' is just the same as 'committing adultery'; and there is nothing in what he says to suggest that he thinks there are no morally relevant differences between the two. And again, in the quotation from Mark, although Christ emphasizes the importance of the 'coming from within', he does this in the context of *what comes* from within: *that* is what he says defiles a man. Now what comes from within a murderer is a murder; what comes from within one who attempts a murder is an attempt at murder.—My use of this language should not of course be taken to mean that I think of the action and the attempt as 'inside' and emerging from the agent in some quasi-physical sense. That would have the absurd consequence that a man who had it in mind to attempt something would be disappointed, and therefore perhaps fail, if he actually succeeded in accomplishing what he attempted! How we characterize what 'comes from within' will depend on what actually happens, or does not happen, at the level of action.—Now while no doubt a man is defiled both by murdering another and by trying to murder him, we have still been given no reason to think that they defile him in the same way. Turning once more to first-person judgments we might, at this point, go back to what Molly Parkin quoted her friend as saying and see what happens if we add the words 'try to' thus: 'To (try to) end another person's life is a shocking thing. The most profoundly disturbing experience that can happen to anyone.' While we may still want to agree with what is said in the first sentence, our inclination will surely be to reply to the second that there is at least one more profoundly disturbing experience that can happen to anyone, namely to end another person's life (as in the original version). One who fails in his attempt to commit a murder and who undergoes a change of heart might subsequently come to thank God that he failed. It is pertinent for us to ask what precisely he has to thank God for. I cannot take this any further without turning explicitly, at this point, from judgments about the act, or attempt, to judgments about the agent. Once again I shall start with the case of the agent who has actually done something, say a murder, and move on to the case of someone who has tried to do such a thing. And I shall continue to observe a distinction between first- and third-person judgments.

In saying, 'Judge not and you will not be judged', Christ was not of course recommending indifference to wrong-doing, but rather, a certain possible attitude which may be taken to wrong-doers. And my purpose here is naturally neither to recommend nor discourage the taking of such an attitude, but to try to see what the possibility amounts to. Here I think the first/third-person distinction crucial. It seems to me that what is enjoined here is that, while an offence committed by someone else is to be condemned and while, indeed, this may involve taking punitive measures against the offender, all of this should be accompanied by *compassion* for the offender.[12] And this compassion is to be directed not merely, or chiefly, at the perhaps terrible causal consequences to him ensuing from his offence and its detection, but rather at *what he has become* simply by virtue of his having committed that offence. I am thinking here of a conceptual link between the commission of the offence and what its committer thereby becomes (though without deny-ing that a consideration of what I have called 'causal con-sequences' may be relevant to that link). This conception of 'what a man becomes' is, I am sure, absolutely central to the main subject under discussion in this essay, though I am very conscious of my inability to give any remotely satisfying account of it.

My reason for saying just now that the first/third-person distinction is crucial here is that certain attitudes which we can understand as possible as between one man and another cannot be brought into play in the same way in considering a man's relation to his own life. 'Self-compassion', for example, is a nonsense term.[13] There is, notoriously, such a thing as *self-pity*, but this seems to be incompatible with, or at least corrupting of, a devaluation of, the agent's condemnation of his offence, of his remorse.

What does a man become in committing a murder? Well, obviously the first part of the answer must be that he becomes a murderer; but, equally obviously, merely to say this would be quite unilluminating. It is perhaps important that there can be no real distinction between a man's reflecting on the fact that he has committed a murder and his reflecting that he is a murderer. If he feels remorse for the murder that he has committed, he condemns himself for being a murderer; and as I have suggested, there is at least some logical tension between this and his pitying himself, while there is not the same tension (though there is psychological difficulty) in blaming another man for having committed a murder and feeling compassion for him in respect of what he has thereby become.

Remorse is backward-looking in relation to the offence committed; but it is also forward-looking. Part, but not the most important part, of what I mean by this concerns reflection by the agent on what reparation he can make. This can be a matter for inter-personal discussion and here the distinction between first- and third-person judgments may not be particularly important. Anyway, there are certain offences (e.g., murder) for which any real or adequate reparation is out of the question. Especially in such cases a man's remorse may include reflections of the form: 'How can I live with myself now, considering what I have become in doing that act?' *This* question cannot be a matter for public discussion in the same way. For one thing, it does not concern *techniques*: consider the insensitivity which would be involved in someone's saying to such a man who raised this question seriously, 'Well, you must just try to forget it'. The question can hardly be asked at all by one man on another man's behalf. Of course, another may ask, 'How can *I* live with *him*, who has done such a deed?', but this is something quite different. Revulsion (for oneself and for the other) comes into both cases, but differently. Another *may* feel that he ought to try to overcome his revulsion and treat the offender with compassion. But I think if the offender tries to think in this way the genuineness of his remorse is to that extent devalued. Moreover, there obviously are techniques which another may use: he doesn't *have* to go on living with the offender—he can break off relations. But the offender cannot 'break off relations' with himself in the same way. There are, of course, certain forms of withdrawal: cases in which we may feel inclined to say of a man, 'It's as if he were already dead. Life can hold nothing more for him'. Or there is suicide. But it must surely be pretty obvious that such things are very different from what can arise in the inter-personal cases.

I turn now to what can be said about these issues in the case of someone who has merely tried (and failed) to commit an offence. A man who commits a murder thereby becomes a murderer. What does one who attempts murder become? Again the trivial answer would be that he becomes an attempted murderer. But we need a characterization which makes perspicuous the difference between what can be said, morally, in the one case and in the other. (That there are differences is brought out by the fact that it is perfectly possible to raise *moral* objections to any proposal legally to treat attempted murderers in the same way as murderers.) Such a characterization requires some further account of the difficult notion of 'what a man becomes' in doing certain kinds of things. And a consideration which should, perhaps, have been introduced earlier is the internal connection between the notions of 'what I am' and 'my relations to the world I live in'. This internal connection may be brought out by further consideration of the idea of 'being able to live with myself'. Although 'being able to live with myself' is a different kind of notion from 'being able to live with another' nevertheless my ability to live with myself is certainly not independent of what is open to me with respect to my relations with others. When I speak of 'what is open to me' here, I do not mean simply what is, as a matter of fact, open to me, but wish to refer rather to the framework within which I can make sense of certain alternatives as possible ones but have to see others as ruled out even as capable of being considered. This framework will be deeply affected by what has been done in the past, both by oneself and by others, although what one has oneself done will have a different sort of relevance for the possibilities of one's own future life than will what has been done by others.

Consider, for example, the relations between the former Gwendoline Harleth and her husband Grandcourt in George Eliot's *Daniel Deronda*. Here, Gwendoline's problem: 'How can I live with Grandcourt' was hardly distinguishable from the problem she had of how to live with herself. The horror of the marriage derived, of course, in large part from the horror of the circumstances under which it was agreed to and, as far as Gwendoline was concerned, from the betrayal by her of Grandcourt's former mistress which was involved and all the deceptions which went along with that. It is against this background that everything she could do, or even attempt to do, has to be understood, for that background limits the possible intelligible *descriptions* of what she could do or attempt. She could, of course, and in fact did for a time, try to live her marriage as if nothing of all that had happened. But it *had* happened, and this very fact alone made what she was doing a case of self-deceit and deception of others. This is a conceptual truth although, of course, the nature of the framework which makes it a conceptual truth was shaped by past contingencies. Some, but not all, of those contingencies were her and others' actions which might have been different. But the 'external' social framework, not dependent on the wills of the participants in the novel, was of course also important: considerations like the state of the divorce and marriage laws, currently accepted moral views on what was allowable for a married woman, and so on. It was this whole framework which gave form to her problems and if it had been different, her problems would have been different too. This is not to say that a change in social or legal conditions would have eliminated all problems: it would have made the problems different. (One can convince oneself of this by thinking of the divorcées spending most of their waking hours operating one-armed bandits in Las Vegas in a framework of easy divorce laws.)

In these lamentably sketchy remarks I have tried to indicate the following things. First, that any moral assessment of Gwendoline depends on the notion of what Gwendoline had become by contracting the marriage with Grandcourt in the circumstances which existed. Second, that this notion of 'what she had become' is inseparable from the notion of what would, and what would not, be possible descriptions of her relations with other people, given the framework within which she was living her life. Third, that this framework was shaped, importantly though not exclusively, by her own actions in the past.

Let us try to imagine that *Daniel Deronda* had been a different (and much less interesting!) novel. Suppose that Gwendoline, in trying to escape the humiliating alternative of becoming an indigent governess, had *tried* to marry Grandcourt but failed. Her *actually* marrying Grandcourt was a morally terrible act. Her *trying* to do this would also have been terrible (because of the nature of what she was trying to do). But would it have been *as* terrible, and would she have been properly subject to the same moral assessment, if she had tried and failed? I incline to think not. Certainly her life would have developed differently and she would have become a morally different person. I mean that any moral assessment of her relations with other people would necessarily have been different; and I do not know how to separate *this* from a necessary difference in the moral assessment of *her*. If anybody wants to say that she would nonetheless have been equally 'blameworthy' in respect of her trying as in respect of her trying and succeeding, then it seems to me that the notion of blameworthiness is just being cut off from all the complexities of moral judgment which enter into one's understanding of what a person is; and then I do not understand precisely what sense is being attached to the word.

Let me conclude by trying to put my main point in a general way. In *doing* something evil one *becomes* something evil (one is, in Christ's words, 'defiled'). What one thus becomes is inseparable from the complex network of relations one enters into with other people which imposes limits on what can and what cannot be intelligibly said of one's subsequent life by way of moral assessment. If a man tries to do something evil and fails, then he does not become what his success would have made him and thereby the possibilities of moral assessment of him are different. It is not that the man who fails has nothing to condemn himself for or to be condemned for; but he does not have that to condemn himself for which he would have had if successful. He can later thank God he failed. What he is then thanking God for is that he did not become what he had it in him, and was ready, to become. What was 'within him' was not *realized*. The moral difference between someone who does and someone who merely tries is the difference between embracing Juno and embracing a cloud. I have never, I'm afraid, done either of these things; but I am sure they must be very different.*

NOTES

[1] *Proceedings of the Aristotelian Society*, Supplementary Volume XLV, 1971.

[2] See above, Chapter 6.

[3] Loc. cit., p. 196.

[4] H. A. Prichard, 'Duty and Ignorance of Fact', in *Moral Obligation* (Oxford University Press, 1959).

[5] Loc. cit., pp. 204-8.

[6] *Philosophical Investigations*, I, § 620.

[7] Op. cit., I, § 615.

[8] Oxford: Clarendon Press, 1959.

[9] Wittgenstein, *Notebooks*, 1914-1916, p. 73.

[10] In the *Observer Review*, 31 January 1971.

[11] The fact that this was not a case of murder does not, I believe, affect the point I am trying to make.

[12] Cf. 'Ethical Reward and Punishment'; below, Chapter 11.

[13] But see Simone Weil, *First and Last Notebooks* (translated by Sir Richard Rees, Oxford University Press, 1970), p. 94.

* I owe much to discussions with various people on the issues raised in this paper: especially James Cargile, Jeffrie Murphy, Rush Rhees and B. R. Tilghman.

8

The Universalizability of Moral Judgments

Says a writer whom few know, 'Forty years after the battle it is easy for a non-combatant to reason about how it ought to have been fought. It is another thing personally and under fire to direct the fighting while involved in the obscuring smoke of it. Much so with respect to other emergencies involving consideration both practical and moral, and when it is imperative promptly to act. The greater the fog the more it imperils the steamer and speed is put on though at hazard of running somebody down. Little ween the snug card-players in the cabin of the responsibilities of the sleepless man on the bridge.'[1]

We cannot judge an action to be right for A and wrong for B, unless we can find in the natures or circumstances of the two some difference which we can regard as a reasonable ground for difference in their duties. If therefore I judge any action to be right for myself, I implicitly judge it to be right for any other person whose nature and circumstances do not differ from my own in certain important respects.

If a kind of conduct that is right (or wrong) for me is not right (or wrong) for someone else, it must be on the ground of some difference between the two cases, other than the fact that I and he are different persons.[2]

While these two quotations do not, perhaps, directly contradict each other, it is clear that they represent two very different approaches to questions of morality. In this essay

I want to present a view of a certain kind of moral judgment, made in a certain sort of situation, which contests what Sidgwick says here and which involves, I think, a drawing out of some of the consequences of Melville's position.

How should we characterize the conflict between Melville and Sidgwick? It has to do, obviously, with the importance to be attached to the peculiar position of a certain sort of moral agent. Melville wishes to emphasize the uniqueness of this position, while Sidgwick argues that the fact that a moral judgment is made by an agent about a contemplated action of his own in no way affects what can be said about the rightness or wrongness of this judgment.

In his premiss Sidgwick asserts that if in certain circumstances I judge an action right for a third party, A, then I am committed to judging the same action right for any other third party, B, given circumstances not relevantly different. In other words, Sidgwick's premiss concerns the way in which one judgment, made by me as a spectator of another's situation, commits me to other judgments, also made by me as a spectator. In this paraphrase, I have given prominence to the fact that Sidgwick's premiss concerns the relation between judgments made by one and the same person and that that person is in the position of a spectator: two facts which are not considered important by Sidgwick himself in relation to the point he is making.

Sidgwick's conclusion treats of what a judgment made by me about the rightness of an action for myself[3] commits me to concerning judgments about the rightness of similar actions for other people in similar circumstances. It is clear that he would take this conclusion to cover the following case: I decide that a certain action is right for myself and act accordingly; another agent is then confronted with a situation not relevantly different and decides that for him the action I had regarded as right would be wrong; then, according to Sidgwick's conclusion, unless I have changed my mind about the rightness of the action for me in the earlier situation, I am committed to saying that the other agent decided wrongly.

For Sidgwick, ethics is a sort of calculus of action,[4] in which actions are considered as events merely contingently attached to particular agents. What determines the rightness or wrongness of an action is the situation in which it is to be performed; the nature of the agent can be taken into account only insofar as it affects the nature of the situation. In the final sentence of the passage I have quoted, Sidgwick speaks of 'a kind of conduct that *is* right (or wrong) for me' and 'a kind of conduct that *is* right (or wrong) for somebody else'[5] as though, as in the case of mathematical propositions, the question who is making this judgment is of no logical interest. That is what I wish to call in question.

My attention will be concentrated mainly on a certain class of agents' judgments. But first I shall say a few words about the relation of spectators' judgments to these. Very often, to think about the moral decisions and actions of other people, actual, hypothetical or fictional, is to think about general moral issues. A person's thought about these is related to his own agent's judgments in two ways. First, what he thinks about general moral issues will affect his own moral decisions; and this 'affecting' is not just a contingent relation, since to *call* a man's decisions 'moral' decisions is to put them in the context of his thinking about general moral issues. A person *can* (logically) only decide morally insofar as he decides in the light of moral considerations; and discussion and thought about general moral issues—often in the form of discussion about the actions and decisions of other people —play a central part in the development of a man's grasp of moral considerations. As Melville suggests, it may well happen that when I am confronted with an actual situation demanding a delicate moral decision from me, I find that things strike me rather differently from the way they struck me when I was thinking only generally, or as a spectator. But that does not mean that the direction which such thinking of mine in the past has taken can be left out of account in trying to understand what my view as an agent in such a situation turns out to be.

But secondly, when I think about the moral decisions and

L

dilemmas of others, it seems to me that I am very often asking: 'What would *I* think it right to do in such a situation?' That is, I am making a hypothetical agent's judgment of my own. Thus, only a man who is himself a moral agent, who is capable of making moral decisions of his own, is capable of making and understanding spectators' moral judgments about the actions of other people. In this respect moral judgments are analogous to statements of intention or statements about pain. The grammar of my attributions of intentions or of pains to other people is quite different from that of my own expressions of intention or pain-complaints; but I have to understand the grammar of first-person expressions of intention or pain-complaints, if I am to be able to make and understand such third-person attributions; and my ability to operate with such first-person expressions is an essential part of such understanding.

Because of this convergence of spectator's judgments, made by one and the same person, on his own actual and possible agent's judgments, I accept Sidgwick's thesis about universalizability, *as applied to the relation between such judgments*, which is what he refers to in the premiss of his argument. For, of course, considerations of consistency, intelligibility, and rationality do apply in moral matters; and if a man were to make different spectator's judgments of his own about the moral conduct of agents in situations which he agreed contained no relevant moral differences, there would, I think, be serious difficulty in understanding what he was saying. But to insist that, to speak intelligibly, he must *also* be prepared to say: 'And other people too, if they are to judge rightly, must make the same judgments as I have made concerning these situations', is to make a much more sweeping claim and one which seems to me highly questionable.

In moral as in other branches of philosophy good examples are indispensable: examples, that is, which bring out the real force of the ways in which we speak and in which language is not 'on holiday' (to adapt a remark of Wittgenstein's). It is needful to say this in opposition to a fairly well-established, but no less debilitating, tradition in recent Anglo-Saxon moral philosophy, according to which it is not merely permissible, but desirable, to take *trivial* examples. The rationale of this view is that such examples do not generate the emotion which is liable to surround more serious cases and thus enable us to look more coolly at the logical issues involved. On such a view what is characteristic of the ways in which we express our moral concerns can be examined quite apart from any consideration of what it is about these concerns which makes them important to us. But 'a moral issue that does not matter' is a mere chimera. The seriousness of such issues is not something that we can add, or not, after the explanation of what those issues are, as a sort of optional emotional extra: it is something that 'shows itself' (again I deliberately echo Wittgenstein) *in* the explanation of the issues. And an issue the seriousness of which does *not* show itself will not be one that presents for our scrutiny those features of morality that we find philosophically puzzling.

For an example of the sort of agent's moral judgment on which I want to focus attention I shall use the story of Melville's from which comes my earlier quotation: *Billy Budd*. I shall consider the moral dilemma of Captain 'Starry' Vere, R.N., captain of H.M.S. *Indomitable*, on active service against the French in the period immediately following the Nore mutiny, when further mutinous outbreaks aboard H.M. ships were feared at any time: a situation 'demanding', Melville writes, 'two qualities not readily interfusible— prudence and rigour'.[6] Billy Budd, a foretopman of angelic character, is impressed into service on the *Indomitable* from the merchantman *Rights of Man* on the high seas. He is persecuted by the satanic master-at-arms of the *Indomitable*, Claggart, in a campaign which culminates in Claggart's falsely accusing Billy, before Vere, of inciting the crew to mutiny. In the stress of this situation, Budd is afflicted with a speech-impediment which prevents him from answering the charge. Frustrated, he strikes Claggart, who falls, strikes his head and dies.

In the jugglery of circumstances preceding and attending

the event on board the *Indomitable*, and in the light of
that martial code whereby it was formally to be judged,
innocence and guilt, personified in Claggart and Budd, in
effect changed places.

   In the legal view, the apparent victim of the tragedy
was he who had sought to victimise a man blameless; and
the indisputable deed of the latter, navally regarded,
constituted the most heinous of military crimes. Yet
more. The essential right and wrong in the matter, the
clearer that might be, so much the worse for the responsibility of a loyal sea commander, inasmuch as he was
authorised to determine the matter on that primitive
legal basis.[7]

We might at first be inclined to say that this situation
involves a simple conflict between morality and military law.
But whilst the example does raise such questions, I do not
want to consider them here; neither are they the questions
which are at the centre of Melville's further treatment of the
story. This is already hinted at in the above description of
Vere as a 'loyal' sea commander: the point is that Vere, while
he sees the military code as opposed to *certain* of the demands
of morality, does not see it as to be contrasted with morality
sans phrase, but as something to which he himself is morally
committed. For him the conflict with which he is faced is an
internal moral one, and as such I shall treat it in what follows.
That a different agent in similar circumstances might regard it
differently, I am well aware, but this is a fact which supports
rather than undermines the general position that I wish to
maintain.

   Vere charges Budd before a summary court-martial with
the capital offence of striking his superior officer; first he
speaks as a witness to the events giving rise to the charge.
This done, he makes a speech that will repay study.[8]

'Hitherto I have been but the witness little more; and I
should hardly think to take another tone, that of your
coadjutor, for the time, did I not perceive in you—at the
crisis too—a troubled hesitancy, proceeding, I doubt not,

from the clashing of military duty with moral scruple—scruple vitalised by compassion. For the compassion, how can I otherwise but share it? But mindful of paramount obligation, I strive against scruples that may tend to enervate decision. Not, gentlemen, that I hide from myself that the case is an exceptional one. Speculatively regarded, it might well be referred to a jury of casuists. But for us here, acting not as casuists or moralists, it is a case practical and under martial law practically to be dealt with.[9]

But your scruples! Do they move as in a dusk? Challenge them. Make them advance and declare themselves. Come now: do they import something like this: If, mindful of palliating circumstances, we are bound to regard the death of the master-at-arms as the prisoner's deed, then does the deed constitute a capital crime whereof the penalty is a mortal one? But in natural justice is nothing but the prisoner's overt act to be considered? Now can we adjudge to summary and shameful death a fellow-creature, innocent before God, and whom we feel to be so?—Does that state it aright? You sign sad assent. Well, I too feel that, the full force of that. It is Nature. But do these buttons that we wear attest that our allegiance is to Nature? No, to the King . . .

But the exceptional in the matter moves the heart within you. Even so, too, is mine moved. But let not warm hearts betray heads that should be cool. Ashore in a criminal case will an upright judge allow himself off the bench to be waylaid by some tender kinswoman of the accused seeking to touch him with her tearful plea? Well, the heart here is as that piteous woman. The heart is the feminine in man, and hard though it be, she must here be ruled out.'

He paused, earnestly studying them for a moment; then resumed.

'But something in your aspect seems to urge that it is not solely that heart that moves in you, but also the conscience, the private conscience. But tell me whether or not, occupying the position we do, private conscience should not yield to that imperial one formulated in the code under which alone we officially proceed?'

The first point to notice is that Melville is at pains to emphasize the moral side of the court-martial's dilemma. For instance he has Vere distinguish carefully and tellingly between a conflict between moral obligation and inclination, in the shape of 'the heart', which is as 'some tender kinswoman of the accused', and on the other hand a conflict between two moral obligations: that to enforce the military code and that to follow the 'private conscience'. It is hard to act in accordance with the code, not just because this goes against the grain of natural compassion, but also because it seems morally outrageous to do so.

Again, and this is very important, the demands both of the code and of 'private conscience' are displayed with genuine moral feeling. What I mean is this. It would be quite possible for someone to state the requirements of military law in a purely descriptive way: according to King's Regulations, etc., this is what ought to be done.—Here the 'ought' need have very little evaluative force; we may have simply a statement of the facts about what is contained in the code. This is not how Vere puts the case. 'Our vowed responsibility is in this: That however pitilessly that law may operate, we nevertheless adhere to it and administer it.' The same point can be made about Vere's attitude to the way of thinking which he calls 'private conscience'. This, too, might have been presented 'descriptively', as perhaps: what we ought to do according to the law is clear; the prisoner is guilty of a capital offence; many would say that Budd, in natural justice, is innocent and ought to be acquitted, but natural justice is irrelevant here.—But that is not how Vere talks. 'Now can we adjudge to summary and shameful death a fellow-creature innocent before God, and whom we feel to be so?—Does that state it aright? You sign sad assent. Well, I too feel that, the full force of that.' And of course this attitude of Vere's is an essential part of the moral tragedy which is the central point of the story.

I have laboured these points because it is important to my purposes to establish that Vere is faced with a conflict between two genuinely moral 'oughts', a conflict, that is, *within* morality. I can best bring out my reason for attaching importance to this, by considering here one set of very serious considerations that writers like Sidgwick, especially from Kant onwards, have had in mind in talking as they have done about the universalizability of moral judgments. They have wanted to guard against the temptation to which we are all prone of making an exception in our own case, for no good moral reason, in order to evade a distasteful duty. For obvious reasons a view such as the one I am presenting here, which puts a certain class of *first-person* moral judgments in a special position as not subject to the universalizability principle, is liable to be regarded with special suspicion by such writers.

At this juncture it is necessary for me to emphasize the very wide variety of situations, arguments and judgments to which it is natural to apply the term 'moral'. These should be distinguished with care and it should not be assumed that logical considerations which hold of one category of moral judgment will also hold of others. It is easy to make this platitudinous remark, less easy to apply it, especially when one is in the grip of a compelling philosophical doctrine. The following passage by Singer, for instance, is by no means untypical of writers on the subject.[10]

> Hence to give a reason in support of the judgement that a given individual ought or has the right to do some act presupposes that anyone with the characteristics specified in the statement of the reason ought, or has the right, to do the same kind of act in a situation of the kind specified.

Here we find the unargued assumption that all statements of the verbal form 'X ought to do so and so' behave in the same way in this respect; that all statements of the form 'X has the right to do so and so' behave in the same way; and that all statements of the one form behave in the same way as all statements of the other form: a very large assumption. A. I. Melden[11] has shown some important differences between certain typical 'ought' statements and certain typical 'has the right to' statements. Now it seems to me likely that what

Singer says here is true of the majority of statements about rights. This fact, if it is one, is connected with the quasi-legal character of most such statements: their concern with what demands on a person may or may not legitimately be made by other persons; with social roles and spheres of influence. It is fairly easy to see the importance of having generally agreed and settled methods of settling such matters. There would certainly be something both morally suspect and logically strange in saying: 'Because of factors x, y, and z, I have the right to do such and such; but A, to whom just the same considerations apply, no more, no less, does not have the right to do it'.

There are many instances of 'ought'-statements to which similar considerations apply: notably where an obligation attaches to a person by virtue of his social role. The way Vere speaks in the penultimate paragraph of my quotation from his speech is a case in point. Though he does not appeal explicitly to the universalizability principle, it is perhaps involved in his insistence that his brother officers regard their position as analogous to that of a judge whose private sentiments are appealed to by a kinswoman of the accused. Vere's argument has the form: 'It is clear to you what the judge's duty would be in such a case. Well, just the same considerations apply to us in the present situation.' It is noteworthy that, at this stage of Vere's argument, what raises the question about what the members of the courtmartial ought to do is that they feel an *inclination* to do something different. Writers like Singer (Hare is another example[12]) are particularly interested in this sort of case; and it is true that here the universalizability principle can often be used very cogently, as Hare, I think, shows very well.

But Vere's next words put the matter in quite another context and change the sense of the problem. 'But something in your aspect seems to urge that it is not solely that heart that moves in you, but also the conscience, the private conscience.' The conflict is now no longer between the demands of morality and the promptings of however praiseworthy an inclination; it is between two conflicting sets of equally moral demands. In this paper I am confining what I have to say to agents' moral judgments made as the outcome of such situations, without claiming that it either does or does not apply to judgments made in other situations.

One important consequence of this limitation is that it should eliminate any suspicion that I wish to make possible special pleading or the making of an exception to a moral principle in one's own case. Such a suspicion would really make sense only in the context of a presumption that a person is going to evade doing what he ought to do if he can persuade himself that he is justified in doing so. Here, however, I am interested in the position of a man who, *ex hypothesi*, is completely morally serious, who fully intends to do what he ought to do but is perplexed about *what* he ought to do. He feels the force of conflicting moral demands on him. 'On the one hand I ought to do this, on the other hand I ought to do that. So what ought I really to do?' I am interested here in the force of the word 'ought' in the last question and in the answer given to it. And I shall argue that when, in answer to such a question, a man says, 'This is what I ought to do', there is nothing in the meaning or use of the word 'ought' which logically commits him to accepting as a corollary: 'And anyone else in a situation like this ought to do the same.' I am not denying that some men, in some situations, may want to go on like this; I am not claiming that those who do are speaking unintelligibly; I am not claiming that there are no cases in which anyone would be morally justified in going on like this. I am denying only that, in all cases, a man who refuses to accept such a corollary is thereby misusing the word 'ought'.

I now resume my examination of Vere's argument. As far as I can see, the two 'oughts' which set the limits of the conflict Vere is considering are, as Vere uses them, universalizable in the sense of my original quotation from Sidgwick. This is particularly obvious in the case of the military code, the whole point of which is to lay down what should be done in a certain type of case and which also contains provisions—Hart's 'secondary rules'—for obtaining an authoritative and binding decision in cases of doubt. This is not in the same sense true of the demands of natural justice about which, notoriously, opinions can differ considerably. But this complication need not concern us here since, in the context of Melville's story, no doubt at all is raised by any of the participants concerning what natural justice, or 'private conscience', demands.

Melville's use of the term 'private conscience' is somewhat misleading in relation to the point I am discussing. It is 'private' as opposed, perhaps, to 'official'; but it is quite clear that Vere is to be taken as appealing to a well-established and agreed system of ideas, according to which such cases as this are to be judged. It is misleading, though, in that Vere's speech might naturally be described as itself an appeal to the private consciences of his hearers to *choose between* what *he* has called the demands of 'private conscience' and the demands of military law. It is also an expression of the way he has come to make this choice, of the workings of his own conscience. Faced with the demands of two incompatible 'oughts', Vere reflects what he ought to do; and the outcome of his reflection is that he ought to ensure that the law takes its course. It is with the force of the word 'ought' in this conclusion that I am now concerned.

The first point to notice about it is that the admitted universal application of the two 'oughts' which have made a decision necessary cannot be deployed in order to resolve the conflict. Indeed, it is precisely because they are both taken as *uncompromisingly universal* in their application that it has been necessary to ask the question, 'what ought I to do?' If either of them were felt to swallow up or supersede the other on their own level we should not have the moral tragedy that in fact we do have. It is true that Vere's argument takes the form of putting the claims of the military code in a peculiarly impressive and compelling light; but it is not that he simply accepts the one and rejects the other, nor is it that he regards the one as extinguishing the other. After his decision the demands of natural justice remain as real for him as they were before, as is quite clear from his demeanour in the remainder of the story (a matter to be discussed presently). The agent's judgment 'I ought to enforce the law', says that I ought to do what the law says ought to be done; and this judgment is what it is only by virtue of its having been arrived at through a consideration of the real claims of the law and 'private conscience'. 'But tell me,' Vere says, 'whether or not, occupying the position we do, private conscience *should* not yield to that imperial one formulated in the code under which alone we officially proceed.' The 'should' which I have italicized is quite unintelligible if we try to identify it with the 'shoulds' appearing in either the imperial code or that of 'private conscience'.[13] And it is only because the latter are recognized by Vere as having the force proper to them that he can enunciate his 'should' with the force proper to it.

I want now to ask whether Sidgwick's thesis holds of Vere's 'This is what I ought to do' in this situation. That is, is Vere logically committed to the corollary, 'And anyone else in the same situation ought to act likewise'? To answer this I first ask myself what I would have said and done if faced with the same circumstances as Vere.[14] I try, as does Melville in depicting Vere's line of thought, to discount the possibilities of failure of nerve and softness in the face of a terrible duty; I try, that is, to confine myself to the genuinely moral features of the situation. Having done this, I believe that I could not have acted as did Vere; and by the 'could not', I do not mean 'should not have had the nerve to', but that I should have found it morally impossible to condemn a man 'innocent before God' under such circumstances.[15] In reaching this decision I do not think that I should appeal to any considerations over and above those to which Vere himself appeals. It is just that I think I should find the considerations connected with Billy Budd's peculiar innocence too powerful to be overridden by the appeal to military duty.

According to Sidgwick, and those who think like him, this must mean that I think Vere acted wrongly, made the wrong decision. However, I do not think this.[16] The story seems to me to show that Vere did what was, for him, the right thing to do. But what makes me say this is not anything that I see in his situation different from what I have imagined myself to be faced with. Before I examine what kinds of consideration I would appeal to in making this judgment, something must be said about the philosophical issue which is here at stake.

I wrote earlier of the universalizers' *moral* concern with disallowing the possibility of an agent's making an exception in his own case to a moral principle. But perhaps even more important for most of them has been the *logical* concern with drawing a distinction between sense and nonsense in moral discourse, with allowing for an intelligible relation between moral judgments and the reasons offered for them. To them it will seem that to speak as I have just spoken is to concede that anything goes in matters of morality, that morality is not a rational universe of discourse at all. One line of attack might be directed against my use of the expression 'for him' in the phrase 'the right thing for him to do'. It will be said that if I do not admit that the right thing for him to do would be the right thing for anyone to do in the same circumstances, I am ruling out any possible distinction between what a man thinks he ought to do and what he in fact ought to do. And if that is so, how can it matter to a man *what* he thinks is right; since whatever he thinks is right will *be* right.

This objection treats my position as a version of the Protagorean 'Man is the measure of all things', according to which if A asserts p and B asserts not-p, we cannot ask who is right, but only say that p is true-for-A and not-p is true-for-B. But of course to say that p is true-for-A is simply to say in a misleading way that A believes that p, i.e., that A thinks that p is *true* (not: true-for-A); so that the notion of a truth which does not depend on what anybody happens to think has not really been eliminated at all.

But this Protagorean position is not mine. I am holding that if A says 'X is the right thing for me to do' and if B, in a situation not relevantly different, says 'X is the wrong thing for me to do', it can be that both are correct. That is, it may be that neither what each says, nor anything entailed by what each says, contradicts anything said or implied by the other. But this certainly does not mean that, if A believes that X is the right thing for him to do, then X is *made* the right thing for A to do by the mere fact that he thinks it is. It was clearly important to Vere that he did the right thing and he did not think that whatever he thought would be the right thing would in fact be so.

One way of expressing what is puzzling about the class of expressions we are examining is to say that they seem to span the gulf between propositions and expressions of decisions. And, we feel inclined to ask, how *can* a gulf like that be spanned? A man in a situation like Vere's has to decide between two courses of action; but he is not merely concerned to decide to *do* something, but also to *find out* what is the right thing for him to do. The difficulty is to give some account of what the expression 'find out' can mean here. What I have suggested is that the deciding what to do is, in a situation like this, itself a sort of finding out what is the right thing to do; whereas I think that a writer like Sidgwick would have to say that the decision is one thing, the finding out quite another. It is because I think that deciding is an integral part of what we call 'finding out what I ought to do' that I have emphasized the position of the agent in all this. For it makes sense to say that a man has decided what *he* will do, not that he has decided what somebody else will do— unless this latter means that he is *predicting* what somebody else will do, or has decided to do something himself which will bring it about that somebody else does what he says.

If, as I have said, a man who decides what he ought to do has in a sense found something out, then we must have ways of distinguishing correct from incorrect judgments of this sort. A thorough treatment of this question is hardly possible here, but I shall offer some suggestions about where I think we ought to look, by considering one way in which the expression 'I acted rightly' may be used by a man who has taken a decision like Vere's. How are we to judge whether what such a man says is to be accepted or rejected? It seems to me that there are at least three sorts of circumstances in which we might want to reject it.

Firstly, it may be that the circumstances surrounding the utterance and the action to which it refers are such as to make us want to say that the agent was not really bothered about moral questions at all. A different sort of commander from Vere, for example, might have been quite unmoved by Billy Budd's 'innocence before God' and have applied military law mechanically and without torment. Of course, in making judgments of this nature we shall have to take care that their object really is as morally insensitive as he appears and also that he has not been struck by moral features of the situation quite different from those which have impressed us. But these complications, difficult though they may be to give an account of in their own right, need not be taken as affecting the present issue. The important point is that we have here a consideration which limits the acceptability of the utterance, 'I acted rightly', by insisting that it can only properly be made in a genuinely moral context—our common understanding of moral ideas enabling us to judge what is and what is not a genuinely moral context.

Secondly, there are cases where a man acts with every sign of moral concern, but where his ideas of right and wrong differ so profoundly from our own, that we are unwilling to accept his claim that he acted rightly. The difference between this case and that described in the previous paragraph is that whereas our rejection of the first 'I acted rightly' is a sort of *logical* protest, a claim that the speaker is misusing moral terms, in the present case it is an expression of our *moral* disagreement with him. One aspect of my dispute with Sidgwick is that he would want to include far more cases within this class than seems to me proper.

Thirdly, an agent may say, 'I acted rightly', in circumstances which show that he was and is genuinely concerned with the morality of what he has done, but his way of saying this, his demeanour and accompanying conduct, show that he is being insincere. Raskolnikov, for instance, after his murder of the moneylender, is faced with the bloodstains on his clothing, while getting dressed.[17]

> 'If I'm lost, I'm lost! Makes no difference! Put on the sock?' he suddenly thought to himself. 'It'll get even dirtier with the dust and there won't be any trace of bloodstains left.' But no sooner did he put it on than he at once pulled it off again in horror and disgust. He pulled it off, but realizing that he had no other, he picked it up and put it on again—and again he laughed. 'All this is just a matter of convention, it's all relative, just a matter of form,' he thought for a fraction of a second, the thought just peeping out in his mind, while trembling all over. 'I've put it on all the same! Finished by putting it on!' His laughter, though, immediately gave way to despair.

It is instructive to contrast this with Vere's behaviour after Billy Budd's execution. He is mortally wounded in an engagement with the French ship, *Athéiste*.[18]

> Not long before death, while lying under the influence of that magical drug which, soothing the physical frame, mysteriously operates on the subtler element in man, he was heard to murmur words inexplicable to his attendant —'Billy Budd, Billy Budd.' *That these were not the accents of remorse*, would seem clear from what the attendant said to the *Indomitable*'s senior officer of marines, who, as the most reluctant to condemn of the members of the drumhead court, too well knew, though here he kept the knowledge to himself, who Billy Budd was.

It is over the interpretation that I want to give this sort of consideration that the main difference between a follower of Sidgwick and myself probably lies. Whereas I want to say that such considerations have a bearing on the question, 'Did the agent act rightly?', he would limit its relevance to the question, 'Does the agent think he acted rightly?' Certainly, he would argue, Vere's death-bed demeanour shows that he did *not* feel remorse for what he had done; but this has a bearing only on whether he thought that he had done the right thing, not whether he had in fact done so. Now, as I pointed out earlier, I certainly do not want to identify doing what is right with thinking that one is doing what is right. Equally, not feeling remorse is certainly not a sufficient condition of having acted rightly; and again, feeling remorse is not a sufficient condition of having acted wrongly. However, I have not said that either of these things is the case. Vere's lack of remorse has to be put alongside his whole course of conduct during and after the trial and with the moral ideas in terms of which he was shown to be thinking during the trial. We also have to remember that it is not a *mere* lack of remorse, not a simple lack of feeling about what he had done to Billy Budd: he is, after all, murmuring Billy's name on his death-bed. Analogous points, *mutatis mutandis*, could be made about Raskolnikov's case, if anyone were to charge me with making the mere feeling of remorse a sufficient condition of having acted wrongly.

If, as I have argued, deciding what one ought to do is not a matter of finding out what anyone ought to do in such circumstances; and if, as I have also suggested, there is a genuine sense in which it does involve the notion of 'finding something out', what account am I to give of this latter? It seems to me that what one finds out is something about oneself, rather than anything one can speak of as holding universally. However, this point has to be made with great caution, since I certainly do not wish to endorse any 'self-realization' theory of morality. The important point to make is that what a man finds out about himself is something that can be expressed only in terms of the moral ideas by consideration of which he arrives at his decision. Thus Vere, faced with Billy Budd's military offence, considers the conflicting claims of his duty as a naval commander and considerations of natural justice. This leads him to an understanding of what he must do: that is, of what is and is not morally possible for him in these circumstances. But these are moral modalities. If he were asked to give an account of what the possibility or impossibility consisted in, he could only again rehearse the moral arguments which led him to his decision. But somebody else in such a situation, considering those very same arguments, might conclude that the moral possibilities were different for him without necessarily making any further judgment about what the corresponding possibilities were for Vere or for anybody else and without being committed to any such further judgment.

Hare, it seems to me, comes very close to admitting what I am saying in the following very revealing remark, made in the course of a warning that acceptance of the universalizability principle should not be taken as an encouragement to brash officiousness.[19]

> Since we cannot know everything about another actual person's concrete situation (including how it strikes him, which may make all the difference), it is nearly always presumptuous to suppose that another person's situation is exactly like one we have ourselves been in, or even like it in the relevant particulars.

So much has to be admitted by anyone who approaches the facts of moral experience with any sensitivity. But it is to admit that, within the class of moral judgments to which this remark applies,[20] the universalizability principle is *idle*.

'We cannot know everything about another person's concrete situation (including how it strikes him, which may make all the difference).' But if we want to *express*, in a given situation, how it strikes the agent, we cannot dispense with his inclination to come to a particular moral decision. Thus the situation at the courtmartial clearly struck Vere very differently from the way it struck the senior officer of marines, who was for acquitting Billy. But what did this difference consist in? Surely in the fact that, faced with two conflicting sets of considerations, the one man was disposed to give precedence to the one, and acquit, the other to give precedence to the other, and convict. If such dispositions as this have to be taken into account in applying the notion of 'exactly the same circumstances', surely the last vestige of logical force is removed from the universalizability thesis.

M

NOTES

[1] Herman Melville, *Billy Budd, Foretopman*, in *Four Short Novels* (New York: Bantam Books, 1959), p. 264.

[2] Henry Sidgwick, *The Methods of Ethics* (7th edition, London: Macmillan, 1907), pp. 384-5; quoted by Marcus Singer, *Generalization in Ethics* (London: Eyre and Spottiswoode, 1963), p. 17.

[3] For brevity's sake I shall, in this essay, speak as if all such judgments are agents' judgments. This is not in general true, since I can look on my own actions with the eye of a spectator. But this complication does not, I fancy, affect the issues that I shall be discussing.

[4] Cf. Singer's remark that the establishment of Sidgwick's thesis is necessary 'to lay the groundwork for a rational and normative system of ethics' (op. cit., p. 6). In what I say I am, of course, implicitly questioning the possibility of such a system; though this does *not* mean that I wish to deny that ethics is either 'rational' or 'normative'.

[5] My italics.

[6] Op. cit., p. 253.

[7] Op. cit., pp. 253-4.

[8] Op. cit., p. 260 ff.

[9] It should be noted that, though Vere here talks as if the issue lay between morality and military law, the appeal he makes to give military law precedence is an unmistakably moral appeal.

[10] Op. cit., p. 367.

[11] A. I. Melden, *Rights and Right Conduct* (Oxford: Basil Blackwell, 1959).

[12] R. M. Hare, *Freedom and Reason* (Oxford: Clarendon Press, 1963).

[13] I do not think it would be quite right to call these 'spectator's "oughts" '; but they are not agent's 'oughts'.

[14] Ignoring here, as far as is possible, the very considerable difficulties connected with the notion of the 'same circumstances'.

[15] Cf. Vere's locution: 'Now *can* we adjudge to summary and shameful death a creature innocent before God . . .?'

[16] The issue between a follower of Sidgwick and myself is not, of course, whether he would happen to agree with this particular moral judgment of mine, but whether I am saying anything intelligible and coherent at all, whether I am in fact making any genuine moral judgment, in speaking thus.

[17] F. Dostoyevsky, *Crime and Punishment*, Part II, Chapter 1. This case also perhaps falls into my second class; but I ignore this aspect of it here.

[18] Op. cit., p. 278. The italics are mine.

[19] *Freedom and Reason*, p. 49.

[20] That is, pre-eminently, an agent's judgment about what he ought to do.

9

Moral Integrity

In view of the title of this lecture, and so that you do not find yourselves on the edge of your seats waiting for me to start talking about moral integrity, I must explain that I shall not be attempting an 'analysis' of this concept. In fact I shall not use the expression 'moral integrity' again in this lecture. What I have to say, though, does have a lot to do with this concept, as I hope will be clear. My subject is the relation of a man to his acts, and I discuss it in connection with certain very fundamental difficulties facing a philosopher who wishes to give an account of morality. But of course much more than this is involved in asking what it is to act and there are very many relevant issues which I cannot possibly claim to discuss. But to give what follows a perspective, I want to sketch a caricature of a certain way of looking at the relation between a man and his acts, which I suspect is secretly at work in the writings of many philosophers who would certainly disclaim my caricature, if it were explicitly put to them. It is a view which the considerations that I shall try to develop count against, though I shall not have time to make this point very explicit.

The idea is of an action as a change in the world which the agent brings about. This may involve changes which are brought about 'indirectly' by a movement of the agent's body, or it may simply *be* a movement of the agent's body. Even in the latter case, though, this movement is thought of as 'brought about' by the agent. The picture of the agent involved here is, as it were, of a spectator of a world which includes his own body; though this spectator is also able, to a limited extent, to effect changes in the world he observes. So he needs to be presented with considerations which will show him why he should initiate one set of physical changes rather than another, or rather than none at all; he needs guidance, that is, in the exercise of his will. Morality is thought of by many philosophers as one such guide.

I shall approach the difficulties I think I see in this whole picture by first considering some objections to this way of conceiving morality. I shall go on to examine some examples of human situations which I think point towards a wholly different account of what it is for a man to act, though, as I said, this is not something I shall be able to develop here.

To doubt the helpfulness of an account of morality as a guide to conduct is, of course, not to deny the existence of moral guidance. But our understanding of this term presupposes our understanding of the nature of the difficulties which occasion the need for guidance. Now these difficulties would naturally be conceived as obstacles between a man and some goal he is trying to attain. And of course, men do try to attain goals and they do encounter obstacles in their way: lack of money, lack of various kinds of natural ability, lack of friends, opposition by other men, to name just a few. But morality has nothing much to do with helping people to overcome any of these. On the contrary, were it not for morality, they would often be a great deal easier to overcome. What are the difficulties, then, which morality can show us the way round? I do not know what answer can be given except to say that they are moral difficulties. For instance, a man devotes himself to building up a business and then finds that the whole enterprise will founder if he does not do something morally questionable—something perhaps that does not amount to legal fraud, and involves him in no risk of suffering ill repute amongst his fellows, but something nevertheless which he regards as morally inadmissible. Morality, we are told, is a guide which helps him round his difficulty. But were it not for morality, there would be no difficulty! This is a strange sort of guide, which first puts obstacles in our path and then shows us the way round them. Would it not be far simpler and more rational to be shot of the thing altogether? Then we could get on with the matter in hand, whatever it is.

This is in fact the substance of Glaucon's case in Book II of *The Republic*. The most desirable state of affairs for any individual would be to pursue his own concerns without any regard to morality. However, since to the extent that any individual does this, *other* individuals are going to be hindered from pursuing *their* own concerns, conventions are established to balance out opposing interests and promote the greatest happiness of the greatest number. To these conventions sanctions are attached, whether in the form of explicit legal penalties for infringements or, more informally, in the form of loss of friendship, co-operation and respect towards the delinquent on the part of his fellow citizens. Given this sort of social structure, Glaucon agrees, it is in fact for the most part in a man's best interests to toe the line and therefore reasonable for him to do so. But suppose conditions were such that this were not so—conditions which Glaucon pictures dramatically with the story of the magical Ring of Gyges, which enables its owner to become invisible and thereby to do wrong with impunity—then, Glaucon argues, people would think the owner of the ring 'a miserable fool if they found him refusing to wrong his neighbours or to touch their belongings, though in public they would keep up a pretence of praising his conduct, for fear of being wronged themselves'.

Glaucon's challenge has haunted moral philosophy ever since, obviously in the case of those philosophers who have accepted the terms of his challenge, but also, as I shall try to show, in the case of others who, having seen that the challenge is unanswerable, have just ignored it.

Consider the case of John Stuart Mill. Mill accepts the starting point of his mentor, Jeremy Bentham, that since morality is a guide to conduct, the task of moral philosophy is to make it clear *towards* what morality is guiding men, then to show what is required in order to lead men safely to this goal. Hence Mill's first question concerns 'the *summum bonum*, or, what is the same thing . . . the foundation of morality' and he immediately expands this into a question about the *ends* of human action. 'All action is for the sake of some end, and rules of action, it seems natural to suppose, must take their whole character and colour from the end to which they are subservient.'[1] Mill sees, quite rightly, that to make his case he has got to find an end which will recommend itself to any individual—since otherwise he will have produced no good reason to convince that individual that he *should* adopt morality as a guide to his conduct—and he therefore asks what it is that is required in order to move any agent to action. His answer is that it is pleasure or the avoidance of pain and, on the basis of this result goes on to produce his famous (or perhaps notorious) 'proof' that the greatest happiness of the greatest number provides the supreme principle of morality.

I am not concerned here with the details of Mill's argument and want only to point out that, and why, it rests on the assumption that what is required is some consideration which any agent can see will make it worth his while to act (i.e. to initiate changes in the world) according to the requirements of morality. If action is interpreted thus, this issue has to be raised. For surely, if to act is to decide what changes I should bring about in the world I observe, then some considerations must be brought to bear which will, as it were, bring the various possibilities of change and nonchange into relation with me, so that I can see that I have a reason for preferring one state of affairs to another. The initial interpretation of action—developed more explicitly by Mill in his *System of Logic*—separates the agent from the world in which he acts and, to make action intelligible, this gap has first to be bridged. And the concept of the agent's *interests* is the natural bridgehead on his side of the gap.

The terms of the question having been accepted, it is almost inevitable that the answer will be sought in the idea that, whereas in particular situations acting morally may be contrary to a man's interest, nevertheless, the general policy of thus acting cannot be. Mrs Philippa Foot is one of the most recent of a long line of philosophers who have treated the question in this way.[2] She argues, with some force, against the Glauconian possibility of a man's making it a general policy to pay lip-service to morality, to present the appearance of respecting it, whilst actually having his eye purely on the main chance. Her argument is, roughly, that whilst morality is adopted as a guide out of self-interest, once it is adopted self-interest becomes subservient to considerations internal to morality. In fact this argument is a filling out of Mill's thesis that virtue, having initially been a means to a further end, namely happiness, becomes a part of that end.

In so far as Mrs Foot is arguing that such a Glauconian policy would be extremely difficult, I think she is undoubtedly right. But here Glaucon would have agreed with her: for his thesis is put forward in the context of a discussion about what would be rational for the strong man as opposed to the averagely weak. It is agreed that most men are not in fact strong enough to free themselves from the shackles of convention and the question is: But suppose that somebody could, what then? And anyway situations in which men actually can and do act in ways which they know to be wrong and get away with it are not, after all, far to seek. What can be said to show them that they would not be fools not to do so? *Moral* reasons can clearly not be used here as that would beg the question at issue. As Adeimantus puts it in his supplement to Glaucon: 'When children are told by their fathers and all their pastors and masters that it is a good thing to be just, what is commended is not justice itself, but the respectability it brings.'

Adeimantus's remark brings out very clearly the impossibility of answering Glaucon's question. For the question is: What advantage does morality bring? And the form of the question suggests that we must look *outside* morality for something on which morality can be based. But the moment we do this, then 'what is commended is not morality itself', for surely if the commendation is in terms of some further advantage, the connection between that advantage and morality can only be a contingent one. And it does not matter how strong a contingent connection it is; it will still not be 'morality itself' which is being commended.

Now it may with justice be said here that the impossibility in principle of answering Glaucon's question simply shows that it is a pseudo-question. And there is indeed confusion in the way Glaucon expresses himself. Nevertheless, what has brought him into this confusion is a perception, an insight into where men stand with regard to morality, which those who avoid his confusion may miss.

This point can be filled out by considering the case of some philosophers who have not followed Mill in attempting a 'proof of the supreme principle of morality'. This is true, for instance, of Sidgwick, Moore and Prichard. Indeed, Prichard argues very incisively against the possibility of any such proof in 'Does Moral Philosophy Rest on a Mistake?' What is note-worthy about these philosophers, however, is that they have tried to replace such a 'proof' with notions like 'self-evidence' and 'intuition'. They have shown thereby that, clearly as they may have seen the hopelessness of trying to answer Glaucon on his own terms, they have not quite grasped the radical worry which underlay his question. For the effect of words like these is to suggest a sort of justification, whilst freeing oneself from the burden of actually supplying any. And if a rationalistically-minded philosopher thinks that my attitude to Glaucon's question is obscurantist, my retort is that this 'intuitionist' move is much more so.

The case of G. E. Moore is particularly relevant. In *Principia Ethica* Moore argues that there are three great divisions of ethical inquiry. The first concerns the question: What is the meaning of the word 'good'?; the second: What things are good in themselves?, and the third: What things are related as causes to that which is good in itself? It is only with the third question that Moore thinks we reach considera-tion of human conduct. Thus Moore does not see morality as a device for enabling men to reach non-moral ends; but rather as involving ends of its own peculiar sort—goods. Now this approach does indeed evade part of the objection which I raised at the start of this lecture to the conception of morality as a guide to conduct. For along with the idea that morality involves the pursuit of ends peculiar to itself goes the possibility that there may be difficulties in the way of attaining those ends which are peculiar to morality, in so far, for example, as the attainment of one moral end may conflict with the attainment of another. But Moore's account involves difficulties of its own, of which perhaps the most fundamental is this. If, as Moore says, to say that something is good is simply to state a fact about it, then surely some further argument is needed in order to show why a man should aim at producing something of that kind. This demand is likely to be made especially strongly by someone to whom it seems—not obviously falsely—that the difficulty and distress involved in morality considerably outweighs the satisfaction involved in the so-called 'attainment of moral ends'. It is plainly not enough for Moore to rest his case on the contingent fact that men happen to want to produce things which are good, and indeed he does not do so. He thinks rather that it is just self-evident that men ought to do what will produce good things. As John Anderson has pointed out,[3] in the most incisive criticism of Moore's ethics that I know, Moore fails to see the difficulty here because of the way he talks about the intrinsically good as that which is 'desirable in itself'; that is, as Anderson puts it, he smuggles into what is supposed to be simply a property of something the idea of an essential relation which that thing is supposed to have to something else: namely, being desired by, or required of, human beings. So he gives the impression of having offered a reason why men should behave morally without in fact having done so.

It is characteristic of many of the philosophers I have mentioned that they think of the relation of morality to conduct in terms of the reason a man has for doing one thing rather than another. A philosopher of very different style who has sharply criticized this conception is Jean-Paul Sartre who said, perhaps with exaggeration but still with point, that when I come to deliberate—to consider reasons for and against doing something—'*les jeux sont faits*' ('the chips are down').[4] If we wish to understand the moral character of a particular man and his acts it is, often at any rate, not enough to notice that, for such and such reasons, he chooses a given course of action from among those he considers as alternatives. It may be at least as important to notice *what he considers the alternatives to be* and, what is closely connected, what are the reasons he considers it relevant to deploy in deciding between them. Thus one kind of difference between two men is that in which, agreeing about what the issues are with which their identical situations present them, they decide differently in the light of those issues. But an even more important difference—and the kind Sartre is alluding to—is that in which they cannot even agree in their descriptions of the situation and in their account of the issues raised by it. For one man, for instance, a situation will raise a moral issue; for another, it will not.

Let me express this point by saying that a situation, the issues which it raises and the kind of reason which is appropriate to a discussion of those issues, involve a certain perspective. If I had to say shortly how I take the agent in the situation to be related to such a perspective I should say, as I think would Sartre, that the agent *is* this perspective. I should not follow Sartre much further here. I think he is led badly astray by his failure to see clearly that the *possibility* of there being a certain perspective on a situation cannot be led back to any agent's choice. It depends rather on the language which is available, a language which is not any individual's invention—though again Sartre often talks as if it is.

I have avoided equating the perspective from which an action is performed with the notion of an agent's 'will'. My reasons for this can be brought out by considering some difficulties in the account of action implicit in Kant's moral philosophy. What is distinctive about Kant's starting point is his refusal to locate that 'which could be held good without qualification' in any state of affairs which the human will could bring about by its actions, but rather in the 'good will' itself.[5] But Kant is very unclear about how we should conceive the relation between a man's will and his actions. He thinks of the will as a certain sort of *causal* principle and this is a conception he shares with his Utilitarian opponents, even though he and they no doubt give very different accounts of the kind of causality which is supposed to be involved. In line with this conception Kant finds it necessary to produce guiding rules for the will, instructing it as to which phenomenal changes it shall bring about and which not. What he does *not* see is that this project is quite incompatible with his view that the *summum bonum* is located in the will itself. Though he tries to base these guiding rules on the mere concept of the good will, it is clear that he is in fact forced to fall back on precisely that kind of utilitarian consideration which he has rejected as irrelevant to morality. Bentham saw this and concluded that anyone who wishes to produce rules for the guidance of the will in morality cannot but be a more or less disguised utilitarian. There may be some force in this. But it does not follow, as Bentham thought, that Utilitarianism is the only viable moral philosophy. Another possible conclusion is that it is thoroughly misconceived to suppose that philosophy can provide rules for the moral guidance of the will at all.

The difficulties in Kant's conception of the will are closely connected with difficulties in his conception of rationality. (Indeed he identifies the will with practical reason.) From the fact that logical principles cannot be understood as empirical generalizations Kant concludes that rationality must be a purely *a priori* concept—as if the rationality manifested in actual human behaviour were simply an application of principles the validity of which can be understood quite apart from their empirical applications. Since he thinks of moral conduct as a particular sort of application of such *a priori* principles, he supposes that we have a criterion *a priori* for deciding whether any given piece of behaviour is morally right or not. The criterion is to the effect that a piece of behaviour is morally right if and only if it has been performed for the sake of a rational principle itself, that is, according to

Kant's argument, for the sake of duty. But, as I have suggested, Kant is unable to give 'duty' any content without falling back on other, non-formal, considerations so that our recognition of actual kinds of behaviour as cases of 'acting for the sake of duty' are found to depend, contrary to Kant's most fundamental intentions, on kinds of fact which *cannot* be regarded as 'good with qualification'. My conclusion is borne out if we turn from abstract argument to examination of actual cases.

Mrs Solness, in Ibsen's *The Master Builder*, is someone who is obsessed with the Kantian idea of 'acting for the sake of duty'. She does not appear, though, as a paragon of moral purity but rather as a paradigm of a certain sort of moral corruption. No doubt her constant appeal to duty is a defence against the dangerous and evil resentments she harbours within her. For all that, it is possible to think that the situation would have been a good deal less evil if she had occasionally forgotten her 'duty' and let herself go. At least this might have cleared the air and opened the way for some genuine human relationships between herself and her fellow-characters—relationships which are conspicuously lacking in the scene as Ibsen presents it. It may be said that it is unfair to Kant to take such a corrupt case of 'acting for the sake of duty' as this. But my point is that Kant's treatment stands in the way of seeing just what is corrupt about Mrs Solness's case. For Kant has insisted that the good will is the *only* thing of which a corrupt case cannot be found. My argument is that his attempt to give positive criteria of the good will in terms of maxims regarded as universally valid laws of conduct is incompatible with that initial contention. In this matter Kierkegaard is much clearer-headed than Kant. Kierkegaard does not try to say what 'purity of heart' consists in, rather he discusses directly the application of the concept to particular examples. In this discussion the emphasis is on various kinds of corruption, or doublemindedness. Kierkegaard's procedure may be characterized by way of a distinction of Wittgenstein's. He does not attempt to *say* what purity of heart is; he *shows* what it is by portraying various cases.

Kant's position not only forces us to accept as 'good without qualification' kinds of behaviour which we may quite legitimately think are not. It also prevents us from recognizing as 'good without qualification' kinds of behaviour which we may quite legitimately think are. Thus Simone Weil offers as an example of an absolutely 'pure' action the case of a father playing with his child—not out of a sense of duty but out of pure joy and pleasure. Kant would have to classify this as a case of acting from 'inclination' rather than from 'practical reason' and hence as possessing no moral value, though he might perhaps allow that it is aesthetically pleasing. But let us consider the case of a man who finds himself unable to enjoy himself spontaneously with his child; though he goes out of his way to entertain the child out of a sense of his duty as a father. May he not quite well regard his relative lack of spontaneity, *vis-à-vis* the father in Simone Weil's example, as a *moral* failing? Can he not, without confusion, regard himself as 'a worse man' than the other?[6] And would that be an 'aesthetic' judgment?

Now some people will have objections to my way of treating these examples. It may, first, be thought that, in emphasizing the positive value of spontaneity I am offering an alternative to Kant's 'acting for the sake of duty' as that which is good without qualification. And to this it could rightly be objected that there are other cases where I should have to agree that acting as one spontaneously felt inclined to would be quite wrong and where it would be right to curb one's inclinations from considerations of what duty requires. With this I completely agree; but it is not an objection to anything that I want to say. For I am not trying to *replace* Kant's contention that acting for the sake of duty is the only kind of behaviour which is good without qualification with the counter-contention that acting spontaneously is the only kind of behaviour which is good without qualification. On the contrary, my contention is that there is *no* general kind of behaviour of which we have to say that it is good without qualification. Kant's mistake, that is, lies in trying to fill out the view that only the good will can be called good without qualification with a positive account of the kind of behaviour in which a good will *must* manifest itself. All we can do, I am arguing, is to look at particular examples and see what we *do* want to say about them; there are no general rules which can determine in advance what we *must* say about them.

But doesn't this result in making what we happen to say about any particular case entirely arbitrary? No more than many of the things we say in countless other dimensions than the moral are arbitrary. If I am asked what colour this desk is, I shall call it 'brown'. But how should I justify calling it brown? I could not do this; this is just what I call brown. Is it not, though, that there is a general rule laying down that I shall call 'brown' only things which resemble other things in a certain respect? But in what respect? In respect of being brown! To specify the respect in which this desk has to resemble other things if I am to be justified in calling it brown, my willingness to call it brown is already presupposed. And that is no justification at all.

The question of what it is to attribute an action to an agent is one which greatly exercised Kant. His position was that where an action is performed 'from inclination' the cause of the action does not lie in the agent himself and the action is, therefore, not 'autonomously' the agent's. And he mistakenly thought that the idea of 'acting for the sake of something' had to be emphasized if such autonomy were to be accounted for at all. The weight of Kant's case rests on his treatment of the way in which two outwardly similar pieces of behaviour may nevertheless differ completely in moral significance.

A man who repays a debt to avoid criminal proceedings may happen to act 'in accordance with duty' but he is very differently related to his act from the man who repays the debt simply because he owes it, without thought of any unpleasant consequences to him ensuing from his not paying it. The obvious importance of the distinction between these two cases should not blind us to the possibility that Kant's account of it is faulty. His account consists basically in seeing the relation of the act to the agent in terms of the principle, or 'maxim', according to which the agent is supposed to be acting. But this account will not cover all cases.

Is it right to say that the man who repays the money because he owes it, and not out of fear of the debtor's prison, is acting 'for the sake of duty'? Well, I feel like saying that the man whose guiding thought is 'He lent me this money and I must repay it', different as he is from the man whose thought is 'If I don't repay it I shall be sent to prison', is just as importantly different from the man whose thought is 'I must repay this money in order to fulfil my duty.' Perhaps the distinction is clearer if we return to the case of Mrs Solness. When Hilda Wangel arrives at the Solnesses' house as a guest, Mrs Solness, in splendid Kantian tones, says: 'I'll do my best for you. That's no more than my duty.'[7] How very differently we should have regarded her if she had said: 'Do come and see your room. I hope you will be comfortable there and enjoy your stay.' Certainly in the latter case the conception of the relation between host and guest and the duties involved in that relation would still enter into our understanding of the situation, but not in the form of something 'for the sake of which' the action is performed. Similarly in the case of Simone Weil's example of father playing with child: the force of the example does depend on what we understand of the relation between father and child, which does include, of course, the idea of certain duties and responsibilities; but equally the force of the example depends on the fact that the father is not behaving as he is for the sake of fulfilling his duties. I also want to resist a suggestion that many philosophers would make here: namely that the father is doing what he is doing 'for its own sake'. The trouble with this locution is that it makes his behaviour *too like* that in which a man does what he does for the sake of something else—as if the father thought that a situation in which a parent plays with his child has positive value in itself and played with his child *for that reason*, rather than because he thought that doing so would be conducive to further consequences which he positively valued. That is a possible case too; but it is not the sort of case which Simone

Weil presents us with, nor is it a sort of case which she would have described as having the sort of 'purity' which she does ascribe to her actual example.

We might speak of the father in this example as 'absorbed in' what he is doing and my suggestion is that we do not always need to think of a man's action as performed by him in accordance with some principle ('maxim') in order to think of it as unequivocally *his* act and to attach moral value to it. The case of Oedipus may make clearer what I am saying. Here we might almost want to speak of Oedipus as having been 'absorbed by' what he has done. Oedipus did not intend to kill his father and marry his mother; he would have acted differently if he had known the true nature of what he was doing but was in a position in which, in an important sense, it was not within his power to know this. On Kantian principles what we *must* say here is that Oedipus is in no way responsible for his actions (at least under these descriptions) and that no question of blame can possibly arise.

Now I realize that many people would in fact say this and I have nothing to say here against someone who, as a matter of fact, takes such a view. I do, however, have something to say against a philosopher who argues, on Kantian lines, that this is the only possible coherent view to take. Oedipus undoubtedly blamed himself for what he had done. Was this irrational of him in view of the circumstances? Well, there is one important feature of the situation which we should not lose sight of, namely that Oedipus had *done* those things— married his mother and killed his father, even if he had not intended them. For this reason his perspective on those happenings was quite different from that of an onlooker on natural happenings. I do not find it at all difficult to understand that he should blame himself in these circumstances; neither do I feel inclined to say that it was irrational for him to do so. I do not say this from any facile idea that 'Greek moral concepts were quite different from ours'. My point is that people seem to me over-hasty in asserting that our contemporary moral concepts preclude the possibility of a judgment like this.

When I say 'I can understand Oedipus blaming himself', I do not of course mean that I should want to blame him too. That is a different issue. Blaming oneself is quite a different matter from blaming other people—a difference which is marked by our having a special word for it: 'remorse'. If Oedipus had intended what he did, I might indeed think it appropriate for me to blame him. As it is, the appropriate reaction is surely one of pity, the attitude which Sophocles' play invites from us. But for what are we invited to pity him? Not, I think, just for the terrible consequences which befall him when his deeds are discovered, for though we could indeed pity another man to whom, for quite different reasons, such things happened, it would not be the same sort of pity. The pity we feel for Oedipus is inextricably connected with our realization of what he has *done* and with our understanding that these are actions for which he could not help blaming himself. What makes the consequences so terrible is precisely *what* they are consequences *of*; they are, as it were, the vehicle which carries our understanding of what Oedipus is by virtue of what he has done. But the moral character of Oedipus's situation would have been the same, even if there had been no such consequences; and we could still have pitied him.

Let me consider another sort of case. In a film called *Violent Saturday*, which I saw many years ago, a gang of bank raiders hide from the police on the farm of a strict, Dukhobor-like religious community, one of whose most fundamental guiding principles is non-violence. At the climax of the film one of the gangsters is about to shoot a young girl member of the community in the presence of the community's elder. With horror and doubt on his face, the elder seizes a pitchfork and hurls it into the gangster's back.

How are we to describe the elder's position? According to a neo-Kantian position like Professor Hare's, the elder has had to make a 'decision of principle', which consists in either qualifying, or perhaps even abandoning, the principle of non-violence according to which he has hitherto tried to live. But several features of the situation seem to me to speak against this account. In the first place, it is quite clear that the elder thinks he has done something *wrong* in killing the gangster. It is not that he has abandoned or qualified his commitment to the principle of non-violence. The whole point of this principle, in the context of the religious life of the community, would be lost if it were thought of as subject to qualification in this way; and the life of the community still represents the elder's highest ideal—so he cannot be thought of as having abandoned the principle.

But in the second place, it is equally clear that the elder would think that in some sense he 'had no choice' in the situation. That is how he *had to* act and if he had acted differently he would not have been able to forgive himself. My use of phrases like 'had to' and 'would not have been able to' in that last sentence may encourage some philosophers to think that what is in question here is a conflict between a moral demand—in this case the principle of non-violence—and something 'purely psychological', a Kantian 'inclination'. Now I do not find the concept of the 'purely psychological' as luminous as some appear to, but in so far as there is an implied *contrast* here between the psychological and the moral, I am quite sure that this account will not do. I said that, having killed the gangster, the elder knew he had done something wrong; but I also said that, if he had not killed the gangster, he would not have been able to forgive himself; i.e. that would have been wrong too, though perhaps in a different way. That the modalities involved on the side of killing the gangster are moral modalities is also clear from the fact that, in order to explicate them, notions like that of the innocence of the girl whose life was threatened and that of protecting the defenceless would have to be introduced. But it would be wrong to introduce them in the form of principles for the sake of which the elder was acting. They are involved in what I have called the 'perspective' of the action, but that perspective is not to be understood in the form of Kantian 'maxims' or Harean 'principles'. It will be objected that my account leaves no room for any discovery of, or decision concerning, '*the* right' thing to do in such a situation and thus makes morality useless as a guide to conduct. But my whole point is that there *is* no room for the notion of 'the right thing to do' in such a situation and that this shows yet again that morality is *wrongly* conceived as a guide to conduct.

This case could serve to exemplify a remark by J. L. Stocks. Stocks argued strongly against the possibility of understanding morality in terms of the means-end relationship and said that morality can require that we abandon absolutely any specifiable end, *including the end of one's own moral perfection.*[8] In my example the elder's ideal of moral perfection included adherence to the principle of non-violence. I have been arguing that in acting against that principle he neither abandoned that ideal nor succumbed to a non-moral temptation.

Now in some ways a better way of expressing the truth in Stock's remark might be to say that one's own moral perfection is not a possible end of one's conduct at all and, *a fortiori*, not a possible moral end. This, I think, is made clear in my last example, which comes from Tolstoy's story, 'Father Sergius'. This example may also serve to connect my intervening argument more closely with what I said earlier about Plato's Glaucon.

Sergius is a man who suddenly abandons the brilliant military career which lies before him to become a monk.[9]

By becoming a monk he showed contempt for all that seemed most important to others and had seemed so to him while he was in the service, and he now ascended a height from which he could look down on those he had formerly envied. But it was not this alone, as his sister Varvára supposed, that influenced him. There was also something else—a sincere religious feeling which Varvára did not know, which intertwined itself with the feeling of pride and the desire for pre-eminence, and guided him.

An important point which I must make here is that the 'religious feeling' and the 'desire for pre-eminence', of which Tolstoy speaks, must not be regarded as two quite distinct

motives which are contingently intermingled. It is essential
to understanding the story and to the philosophical point
which I want to make to see that the one is a corrupt form
of the other.

Sergius shines as brightly as a monk as he had as an officer
and eventually becomes a hermit, with a great reputation for
saintliness, and crowds visit him, bringing their sick to be
healed. In the middle of his career a young society woman
visits him alone in the night and tries to seduce him. To
defend himself against temptation Sergius takes an axe and
chops off one of his fingers.

As the years go on and his saintly reputation increases,
Sergius's religious doubts begin to get the upper hand. At the
climax of these doubts an intellectually feeble young girl,
who has been sent to him for healing, offers herself to him
and he succumbs to the temptation.[10]

> 'What is your name?' he asked, trembling all over and
> feeling that he was overcome and that his desire had al-
> ready passed beyond control. 'Marie. Why?' She took his
> hand and kissed it, and then put her arm round his waist
> and pressed him to herself. 'What are you doing?' he
> said. 'Marie, you are a devil!' 'Oh, perhaps. What does it
> matter?' And embracing him she sat down with him on
> the bed.

My reason for quoting that piece of dialogue lies in Marie's
Glauconian question, 'What does it matter?' Sergius's
tragedy was that, from the perspective which he had come
to occupy *vis-à-vis* his religious life, he could no longer see
that it did matter. Earlier in the story there is the following
passage:

> The sources of [his inner conflict] were two: doubts, and
> the lust of the flesh. And these two enemies always ap-
> peared together. It seemed to him that they were two
> foes, but in reality they were one and the same. As soon
> as doubt was gone so was the lustful desire. But thinking
> them to be two different fiends he fought them separately.

I think the point is this. Earlier, Sergius had been able to overcome his lust by chopping off his finger. He could do this because, at that stage, the problem presented to him by his lust was understood by him from the perspective of a genuine religious belief. That is to say it was not then a case of setting the satisfaction of his desire alongside the demands of his religion and choosing between them. The fulfilment of his religious duties was not then for him an object to be achieved. But this is what it *had* become for him at the time he succumbed to temptation and this indeed is precisely why he succumbed. Marie's question 'What does it matter?' invited a judgment explaining why religious purity is more important than the satisfaction of lust, a comparison, as it were, between two different objects. And no such judgment was possible. I do not mean that earlier, at the time of his strength, Sergius *could* have answered the question; the point is that, from that earlier perspective, the question did not arise for him.

All this is brought out superbly well in further passages from the story. Shortly before his fall Sergius has a discussion about religion with (save the mark!) 'a sceptical young professor'. Afterwards he meditates alone.[11]

> 'Can I have fallen so low?' he thought. 'Lord, help me! Restore me, my Lord and God!' And he clasped his hands and began to pray.
>   The nightingales burst into song, a cockchafer knocked against him and crept up the back of his neck. He brushed it off. 'But does He exist? What if I am knocking at a door fastened from outside? The bar is on the door for all to see. Nature—the nightingales and the cockchafers—is that bar. Perhaps the young man was right.'

In a letter to his aunt Tolstoy once wrote, speaking from a perspective very different from that of Father Sergius: 'For me, religion comes from life, not life from religion. You scoff at my nature and nightingales. But in my religion, nature is the intermediary.'[12] Now it would be confused to ask here who is right, Sergius or Tolstoy in his letter. It cannot be demonstrated that nature is either a bar or an intermediary;

but one can see how it may manifest itself as either one or the other according to the perspective of the agent. Sergius looked for a demonstration, much as Glaucon looked for a demonstration that justice is preferable to injustice. To do this he contemplated the religious life as an object and asked what there was about it which made it worth while. But just as Adeimantus noted that when people commend justice, what they commend 'is not justice itself, but the respectability it brings', so Sergius found that if he tried to commend the religious life, what he was commending was not that at all, but the kudos and admiration it brought him.[13]

> They told him that people needed him, and that fulfilling Christ's law of love he could not refuse their demand to see him, and that to avoid them would be cruel. He could not but agree with this, but the more he gave himself up to such a life the more he felt that what was internal became external, and that the fount of living water within him dried up, and that what he did now was done more and more for men and less and less for God ... He thought himself a shining light, and the more he felt this the more was he conscious of a weakening, a dying down of the divine light of truth that shone within him.

I think the situation is something like this. If one looks at a certain style of life and asks what there is in it which makes it worth while, one will find nothing there. One may indeed describe it in terms which bring out 'what one sees in it', but the use of these terms already presupposes that one does see it from a perspective from which it matters. The words will fall flat on the ears of someone who does not occupy such a perspective even though he is struggling to attain it. If one tries to find in the object of contemplation that which makes it admirable, what one will in fact see is the admiration and applause which surrounds it. So one will see oneself perhaps as a prospective object of such admiration. And then what one is aiming at is to be such an object of admiration. 'What was internal becomes external.'

It may now be asked what is so attractive about being an

object of admiration; and this is a pertinent question. Of course, if one is an object of admiration this may as a matter of fact be of assistance to one's further designs by, for example, bringing with it power or money. But it is not just that which one values in admiration; one values it precisely *as* admiration. This too is well brought out in the description of Sergius: the form which people's admiration of him took was positively burdensome to him and yet he could not help feeling pleasure in it. 'He was oppressed and wearied by visitors, but at the bottom of his heart he was glad of their presence and glad of the praise they heaped upon him'.[14] But to understand people's behaviour as constituting admiration is to understand it as directed towards something good, something worthy of admiration. So the thought of something as really worthy of admiration is indeed involved when anyone takes pleasure in being admired. Only this thought is corrupted.

I think it is an important task for philosophy to make clear the distinction between corrupt and non-corrupt forms of the thought that something is worthy of admiration. But neither it, nor any other form of enquiry, can show what *is* worthy of admiration. The idea that it can is itself a form of corruption and always involves an obscuring of possibilities. The reason why I think this should be clear from my treatment of Kant. Philosophy may indeed try to remove intellectual obstacles in the way of recognizing certain possibilities (though there is always the danger that it will throw up new obstacles). But what a man makes of the possibilities he can comprehend is a matter of what man he is. This is revealed in the way he lives; it is revealed *to him* in his understanding of what he can and what he cannot attach importance to. But philosophy can no more show a man what he should attach importance to than geometry can show a man where he should stand.

NOTES

[1] J. S. Mill, *Utilitarianism*, Chapter 1.

[2] Cf. Philippa Foot, 'Moral Beliefs' in *Theories of Ethics*, edited by Philippa Foot (Oxford University Press, 1967); reprinted from *Proceedings of the Aristotelian Society*, Volume 59, 1958-9.

[3] Cf. John Anderson, 'The Meaning of Good' in *Studies in Empirical Philosophy* (Sydney: Angus & Robertson, 1962).

[4] Cf. Jean-Paul Sartre, *Being and Nothingness* (translated by Hazel E. Barnes, (New York: Philosophical Library, 1956), Part 4, Chapter 1.

[5] Immanuel Kant, *Grundlegung zur Metaphysik der Sitten*.

[6] I say that someone *might* think like this; of course it is also possible for someone to make a contrary judgment. But my complaint against Kant here is not that he gets things the wrong way round: rather, that he claims that there is only one way round to get them.

[7] Henrik Ibsen, *The Master Builder*, Act I.

[8] Cf. J. L. Stocks, *Morality and Purpose*, edited with an introduction by D. Z. Phillips (London: Routledge & Kegan Paul, 1969).

[9] Leo Tolstoy, *The Kreutzer Sonata and Other Tales* (London: The World's Classics, 1960), p. 307. All quotations are from this edition.

[10] Ibid., p. 343.

[11] Ibid., p. 342.

[12] Henri Troyat, *Tolstoy* (translated by Nancy Amphoux; London: W. H. Allen, 1968), p. 186.

[13] Op. cit., p. 332.

[14] Ibid., p. 332.

10

Can a Good Man be Harmed?

The idea that it is worse for a man to do than to suffer wrong is not one that plays a very big part in contemporary Anglo-Saxon moral philosophy. It *has* been discussed by writers interested in the question whether it is possible to offer a man any reasons for acting morally. I believe that Prichard was essentially right, in 'Does Moral Philosophy rest on a Mistake?',[1] when he argued that those who have tried to deploy the idea in that connection have been confused. But the idea has a life of its own apart from that context, and I believe that its neglect has led many philosophers to overlook a very important dimension of moral discourse. In this paper I shall attempt to understand something of what it means.

Let me first present various examples, starting with two which are a direct expression of the idea in question, and continuing with some which, while different, have interesting features in common with the first, and for me central, cases.

(1) But you, too, my judges, must face death with good hope, and remember this one truth, that a good man cannot suffer any evil either in life or after death, and that the gods do not neglect his fortunes. (Socrates, in Plato's *Apology*)

(2) I will mention another experience straightaway which I also know and which others of you might be acquainted with: it is, what one might call, the experience of feeling *absolutely* safe. I mean the state of

193

mind in which one is inclined to say 'I am safe, nothing can injure me whatever happens.' ('Wittgenstein's Lecture on Ethics', *Philosophical Review*, January 1965, p. 8)

(3) Now and then someone speaks of 'suffering punishment when one does the Good'. How is that possible? From whom shall that punishment come? Certainly not from God! Is it, then, from the world—so that when in its wisdom the world is mistaken, it rewards the bad and punishes the Good? And yet no, it is not as that word 'world' implies. The word does not mean what it says. It is improperly expressed. For the word 'world' sounds great and terrifying, and yet it must obey the same law as the most insignificant and miserable man. But even if the world gathered all its strength, there is one thing it is not able to do, it can no more punish an innocent one than it can put a dead person to death . . .

How wonderful, here is a limit, a limit that is invisible, like a line that is easy to overlook with the senses, but one that has the strength of eternity in resisting any infringement. (Kierkegaard, *Purity of Heart*, Fontana Books, 1961, p. 85)

(4) *Claudius:* My words fly up, my thoughts remain below,
    Words without thoughts never to heaven go.
(Shakespeare, *Hamlet*, Act III, Scene III)

(5) So I kneeled down. But the words wouldn't come. Why wouldn't they? . . . I was trying to make my mouth *say* I would do the right thing and the clean thing, and go and write to that nigger's owner and tell where he was; but deep down in me I knowed it was a lie—and He knowed it. You can't pray a lie—I found that out. (Mark Twain, *Huckleberry Finn*, Chapter XXXI)[2]

Now a certain sort of 'tough-minded' philosopher, with whom we are familiar (and who is perhaps among my present readers), might make the following move on being confronted with these examples:[3] he might say that if the words in them are being used in their ordinary sense, then they express a straightforward empirical falsehood; that they can only be true by virtue of an eccentric use of such words as 'harm', 'safe', 'punishment', and then they are true 'by definition' and in a merely 'trivial' way. What the tough-minded philosopher says would be partly correct: those who have made such statements cannot be taken as meaning them in a straightforwardly 'empirical' sense. Indeed, one might think that it is just *because* they have seen such statements to be obviously false when taken in that way that they have found them worth making. Clearly, then, these statements have been thought to express necessary truths of some sort; and clearly their necessity *is* connected with the ways in which the words, on which the tough-minded philosopher fastened, are being used. But perhaps we should not be over-ready to join the tough-minded philosopher in thinking these assertions merely trivial; perhaps we should try to suppress, at least initially, our inclination to share his probable feeling of irritation with Kierkegaard's talk about a 'line that has the strength of eternity in resisting any infringement'.

It looks as though Huck, at least, makes a discovery; Claudius perhaps, too. And what is said by Socrates, Kierkegaard and Wittgenstein could certainly strike someone with the force of a discovery. Or, if the word 'discovery' seems too securely tied to the realm of empirical truths, let us try 'revelation'. But what exactly is revealed?

The cases of Huck and Claudius are slightly different from the others. What they become aware of is a necessary truth in a very obvious way. Anyone who uses the concept of prayer at all, we are inclined to say, must use it like this or he will be using it *wrongly*. 'Punish' is different. We *do* speak of men being 'wrongfully punished' and in so doing we say something intelligible. On the other hand, it is a word which does, interestingly, lend itself to use in the way Kierkegaard uses it. What is being said by someone who uses it in this way?

Kierkegaard would say that it is only 'eternally speaking' that an innocent man cannot be punished. He does not *just* mean that this is true 'by definition' when the word 'punish' is used in a certain way; there are other features in the situation and attitude of a man who speaks thus which *give point* to what he is saying. Some of these features can be brought out more easily by considering the example from *Huckleberry Finn*. What Huck sees when he says 'You can't pray a lie' is an analytic truth and perhaps one that he had been taught before in being shown what it is to pray. But now his life is for the first time presenting him with problems—in connection with his relations with the runaway slave Jim—which enable him to see the point of using the word 'pray' like that. The force of 'You can't pray a lie' strikes him for the first time. He sees the practice of prayer in relation to his moral difficulties: how the complete honesty which has to be present if something is to count as prayer makes the role of prayer in relation to such problems what it is. He is hearing Kierkegaard's 'voice of eternity' for the first time.

That this voice should indeed be the voice of eternity it is necessary[4] that he (Huck in the present example) should say what he does on his own behalf[5] and should not be just repeating something he has heard from someone else. This requirement does not, of course, preclude his having arrived at the capacity to say it on his own behalf as a result of having learned things from other people. Kierkegaard expresses this point by saying that the voice of eternity can be heard only in the silence of the individual's own heart; and this 'silence' is to be understood by contrast with the 'busyness' of 'the world'. It is not enough that it is something that I think to myself privately, for my own thoughts can be thought from the world's point of view, too, a situation which is a paradigm of Kierkegaard's 'double-mindedness'. This, I think, is Claudius's condition when he tries to pray,

> ... though still possess'd
> Of those effects for which I did the murder,
> My crown, mine own ambition, and my queen.

He is trying to regard the activity of prayer from the world's point of view. In this case there is a very obvious absurdity, in that prayer quite explicitly involves a relation of the individual to the eternal and really there is no such thing as prayer 'from the world's point of view'. With punishment the situation is interestingly different: here the remark, 'The world cannot punish the innocent', invites the rejoinder from the world, 'Can't I? Just you watch!'

For the very reason that this rejoinder seems to be a possible one it is important to emphasize in the case of this example that the original remark must be understood as having been made 'in the silence of the heart': it expresses the speaker's attitude, his realization of the possibility of meeting the afflictions of life in a certain way. It is an attitude which the concept of punishment makes possible; or, to adapt an image in the *Tractatus*, it is an attitude which is possible in the 'logical space' defined by the concept of punishment, a space bounded by the notions of guilt and innocence. Of course, for precisely parallel reasons, the concept of punishment *also* defines a logical space in which the world's attitude can exist. The point is that the notions of guilt and innocence lead a double life: they enter *both* into the procedures by which it is determined whether or not penal measures of a certain sort are to be taken against a man, and *also* into the attitude of the person against whom such measures are taken. It would be of the utmost interest to investigate the relation between these two aspects of the matter: but that would have to be the subject of a different paper. What I shall try to do here is to spell out in more detail the attitude which 'the voice of eternity' expresses.

I said just now that one who says 'The world cannot punish the innocent' is struck by the possibility of meeting life's afflictions in a certain way. And this brings out—if it needs bringing out—the connection between *this* remark and the idea that a good man cannot be harmed. For the latter idea also expresses a possible attitude to life's afflictions: one that seems more general, in that it comprises afflictions other than those regarded as punishments. I shall first consider the more particular case.

Imagine a man—let me call him Robert—who makes the distinction between what is and what is not a punishment, central in deciding what his attitude shall be to the various afflictions his life brings upon him. This distinction will cut across the parallel distinction made by 'the world', for some of the penal measures taken against Robert by the world will not be regarded as punishments by him, conscious perhaps of his own innocence; and again many of the painful and unpleasant things that happen to him which the world says are just bad luck and undeserved, will be regarded by him as just punishments for what he regards as his own wrong-doing. His application of this distinction will not be just an arbitrary decision whether or not to use the *word* 'punishment' on a given occasion. For, in the first place, his decision will be guided by the concepts of guilt and innocence and the question whether or not he has been guilty or innocent in his actions on a given occasion is not one he can answer by arbitrary *fiat*. Moreover, in the second place, consequences follow from his decision[6] to regard a given affliction as a punishment: to see it in this way is to see it in an internal connection with his own wrong-doing and this is to accept it in a certain spirit and to include it in his thinking about what will be the right course of action for him on future occasions. What this involves can perhaps be seen by contrasting Robert's attitude with that of James, who sees his afflictions as 'punishments' only in the world's sense. James says: 'Well, they (the authorities, public opinion, my friends) have caught me out in something they regard as a crime, or dishonourable, and they are going to make me suffer for it. Can I get out of this? If not, how can I take care that I don't have to suffer such consequences again in the future? Will I have to refrain from acting like this again? Or is there a way in which I can do so without bringing down the wrath of others on myself?' Robert, on the other hand, says: 'What I am suffering is a just punishment for my own wrong-doing. I must face up to this, try to repent, and think how I can best avoid behaving like this in the future.' These attitudes are totally different: they may indeed lead to subsequent actions by James and Robert between which the world will not be able to distinguish; nevertheless, the meaning of those actions will be quite different for James and for Robert respectively. The most striking difference between them is perhaps the following. For James there is no intrinsic connection at all between what *he* regards as the true nature of his acts and the consequences they lead to; there is merely a causal connection between the ways in which his acts strike others and the reactions of others to them. James's thinking is all on the level of appearances. When Robert, on the other hand, says: 'This affliction is a punishment for what I have done', the 'what I have done' means what Robert really thinks *is* what he has done. And the affliction is being regarded by him as connected with *that* and not with the way what he has done appears to anyone.[7] This connection that Robert sees is not a causal one. He may indeed think there is a causal connection between his wrong-doing and his afflictions, but he need not. That is to say, if someone says to Robert: 'But look, there is a complete lack of causal connection between what you did and what is happening to you now', I do not think Robert would be speaking unintelligibly or improperly if he were to reply: 'Yes, I see that is so, but it is a punishment all the same.'

It is an internal feature of Robert's attitude to the afflictions which he calls 'punishments' (or, we might say, part of what he means in calling them punishments) that he regards them as beneficial and not as harmful. That is, they are to be accepted willingly and welcomingly and not to be evaded. We can express this quite strongly: Robert would be acting *inconsistently*, were he to say of a certain affliction that it is a punishment and try to avoid it. For James, on the other hand, such afflictions (all afflictions, indeed) are harmful and to be avoided if possible. What is the nature of the disagreement between them and, in particular, is it possible for us to say that either of them is 'making a mistake'? It is not an empirical disagreement in any ordinary sense. Robert does not deny that these afflictions are really afflictions, are unpleasant and painful. Indeed, their painful character is a necessary condition for their being beneficial to him in the way he thinks they are. What I think James might say is that

he 'doesn't see the sense' of Robert's way of speaking. He is
unable to make the connections that Robert makes and
perhaps believes that they are not real connections at all, but
'illusory'. Robert likewise may say that James is under an
illusion, is deceiving himself. But it seems to me that there
is not complete symmetry between the two cases: Robert
may understand very well what is involved in James's thinking about his afflictions—being human, he will certainly be
under the temptation to think of them in that way himself.[8]
But he will say that James has only a superficial grasp of his
situation, that he does not see the deeper connections. But
in what sense are the connections that Robert sees 'deeper'
than those that James sees? I do not see that there is much
more that a philosopher *qua* philosopher can say about this
(though certainly philosophers like Plato have *tried* to say
more). It seems to me that it is only *within* Robert's moral
outlook that the sense of 'deeper' can be seen. All a philosopher can do is to try to display what is involved in that
outlook and how it differs from James's. He cannot 'prove'
that either of them is the one anyone 'ought to adopt'; he
can only say: 'there are these two possibilities'. It would be
equally wrong, I think, for a philosopher to say that Robert's
is the 'only truly moral' outlook, though there may be a
strong temptation for some to say this. If Robert says this,
this is itself an expression of his own moral outlook. But it is
important for a philosopher to see that there are other
possible outlooks and that the concept of the moral that we
do have makes it correct to call these outlooks 'moralities'.
To say this, of course, is not to commit oneself one way or
the other to any particular moral view; and that, it seems to
me, is philosophically as it should be.

So far I have confined myself to one side of the question,
'Can a good man be harmed?': namely, to those kinds of
putative harm which fall under the concept of punishment. I
have tried to show something of what may be involved in
saying of *these* that they are not truly harmful. I must now
turn my attention to other types of affliction. Suppose that
Robert says of these, too, that, even though he does not see

them as punishments, they are still not genuinely harmful to him. What sense might we make of this? The difficulty here is that, whereas in the preceding case the concept of punishment itself contains the possibility of seeing afflictions regarded as punishments as positively beneficial, to say, 'I am absolutely safe. Nothing can harm me whatever happens', is 'a distortion or destruction' of the meaning of 'safe'.[9] 'To be safe essentially means that it is physically impossible that certain things should happen to me and therefore it's nonsense to say that I am safe *whatever* happens'.[10] This, together with other examples of parallel difficulties, led Wittgenstein to say:[11]

> My whole tendency and I believe the tendency of all men who ever tried to write or talk Ethics or Religion was to run against the boundaries of language. This running against the walls of our cage is perfectly, absolutely hopeless. Ethics so far as it springs from the desire to say something about the ultimate meaning of life, the absolute good, the absolute valuable, can be no science. But it is a document of a tendency in the human mind which I personally cannot help respecting deeply and I would not for my life ridicule it.

At this point I must consider another example of what Wittgenstein, at the time of delivering this lecture (between 1929 and 1930), regarded as manifesting the same tendency.[12]

> Supposing that I could play tennis and one of you saw me playing and said: 'Well, you play pretty badly' and suppose I answered 'I know, I'm playing badly but I don't want to play any better', all the other man could say would be 'Ah then that's all right.' But suppose I had told one of you a preposterous lie and he came up to me and said 'You're behaving like a beast' and then I were to say 'I know I behave badly, but then I don't want to behave any better', could he then say 'Ah, then that's all right'? Certainly not; he would say 'Well, you *ought* to want to behave better'. Here you have an absolute judgment of value, whereas the first instance was one of a relative judgment.

Wittgenstein went on to say that whereas a 'relative' judgment of value 'is a mere statement of facts and can therefore be put in such a form that it loses all the appearance of a judgment of value', this is not true of an 'absolute' judgment of value.

Discussing developments in Wittgenstein's views in subsequent years, Rush Rhees draws a distinction between the two examples of 'absolute' judgments of value I have just sketched. He says that whereas the qualification of the word 'safe' with 'absolutely' *does* involve a misuse of 'safe', this is not true of the word 'ought', as used in Wittgenstein's 'Well, you *ought* to want to behave better.' This latter remark is the only thing the speaker *could* say in the circumstances sketched; it has a perfectly intelligible sense in that context, in the moral language game. Thus the one example is, and the other is not, a case of 'running one's head against the limits of language'.

I want now to raise the question whether anything similar can be said of the other kind of example; whether judgments like Wittgenstein's 'I am absolutely safe; nothing can harm me, whatever happens' or like Socrates' 'a good man cannot suffer any evil either in life or after death' can be seen as having an intelligible sense as part of a moral language game. Now it is clear that such judgments, as much as the 'Well, you *ought* to want to behave better' in a certain sense express the values of the speaker. I think it is nearly as clear that something analogous is true of certain judgments involving the notions of 'harm' and 'safety', which are *not*, in quite the same sense, *absolute* judgments of value; and that, therefore, Wittgenstein was wrong to say that all such judgments amount to assertions that 'it is physically impossible that certain things should happen'. An example, due originally to Rush Rhees, is Brentano's blindness.[13]

> When friends commiserated with him over the harm that had befallen him, he denied that his loss of sight was a bad thing. He explained that one of his weaknesses had been a tendency to cultivate and concentrate on too many

diverse interests. Now, in his blindness, he was able to concentrate on his philosophy in a way which had been impossible for him before.

Or again, two people might disagree whether a government's policy of support and protection of scientific enquiry would be harmful or beneficial to that enquiry. Their disagreement need not be about the empirical consequences of such a policy, but might be the expression of different conceptions held by them of the value of such enquiry. But these judgments are still contingent on what happens. Brentano could say what he did, while still agreeing that *some* things that might happen would be harmful to him; and so, *mutatis mutandis*, for the other example. The 'absolute safety' of Socrates, Wittgenstein or Kierkegaard on the other hand expresses a judgment of eternity; it is not at all (or not at all in the same way) contingent on what may happen in time.

The sense of such a judgment, if it has one, must clearly be seen as an expression of the values of a man who, in Kierkegaard's phrase, 'wills the Good'. It seems to me that Kierkegaard's discussion of this concept, in *Purity of Heart*, brings out very strikingly the formal parallel between the notion of absolute safety on the one hand and that of willing the Good on the other. I shall lean heavily on this discussion in what follows.

To will the good is to see a limit beyond which one cannot (or will not—I do not think it matters which one says here) go. There are certain actions which such a man could not (would not) perform, whatever the considerations in their favour.[14] It is the observance of such a limit, Kierkegaard argues, which alone can give a man's life a certain kind of unity. The various kinds of 'double-mindedness' on the other hand, which Kierkegaard opposes to willing the Good, make possible at best a spurious and contingent unity. If circumstances change, the double-minded man finds himself constrained to act in a sense quite opposed to that which his actions had before the change. This is most strikingly brought out in Kierkegaard's discussion of what is involved in acting out of a regard for wordly reputation, which is notoriously subject to sudden changes of opinion.

There have been critics of Kierkegaard who have taken him to be overlooking the importance of socially established and conditioned moral concepts in determining what *constitutes* the good in a particular context. I do not myself find this criticism well-founded. Kierkegaard seems to me to be making a point about the role which such concepts may play in a man's life. When one has described how moral concepts operate in the social sphere, what criteria, if any, are relevant to their application in particular contexts, there is still something more to say—concerning what they may mean to an individual man who cares about morality. This question requires a quite different kind of discussion.[15]

What in particular a man must do on a given occasion will depend on his particular circumstances, the sort of man he is, the position he is in, whether he is old or young, and so on, but what holds all these situations together and gives them the significance they may have in a man's life, is their relation to a central enduring concern to act decently and justly. 'If there is, then, something eternal in a man, it must be able to exist and to be grasped within every change . . . As for the Eternal, the time never comes when a man has grown away from it, or has become older—than the Eternal'.[16] In his treatment of what Wittgenstein says about the 'absolute' character of 'You ought to want to behave better', Rhees remarks (*a*) that this would be said in connection with what the person addressed had done in these *particular* circumstances; but (*b*) that the speaker would be claiming that the significance of the behaviour in question 'goes beyond' those particular circumstances. Expanding the meaning of the phrase 'goes beyond' here, Rhees says the matter under discussion isn't something trivial for the speaker; it 'goes deep' for him: and this will be shown both by the nature of the occasion on which it is said and by the behaviour and demeanour of the speaker which surrounds that occasion.

These remarks of Rhees seem to me closely connected with

what Kierkegaard says about the unity and sense which, he claims, are only to be found in the life of a man who wills the Good. Where Rhees says that the moral question 'goes beyond the immediate circumstances' for the man in Wittgenstein's example, Kierkegaard would say that what this man says is the expression of an attitude he has to life as a whole, or a relation he has to eternity. Moreover, Kierkegaard also argues—and this is of the very first importance for the subject of this paper—such a 'relation to eternity' *can* only manifest itself in extended time, in how a man lives his life. (This remark must clearly be regarded as a contribution to the *grammar* of the word 'eternity'.) Thus, the characteristic expression of a man's relation to eternity is *patience*.

Now it seems to me that someone who says, 'I am absolutely safe; nothing can harm me whatever happens', is attempting to give expression to the ethical attitude of patience, as Kierkegaard understood this. *Part* of what is philosophically puzzling about such an utterance is that patience cannot be expressed in that way: this, I think, is what lies behind Wittgenstein's feeling that such an expression is an attempt to go beyond the limits of language. I shall try to say more about this shortly. But also, part of the puzzlement surrounds the concept of patience itself, as Kierkegaard's discussion of it brings out. He is not speaking of an attitude of quiescent acceptance of *avoidable* evils, but of an attitude which it is possible to adopt in the face of evils which are seen as *un*avoidable. And I think no questions are being begged concerning what evils are and what are not unavoidable; the ways in which this is to be decided are not here under discussion. Kierkegaardian patience is the *voluntary* acceptance of *unavoidable* suffering: both the inevitability of the suffering and the voluntariness of the acceptance are essential to it, and this is just what constitutes its paradoxical character.[17]

Is patience not precisely that courage which voluntarily accepts unavoidable suffering? . . . Thus, patience, if one may put it in this way, performs an even greater miracle than courage. Courage voluntarily chooses suffering that may be avoided; but patience achieves freedom in unavoidable suffering. By his courage, the free one voluntarily lets himself be caught, but by his patience the prisoner effects his freedom—although not in the sense that need make the jailer anxious or fearful . . . One can be forced into the narrow prison, one can be forced into lifelong sufferings, and necessity is the tyrant; but one cannot be forced into patience . . . When the victim of unavoidable suffering bears it patiently, one says of him, 'to his shame, he is coerced, and he is making a virtue out of a necessity'. Undeniably he is making a virtue out of a necessity, that is just the secret, that is certainly a most accurate designation for what he does . . . He brings a determination of freedom out of that which is determined as necessity. And it is just there that the healing power of the decision for the Eternal resides: that the sufferer may voluntarily accept the compulsory suffering.

A way of expressing the paradoxical character of patience which would be more acceptable in terms of contemporary philosophical idiom, might be the following. When we reflect on the concepts of voluntary choice and inevitability, we feel inclined to say that they are mutually exclusive, that what is seen as inevitable cannot be voluntarily chosen. The concept of patience shows that this is not so. It would be a mere philosophical prejudice to argue in the opposite direction: that because inevitability excludes voluntary choice, patience is impossible. Patience clearly does exist.

The concept of patience enables us to see the connection between the two 'moral absolutes' cited from Wittgenstein's Lecture: the absolute demand of the moral 'ought' and the absolute impossibility of harming a good man. A man who accepts the first of these *is* a man who accepts the second. For to accept the first is to think that, compared with the importance of acting honourably and justly (for instance), nothing else matters. And this *is* to bear the afflictions that life brings patiently—i.e., not to be deflected from acting decently even under the pressure of misfortune. A man who has such an attitude to life sees that as long as afflictions do not thus deflect him, they do not harm him—not in relation to what he regards as really important in his life.

However, the biggest hurdle of all in the way of understanding this question remains unsurmounted. I do not really think it can be surmounted; all we can do is to try to discern the nature of the hurdle. A man who is patient in Kierkegaard's sense still thinks that *something* could harm him, namely, for him to cease to 'will the Good'; and it is clear that this *may* befall him as a result of afflictions which he has to suffer. Thus, if he says 'nothing can harm me', there *is* still a predictive element in what he says; so he is not really entitled to add 'whatever happens' and if he cannot do this, then his utterance does not have the absolute character it was intended to have. Kierkegaard might say that such a man thinks he can take the Eternal by storm, which involves misunderstanding the relation of man to the Eternal. The same point was being made by Simone Weil in a different way in the following remark: 'To say to Christ as Saint Peter did: "I will always be faithful to thee", is to deny him already, for it is to suppose that the source of fidelity is in ourselves and not in grace. As he was chosen, this denial was made known to all men and to himself. How many others boast in the same way—and never understand.'[18]

I have the impression in reading Kierkegaard's *Purity of Heart* that he is not always willing to concede to affliction the power to overcome even the Good—a concession that I find one of the most impressive features of Simone Weil's writings on this subject. On the other hand, Kierkegaard's insistence that the ethical requires completion by the religious is surely the result of the pressure of just this sort of point. And he makes the point very clearly indeed in §7 of *Purity of Heart*, where he speaks of the self-deception involved in the idea that one can grasp the Eternal in a moment of contemplation.

The moment of contemplation has something in common with the falsified eternity. It is a foreshortening that is necessary in order that the contemplation may take place.

It must foreshorten time a good deal. Indeed, it must actually call the senses and thoughts away from time in order that they may complete themselves in a spurious eternal well-roundedness.

Can a good man be harmed? The answer to the question cannot be formulated, and this means that there is something wrong with the question. It is an attempt to get something said that can only be shown.

NOTES

[1] H. A. Prichard, *Moral Obligation*. Cf. also D. Z. Phillips, 'Does it Pay to be Good?', *Proceedings of the Aristotelian Society*, 1964-5.

[2] I wish to thank Mr Lloyd Reinhardt for drawing my attention to this example.

[3] With the first three anyway; (4) and (5) are not susceptible to the same treatment.

[4] I do not know if Kierkegaard would say it is sufficient; I should not.

[5] Cf. Wittgenstein's remark to Waismann: 'At the end of my lecture on ethics, I spoke in the first person. I believe that is quite essential. Here nothing more can be established, I can only appear as a person speaking for myself.' *Philosophical Review*, January 1965, p. 16.

[6] Of course, 'decision' will not always be the appropriate word. There will be occasions on which a man *cannot but* regard his afflictions as punishments.

[7] Of course, there may sometimes be a possibility of somebody else's saying that Robert is mistaken in thinking that he has done anything wrong, that it only *appears* to him that he has done so. But I do not believe that this in any way contradicts the account I have given in the text of the way in which the distinction between appearance and reality enters into the difference between the *thoughts* of James and Robert respectively.

[8] There are connections here with the questions J. S. Mill raises about how we are to distinguish qualitatively 'higher' and 'lower' pleasure, though I do not believe Mill sheds much light on these questions.

[9] Rush Rhees, 'Some Developments in Wittgenstein's View of Ethics', *Philosophical Review*, January 1965, p. 18.

[10] Wittgenstein, loc. cit., p. 9.

[11] Ibid., p. 12.

[12] Ibid., p. 5.

[13] D. Z. Phillips and H. O. Mounce, 'On Morality's Having a Point', *Philosophy*, October 1965, p. 316.

[14] Jonathan Bennett (in 'Whatever the Consequences', *Analysis*, January

1966) makes some interesting criticisms of one form of this position. I am not sure how far his criticisms really do apply to the sort of position Kierkegaard develops, and there is no time to go into this question here.

[15] I think there is an important analogy here with the remarks Rhees makes (in his Preface to *The Blue and Brown Books*) about the importance Wittgenstein came to attach to the problem of 'meaning-blindness' in the later parts of the *Philosophical Investigations* and about the reasons why his earlier emphasis on language games was unhelpful here. But this again is something I cannot develop further now.

[16] *Purity of Heart*, p. 31.

[17] *Purity of Heart*, pp. 152-3.

[18] Quoted by Gustave Thibon in his Introduction to Simone Weil's *Gravity and Grace* (Routledge & Kegan Paul paperback, 1963), p. xxii.

11

Ethical Reward and
Punishment

Towards the end of the *Tractatus Logico-Philosophicus* (6.422) Wittgenstein wrote:

> When an ethical law of the form, 'Thou shalt . . .' is laid down, one's first thought is, 'And what if I do not do it?' It is clear, however, that ethics has nothing to do with punishment and reward in the usual sense of the terms. So our question about the *consequences* of an action must be unimportant.—At least those consequences should not be events. For there must be something right about the question we posed. There must indeed be some kind of ethical reward and ethical punishment, but they must reside in the action itself.
>
> (And it is also clear that the reward must be something pleasant and the punishment something unpleasant.)

In this essay I want to examine the distinction between punishment and reward 'in the usual sense of the terms' and 'ethical' reward and punishment, paying particular attention to the view that ethical reward and punishment 'must reside in the action itself' and cannot be understood as *consequences* of the action, at least so long as consequences are conceived as events which are causally connected with the action. In particular I want to ask in what kinds of case one can speak of a man's action as being rewarded or punished without speaking of the action's 'consequences' in this sense. And I also want to ask what the relation is between these cases and the others where the consequences of an action belong to what we are talking about when we use the words 'reward' and 'punishment'. Is Wittgenstein right in suggesting that we have to do here with two different senses of the terms 'reward' and 'punishment'? And is he right in the further faint suggestion of a *priority* in the use of the terms in the latter sort of case conveyed in his phrase 'the usual sense of the terms'?

Philosophers have tended to concentrate on questions about the 'justification' of punishment. Such questions are important, but should not obscure the necessity of asking other kinds of question as well. One consequence of this too exclusive attention to questions of justification has been a concentration on the position of an observer contemplating the infliction of punishment by an authority on a third person. This point of view has been the starting point even in those recent discussions which have, quite rightly, insisted on the distinction between questions about the principles which may be appealed to in a (moral) justification of the infliction of punishment and questions about the criteria which (logically) justify one in *calling* the taking of various kinds of measures against a person cases of 'punishment' at all. Much less attention has been paid to the ways in which the concept of punishment may enter into the understanding of what is happening to him of a person being punished. It is this point of view which occupies, e.g., the attention of Plato in his argument (in the *Gorgias*) that it is beneficial for a person who has committed a wrong to be punished. And it is central too to the issue Wittgenstein raises in the passage I have quoted, as is evident from the close connection between what he says in that passage and his treatment in the *Tractatus*, of 'the will as the subject of ethical attributes.'[1] This point of view will be the main focus of my interest in much of this essay.

Let me try to say a little more about the importance of distinguishing an agent's from a spectator's point of view for an understanding of the place of the concepts of reward and punishment in ethics. From the point of view of a spectator seeking to understand the role which the threat of punishment or the offering of a reward plays in the behaviour of a third party, what is most immediately striking is their role as deterrents from or inducements to certain future actions. But taking this aspect of rewards and punishments as central makes their relevance for ethics problematic. For we shall be considering inducements to conformity with some externally imposed standards. And we shall then have to meet Kantian arguments about the autonomy of the will in ethics, arguments which Kant and many others express in terms of the distinction between acting 'in accordance with' and 'for the sake of' a principle.[2] Fear of punishment and hope of reward might in principle, perhaps, be an inducement to a man to conform to any demand whatever, but conforming to demands as a result of inducements is different from acting morally.

My linking of the Kantian distinction between autonomy and heteronomy with the distinction between the point of view of one suffering punishment and that of an observer of one suffering punishment may be questioned. Certainly, the two distinctions do not divide up the cases in at all the same way. I can for example very well consider the prospect of rewards and punishments as inducements to future actions, or refrainings from action, of my own (though here my interest will be not so much in predicting, as in considering reasons for and against, future behaviour). My point is, though, not that considerations about inducements are likely to appear only in third person talk, but rather that they are the only considerations which are likely to appear in third person talk.

This too may be questioned. After all, many of those who have discussed punishment and reward from third-person points of view have emphasized their relation to the guilt or merit of the person on whom they are inflicted or bestowed. The question is, though, whether the words 'guilt' and 'merit' can, from a *purely* third-person point of view, amount to any more than deviance from or conformity to a given standard of what is 'required' or 'to be praised'. And once again the Kantian conception of moral worth will have escaped us. This may help to explain why it has been found so difficult to provide an intelligible role for the concept of retribution alongside utilitarian concepts like that of deterrence or inducement. These concepts exist in different dimensions. 'Retribution' has to be understood in connection with the way in which an agent is related to his own acts, with what those acts are for him. We can see what role the concept of punishment may play in this dimension only by considering ways in which the agent may use it in coming to terms with himself and his actions.

I believe that considerations of this sort underlie Wittgenstein's remark that reward and punishment (in an 'ethical' sense) 'must reside in the action itself' and not in any consequences which may, as a matter of contingent fact, follow from the action. For what matters, ethically, to an agent contemplating his own past actions is, quite simply, what he has done; if his judgment is affected by anything which is merely contingently connected with the character of what he has done (e.g. by the fact that he happens to have been found out), then he is ceasing to think of his action in an ethical way. However, it is easy to go astray here. I am *not* saying that anything which happens subsequently to the time at which the agent performs an action must be irrelevant to his ethical assessment of it. For not every subsequent happening is 'merely contingently connected with the character of what he has done'. If on Tuesday I shoot at a man and wound him and on Saturday he dies as a result of the wound, then what I did on Tuesday (given appropriate further surroundings) was an act of murder; if he had lived and recovered, I would not have committed murder and would not have had to think of myself as a murderer. So my understanding of what I did on Tuesday is here logically affected by what happens on Saturday; and this relation is to be distinguished from the causal relation between what happened on Tuesday (my firing of the gun) and what happened on Saturday (the death of the wounded man). This distinction is extremely important for what I want to say about punishment and reward:

punishment, for instance, will have an 'ethical' sense for me only in so far as the events (e.g. my arrest and imprisonment) which follow from the wrong which I committed enter into my thoughts about that past action in a way which makes a certain sort of difference to my understanding of what that past action consisted in. I will try to explain what I mean with some examples.

Consider the case of a soldier decorated for gallantry for the part he has played in a military engagement. Suppose he is perfectly aware that his actions in the battle were anything but gallant. I assume, for the purpose of the example, that we can take what the soldier thinks about his action as justified. What is important for my purposes is that he thinks it. I want then to ask what views are open to him concerning the decoration which he has been awarded. If the decoration carries with it a cash payment or promotion; if wearing it enhances the soldier's success with women; if other men are more willing to facilitate his schemes because of it; and so on—these are quite intelligible reasons for him to be pleased. But what have they do to with the fact that he has been rewarded for gallantry? It will not quite do to say that they have nothing at all to do with it, since to reward somebody is to do things calculated to please him, things which would be expected to please him quite independently of their being accorded to him as a reward. However, the soldier's pleasure at such things need have nothing to do with the fact that they have come to him under the aspect of a reward for gallantry. He might have been just as pleased had they occurred by pure chance, perhaps from winning a football pool.

But in so far as that were the case his pleasure would be quite unconnected with his thinking in terms of reward. It would then be misleading to describe it as pleasure at being rewarded for gallantry. So I have not yet described what is distinctive in being pleased at a reward. This is further brought out if we note that the decoration need carry no such extraneous benefits with it at all while still giving its recipient pleasure. What, in such a case, is he pleased at? This is by no means an easy question to answer.

Giving someone a reward for what he has done is an expression of admiration or approval for his action. So perhaps his pleasure at the reward is really pleasure at the approval of those who have given it. But what is there to be pleased at here, if we discount the fact that, under some circumstances, the approval of others will carry supplementary advantages along with it of the sort which I described two paragraphs ago? The answer that first suggests itself is that the pleasure is felt at the judgment, involved in the admiration, that the admired action was good.

The precise significance of this answer is still obscure however. Is it that the recipient of the reward is pleased at the fact that others so judge his action, or is it that he judges so too and is pleased at the consciousness that he has acted well? There are difficulties about both these cases, difficulties which both point in the same direction. Where the recipient shares his admirers' judgment that he has acted well there is no great difficulty; for certainly consciousness of having acted well may itself give pleasure. But then the admiration of others seems irrelevant. Important will be only what the agent himself thinks about what he had done. He may indeed be helped to arrive at such a judgment by what other people say (though this may sometimes be a hindrance to him too). But in the end it is what he thinks that matters and there seems to be nothing left in his pleasure which relates specifically to the admiration which others feel for him. And yet it is an undoubted fact about human beings that they may feel pleasure at the admiration of others in a way which is not accounted for by anything I have so far said. That is a further difficulty about this case, and I shall return to it later.

The other case is that of the soldier in my original example. He does not share the belief of his admirers that he acted well in the battle. Their admiration carried no subsidiary advantages with it. And yet, I am supposing, he does feel pleasure at their admiration. What is he feeling pleasure at? Kierkegaard's answer (in 'The Reward Disease', *Purity of Heart is to Will One Thing*, Fontana Books) is that such a man does not know what he is feeling pleasure at, that his pleasure is a symptom of a confused state of mind: what Kierkegaard calls 'double-mindedness' and what we might call 'self-deception'. What arouses pleasure here is the connection between an attitude of admiration and the judgment that the action which is its object is good. Observation of others' admiration as it were brings to the soldier's mind the judgment that he acted bravely, and he feels pleasure at that, half-forgetting for the moment that he cannot share that judgment.

In each of these cases the upshot is that pleasure at being rewarded, indeed, thinking of one's situation in terms of the notion of reward at all, is inseparable from making the judgment that the action for which one is being rewarded is good. The reward in itself, *qua* reward and discounting its incidental characteristics and effects, *is* no more than the judgment that the action was good. And the willingness of the recipient to think of it as a reward is no more than his willingness to think of his action as good. Here we begin to see some of the sense of the idea that the reward must lie 'in the action itself.'

But this result may seem paradoxical. What is the relevance then of practices like the bestowing of benefits on the doer of good which we think of in connection with the notion of reward? My tentative answer would be that these practices are *one* way (but not the only possible way) of filling out, of expressing, the judgment that a good action has been performed. It is a form of expression which emphasizes that the good action is not an isolated event in the life of the agent, but is something which, as it were, spreads out and affects the character of the rest of his life. But someone who thinks about good actions in this way will do so whether or not such actions as a matter of fact attract what are commonly called rewards. The good action will be thought of as having a certain sort of bearing on the rest of the life of the agent anyway, in itself, whether or not this bearing is actually symbolized in the form of tangible benefits. It is what is symbolized that is important to the notion of reward rather than the actual occurrence of the beneficial consequences themselves.

The kind of relationship to a man's life as a whole which I am referring to here emerges more clearly, perhaps, in connection with *bad* actions. I shall try now, therefore, to make some analogous points about the relation between the judgment that a certain action is evil and the notion of punishment.

Let us consider the cases of three convicts, A, B and C, each of whom is serving a prison sentence for a particularly nasty crime. Each of them has a slightly different conception of the relation between the crime he has committed, his confinement in gaol and the bearing of these on his future life. A thinks: 'Next time I shall take good care not to get caught.' B thinks: 'The police are getting much too good. This game is really not worth the candle. When I get out I shall go straight rather than risk another ten years in gaol.' C thinks: 'This is no more than I deserve. I realize now what a despicable life I was leading. When I get out of here I hope I shall be able to live better.'

It is important how we classify these cases. From the point of view of the sociological penologist it may seem that the important division comes between case A on the one hand and cases B and C on the other. After all, A is resolved to continue with his life of crime, whilst B and C are resolved to give theirs up. But from another point of view there is no significant difference between cases A and B and the important division comes between these two cases on the one hand and case C on the other. For both A and B have nothing against the sort of crime they have committed as such; they differ only in the judgments they respectively make about the likely consequences of their repeating it. If B thought he could get away with it, he would, like A, do the same again. On the other hand C's turning away from his crime has nothing directly to do with the chances of his getting caught again if he repeats it. He has turned against it for what it is, rather than for its consequences, though it may be, and this is my supposition in this example, that its consequences—the

P

prison sentence which C is now serving—have been instrumental in helping him to see his criminal action for what it
was.[3]

The way in which C differs from A and B can be further
brought out by considering what the sentence 'I am being
punished because of what I did' might mean in C's mouth as
contrasted with the same sentence uttered by A or B. For
the latter two the 'because' signifies a contingent, causal or
'external' relationship. They have in mind the sequence of
events which followed their criminal acts: their detection
by the police, their arrest and trial, the words of the judge
and the actions of prison officers. They can use the word
'because' in this sense without making any judgment at all
on their own part on whether their actions were evil or
otherwise. For C, on the other hand, while I do not say that
a grasp of this 'sequence of events' is not in any way involved
in his judgment, it certainly does not exhaust the significance
of the 'because' in the same way. For him the key conception
is that of 'desert'. 'I am being punished because of what I
did' means for him principally: 'This miserable existence in
prison is no more than my crime deserves.' And here, of
course, in contrast to the cases of A and B, a judgment on
the crime, made by C himself, is an essential ingredient in the
meaning of what he says. For him, the connection between
the nature of his crime and his sojourn in gaol is an internal
one. I mean that, for him, thinking about his prison sentence
is a way of thinking about his crime. His reflection on his
past crime takes the form of reflection on his prison sentence
and vice versa. We cannot say of him that he is reflecting on
two different things. What his presence in gaol *is* for C can
only be understood through the idea of the wrongness of his
past actions: were he to think of 'it' in another way, without
that connection, he would not, in a certain sense, be thinking
about the same thing. For what he is thinking about is not
just a segment of a sequence of events in time, but something
which has a certain significance in his life (which is also not
just a temporal sequence of events) and whose identification
rests on that significance which it has in his life.

To see this point more clearly consider the question: 'When did C's punishment start?' The prison governor might give one answer, based on the date on which C's body was delivered into his custody. C, however, might have a totally different answer. He might say it started long before he was arrested and tried (Raskolnikov); or he might say it only began some time after his sentence had started.[4] ('Before, I didn't understand what it was all about; it was impossible for me to think of what was happening as a punishment; it was only when I fully realized the vileness of what I had done, that what was happening to me could really be a punishment for me.')

It may be said in objection to thus tying punishment to repentance that it makes punishment otiose ('a mere external addition'). Thus, the argument would go, if the offender truly has repented when he comes to be punished, then there is nothing more for the punishment to achieve in that regard. On the other hand, if the offender is not repentant, then whatever happens to him is not punishment (in the 'ethical' sense of the word which I have tried to develop). In either case punishment can have no ethical sense.

There is something right and important about this objection, but also something important it misses. Something of what I mean is suggested by the following remarks by Simone Weil:[5]

> In the life of the individual, the innocent must always suffer for the guilty; because punishment is expiation only if it is preceded by repentance. The penitent, having become innocent, suffers for the guilty, whom the repentance has abolished.
>
> Humanity, regarded as a single being, sinned in Adam and expiated in Christ.
>
> Only innocence expiates. Crime suffers in quite a different way.

Perhaps the appearance of paradox here is needlessly increased by the equivocal use of the word 'innocence'. I should not myself want to say that the penitent has become innocent, not at least in the same breath as I should want to say of someone who has committed no offence that *he* is innocent. Certainly, the state of the penitent cannot be adequately described if we do not bring in mention of the fact that he has indeed committed an offence: in which, of course, he differs most importantly from the non-offender. At the same time there is an equally big difference (though a different sort of difference) between the state of the penitent and that of the unrepentant offender. Here we are perhaps inclined to say that the guilt of the offender has somehow been 'transcended'—it is difficult to describe such cases except in quasi-Hegelian terms.

But what is important for my purpose in what Simone Weil says is the kind of relation she suggests between guilt, repentance, punishment and expiation. Whereas the objection that I am considering to supposing that punishment can have any ethical dimension treats punishment as merely contingently connected with repentance, Simone Weil is considering a kind of repentance which demands punishment as a vehicle of expiation. That is, the form which repentance takes here cannot be understood apart from the need for punishment experienced by the penitent. It seems to me just to be a fact that some people do sometimes experience such a need, a fact which is made possible by the existence of the concept of punishment and the possibility of applying that concept in a certain way. One of the circumstances which creates difficulty here is that not everybody does think thus—repentance has many forms—and that some even feel considerable repugnance and hostility towards such a way of thinking. The very presentation of such a point of view may be felt by some as an assault on themselves and on their own ethical outlook. But that is not here in question. What *is* in question is that we should recognize the possibility and character of a certain way of thinking and see that it does make a sort of sense, even if it is alien to the way we ourselves may think.

Let me try to take stock of the position I have reached so far. I started from Wittgenstein's distinction between reward and punishment 'in the usual sense of the terms' and 'ethical' reward and punishment: the nerve of this distinction lying in the different significance carried by an action's 'consequences' in the two sorts of case. I then considered various cases of rewards and punishments which did involve the rewarded or punished actions having specific sorts of consequences. I argued that, *even in these cases*, there is a way of using the terms 'reward' and 'punishment', such that the claim that the action has been rewarded or punished is not to be *identified* with recognition of the fact that those consequences have ensued. I suggested that, in these uses of the terms, to think about the action's having been rewarded or punished is a way of thinking about the action itself. The relevance of the action's consequences, according to this way of thinking, is as a 'vehicle' which carries the thought about the action. I must now consider more directly what this means, before going on to ask whether the words 'reward' and 'punishment' can continue to have a significant use even where the action's consequences (in the sense of 'events') have dropped out of consideration altogether.

In the case of the soldier admired for 'gallant' behaviour which he does not think merits that description, I noted as a disturbing and puzzling fact that it is possible for such a man to feel pleasure at the plaudits of others which is neither pleasure at any further tangible benefits to him which such plaudits bring with them, nor pleasure at the consciousness of having acted well.* An analogous point in the case of punishment is that a man may feel wretched at the 'disgrace' involved in the world's condemnation of him in a way which is not to be accounted for either by any further unpleasant consequences which such disgrace may bring with it (for perhaps there are none) nor by consciousness of having genuinely offended (for perhaps he is conscious of not having offended). It seems to me that we must accept as a datum— and one of great philosophical importance—both that these

---

* I am especially indebted to Mr H. O. Mounce for having insisted on this point in the course of a discussion in which I was inclined to overlook it.

are familiar human reactions and also that, considered in themselves, they are reactions for which we can find no rational justification. (It may, of course, be possible to find *explanations*—perhaps of a sociological, or biological type; but such explanations would lead us away from the central issues which are here of interest.) What this way of putting things suggests is that to see any sort of significance in such reactions we must look at them from a point of view outside themselves.

> If I light an electric torch at night out of doors I don't judge its power by looking at the bulb, but by seeing how many objects it lights up.
>
> The brightness of a source of light is appreciated by the illumination it projects upon non-luminous objects.
>
> The value of a religious or, more generally, a spiritual way of life is appreciated by the amount of illumination thrown upon the things of this world.
>
> Earthly things are the criterion of spiritual things.
>
> This is what we generally don't want to recognize, because we are frightened of a criterion.
>
> The virtue of anything is manifested outside the thing.
>
> If, on the pretext that only spiritual things are of value, we refuse to take the light thrown on earthly things as a criterion, we are in danger of having a non-existent treasure.
>
> Only spiritual things are of value, but only physical things have a verifiable existence. Therefore the value of the former can only be verified as an illumination projected on to the latter.[6]

The application of these very striking remarks to our present problem is as follows. There exist ('earthly') institutions consisting in the bestowal of benefits on men whose conduct reaches certain standards generally held to be desirable and in the infliction of unpleasant consequences on men whose behaviour contravenes certain generally required standards. There *also* exist certain characteristic ('earthly')—pleased and distressed—reactions on the part of men thus treated, which cannot be entirely accounted for in terms of the unproblematic reactions of desire and aversion to nice and nasty things respectively. The terms 'reward' and 'punishment' have ('spiritual') connotations which cannot be entirely accounted for in terms of a recital of these earthly facts. What these terms do is to represent a certain sort of understanding—from a point of view 'outside'—*of* such facts: a point of view which brings them into relation with a way of judging the value of actions which would not be possible but for the obtaining of such facts. 'A painter does not draw the spot where he is standing. But in looking at his picture I can deduce his position by relation to the things drawn.'[7] We should add that a painter can only *have* a position relative to something drawable. In *this* sense we can say that the obtaining of these human modes of behaving and reacting are 'prior' to the possibility of the perspective expressed by the terms 'reward' and 'punishment'. But in another sense it is this perspective which has 'priority'. For it is only one who occupies such a point of view who can use the terms to mean anything more than is expressed, e.g., in terms like 'incentive' and 'sanction'.

My tentative conclusion, then, concerning what Wittgenstein says about 'ethical reward and punishment' in contradistinction to reward and punishment 'in the usual sense of the terms' is this. He is right to maintain that these terms are capable of a use in which to talk about rewards and punishments for an action is not just to state that certain events have followed as consequences of the action. What he does not sufficiently take account of, however, is that even in one[8] quite 'usual' sense of the terms, a sense in which consideration of consequences is important, what is being said cannot be exhausted in a description of consequences; more strongly, to confine oneself to a description of consequences even here is to miss the most important aspect of what is being said.

I now have to consider whether the terms 'reward' and 'punishment' can continue to have an intelligible use even in cases where no consequences of the action (in the sense of events) are in question at all. I will approach this question by considering first some intermediate cases in which a conception of 'consequences', while not wholly absent, is drastically attenuated.

One such case is that in which a man sees a natural disaster which afflicts him as a punishment for some wrong which he has committed in the past.[9] There may be a temptation to regard such a way of thinking as superstitious. It *may*, in some circumstances, indeed be superstitious: namely where there is thought to be some (queer) *causal* connection between the offence and the disaster. But this need not be so. Even (or, more accurately, especially) where the disaster is seen as God's punishment for sin, the relation need not be thought of as like that holding between a crime and the infliction of punishment by an earthly authority. To see this, it is only necessary to remember that, for one who thinks of what happens as God's will, *everything* that happens does so according to God's will. That is, that one thing rather than another has happened is not *explained* by referring it to God's will, as being sent to gaol rather than remaining free may be explained by reference to the will of a High Court judge before whom one has been convicted of a crime. For, in the case of God, it would make no sense[10] to suppose that a crime which one had committed might escape His notice.

My earlier discussion should be enough to show that, contrary to what may be thought by some, breaking the causal link between offence and 'punishment' in this way does not drain of all content the judgment that the disaster is a punishment for the offence. I would even contend that it does not damage what is in many ways the most important aspect of a judgment about the relation between a crime and a punishment. We have still a way of thinking about the crime and a way of seeing it in relation to the life of the criminal which has its own logic and which is characteristically different from other ways of thinking about crime. That is, this way of thinking has 'consequences' in a logical sense, even if it does not involve reference to 'consequences' in a causal sense.[11]

A somewhat different kind of intermediate case is that of a man who commits a wrong, who is not punished either legally or more informally by any human authority, and who suffers no natural disaster which he is able to see as a punishment for his offence; who, however, is plagued by intolerable feelings of remorse. It is certainly possible to speak of these feelings of remorse as a 'punishment' for the offence; but it is very easy to go wrong here. Philosophers and others who have a tendency towards a Hobbist conception of human action sometimes talk of the likelihood of an offender's suffering such painful feelings as a sanction against wrong-doing. It is clear, however, that, unlike sanctions imposed by external authorities, such 'sanctions' will only operate on someone who is himself able to see the wrongness of his action. For feeling remorse *is* a way of seeing the wrongness of one's action. A related point emerges if we ask what is so horrible about feelings of remorse; and here some remarks made by Wittgenstein about fear may be adapted.[12]

> If fear is frightful and if while it goes on I am conscious of my breathing and of a tension in my facial muscles— is that to say that I find *these feelings* frightful? Might they not even be a mitigation? (Dostoevsky)

> That there is a fear-syndrome of sensations, thoughts, etc. (for example) does not mean that fear is a syndrome.

The conception of fear is inseparable from that of being threatened by danger; and the frightfulness of sensations of fear is inseparable from the thought of the frightfulness of the dangers by which one is threatened. Similarly, the conception of guilt is inseparable from that of the wrongfulness of what one has done; and the frightfulness of sensations of guilt is inseparable from the thought of the frightfulness of the wrong which one has done.

Considerations like these would help to give some sense to Wittgenstein's remark that ethical reward and punishment are to be found 'in the action itself'. However, there is a last hurdle—and a considerable one—in the way of accepting the full force of what Wittgenstein is suggesting. For Wittgenstein does not say that there *may* be some kind of ethical reward and punishment for wrong-doing, but that 'there *must* indeed be' such a thing. In all the cases I have considered so far, although I have tried to divert attention from the events which followed wrong-doing and to treat these, as it were, only as a platform offering a certain view on the wrong-doing itself, still, it seems to have been a necessary condition for what I have wanted to say that a platform should indeed have existed in the shape of such events: in particular, in the shape of a recognition on the part of the agent of the wrongfulness of his action. But it is, apparently, a purely contingent matter that such recognition, or that any other relevant events, should or should not occur. 'Only spiritual things are of value, but only physical things have a verifiable existence. Therefore the value of the former can only be verified as an illumination projected on to the latter.'[13] Where there are no physical things to be illuminated, the light will be indiscernible, since we are not in a position to look at it directly. What will be our grounds then for claiming that the light does indeed still exist? The same problem is offered by the last sentence from my earlier quotation from Simone Weil: 'Only innocence expiates. Crime suffers in quite a different way.' What kind of suffering, then, can be in question where we are dealing with someone like Socrates's Archelaus?[14]

The terms in which this problem presents itself preclude *ab initio* any attempt to find a solution by looking for relevant events in the life of the offender; for the supposition is that no relevant events are to be found there. Now the only other direction in which we can look is the life of a person who makes such a judgment as 'no crime goes unpunished'. We must try to understand, that is, exactly what such a judgment commits its author to. There is an extremely simple short answer to this question: namely, that one who believes that all wrong-doing is punished is committed in all cases to *pitying* wrong-doers, not merely when they are subsequently visited by worldly misfortunes (including pangs of remorse) but also, and even more especially, when they seem to have escaped any consequences of their crimes.

But this answer, though simple, is not easy to accept or

perhaps even to grasp. Not all the difficulties here are intellectual ones: there are also the moral and psychological difficulties all of us experience in the way of actually taking up a compassionate attitude in the face of really beastly wrong-doing (and of course the beastlier the wrong-doing, the greater the demand for compassion towards the wrong-doer). But I shall confine myself here to the intellectual difficulties. These centre on the apparent impossibility of giving any *justification* for feeling pity for wrong-doers, arising out of the fact that we are supposing such wrong-doers to be subject to no suffering consequential on their wrong-doing. Perhaps, though, this way of putting the difficulty is misleading. It is not that no justification is being offered for pitying a given man in a given situation: the justification is that he has committed a wrong. We go astray if, at this point, we look for some *further* justification in what happens to such a man; our difficulty is rather to see how the fact that a man has committed a wrong can be a justification for pitying him at all. It is a difficulty in attaching sense to a certain way of thinking.

Should there be any difficulty here though? My earlier discussions of cases in which people are rewarded or punished for their actions by 'consequences' (in the sense of events) were designed to show that in so far as the obtaining of rewards, or the suffering of punishments, are regarded as matters for congratulation or commiseration of a kind which takes account of the character of the relevant happenings *qua* reward and punishment, our attention is focused, not on the specific character of those happenings considered in themselves, but on the moral character of the actions which are being thought of as rewarded or punished. In other words, *even in those cases*, the actual character of the consequences drops out of consideration as irrelevant and we are left with the nature of the agent's actions. We still have those actions, together with a certain view of their nature and significance, where no further consequences in fact ensue. That is, we have all that we need to justify congratulations of, or pity for, the agent.

NOTES

[1] I discussed this in 'Wittgenstein's Treatment of the Will'; see Chapter 6.

[2] I have expressed dissatisfaction with this apparatus in 'Moral Integrity', Chapter 9. But this dissatisfaction does not, I think, affect the present issue.

[3] I make no judgment at all here about the likely efficacy of any existing penal system in helping a man to come to terms with the true nature of his life in the way I am trying to describe. In fact my attitude to *that* question is in the highest degree pessimistic. Here I am concerned only with the conceptual possibilities.

[4] Cf. Kafka's 'In the Penal Colony': I must thank Mr Rush Rhees for drawing my attention to the relevance of this story.

[5] Simone Weil, *First and Last Notebooks* (Oxford University Press, 1970), pp. 115-16. I shall comment later on the last sentence of the passage quoted.

[6] Simone Weil, op. cit., p. 147.

[7] Ibid., p. 146.

[8] It is misleading anyway to talk about *the* usual sense of the terms. See, e.g., Nietzsche, *The Genealogy of Morals*, Second Essay, Section XIII.

[9] I discuss such a case in 'Can a Good Man be Harmed?'; see Chapter 10. See also Wittgenstein, *Lectures and Conversations* (edited by C. Barrett, Oxford: Basil Blackwell, 1966), p. 55 ff.

[10] It is of the first importance, and too often overlooked in philosophical discussions of such matters, that this is indeed a matter of what it makes sense to say and not a quasi-empirical imputation of vast knowledge and power to God. God's 'infinite' knowledge and power (if we speak so) is not exceptionally large knowledge and power any more than an infinite series in mathematics is an exceptionally long series.

[11] Cf. Wittgenstein's 'At least those consequences should not be events'.

[12] *Zettel* (Oxford: Basil Blackwell, 1969), nos. 499 and 502.

[13] Simone Weil, loc. cit.

[14] Plato, *Gorgias*.

Index

alienation, 42
Anderson, John, 177
Anscombe, G. E. M., 57, 111, 124
Aristotle, 50–2, 60, 72, 81
Azande, 8–11, 14–26, 28, 35–41

belief, 9, 23, 36, 38, 79
Bennett, Jonathan, 208–9
Bentham, Jeremy, 173, 179
Berlin, Sir Isaiah, 72
blameworthiness, 136–7, 141–2, 149, 184–5
Brentano, F., 202–3

Cargile, James, 150
causality, 6, 27, 38, 110, 113–15, 122, 133, 135–9, 145, 171–2, 176, 179, 182, 199, 210, 213, 218, 224
Christ, 143–5, 149, 190, 207, 219
Christianity, 15, 39, 81
Collingwood, R. G., 14, 85–6
compassion, 145, 157–8, 226–7
Condillac, E. B. de, 92
conscience, 118, 120, 158, 160, 162–3
consciousness, 137–8
contemplation, 190, 207–8
contradiction, 26, 48

death, 43–7, 139–41, 193
description, 28–30, 148–9, 178

Devlin, Lord, 79
Dostoyevsky, F., 166–7
dreams, 20
Durkheim, E., 45
duty, 78, 81, 83, 90, 102, 130, 132–5, 139, 151, 180–3

Eliot, George, 148–9
Evans-Pritchard, E. E., 8–11, 13–28, 37
evil, *see* good and evil

Foot, Philippa, 75, 175
Frazer, Sir James, 37
free will, 113–14, 117

games, 25–6, 67–8, 71
general will, 103, 108
Gillen, F. J., 45
good and evil, 41–4, 47, 60, 75, 96–9, 117–19, 120–1, 150, 174, 176–9, 181, 194, 203–5, 207, 216
grammar, 30, 51, 64, 92, 95–6, 127, 154, 205

Hare, R. M., 76–8, 82, 160, 169, 185–6
Hart, H. L. A., 108–9, 135
Heath, Peter, 130–5, 141
Hegel, G. W. F., 220

Hobbes, Thomas, 59–60, 67, 72, 81, 90–3, 95–108, 225
Holland, R. F., 4–5
Honoré, A. M., 135
Hume, David, 55, 93

Ibsen, Henrik, 180, 183
integrity, 71, 171
Ishiguro, H., 129

Job, 39

Kafka, F., 228
Kant, I., 78, 81–2, 85–6, 116–17, 159, 178–86, 191–2, 212–13
Kellogg experiment, 61
Kenny, A. J., 124
Kierkegaard, S., 118–19, 180, 194–6, 203–9, 215–16

language, 12–13, 22–3, 33–5, 40–1, 54, 59–61, 63–4, 67–8, 76, 78, 82, 92, 116, 123–4, 126, 128–9, 144, 154, 178, 201–2, 205, 209
legitimacy, 6, 104, 107–8
Lévy-Bruhl, L., 9

McCarthy, Senator Joe, 68–9
MacIntyre, Alasdair, 8, 27–38, 40–2, 45, 73, 75–83, 87
magic and witchcraft, 8–11, 15–17, 19–20, 23–6, 36–42
Marx, Karl, 42
meaning, 64–7
Melden, A. I., 49, 58, 72
Melville, Herman, 151–3, 155–8, 160–3, 167–8
Mill, J. S., 173–6, 208
Moore, G. E., 176–7
moral judgments, morality, 2–6, 43–4, 46–7, 50, 54–6, 58–9, 63–4, 66–7, 69–71, 73–83, 87, 96–7, 99–100, 131–2, 134–7, 138–45, 147–93, 200–2, 204, 206, 211, 213, 215–18, 224

Mounce, H. O., 221
Murphy, Jeffrie G., 150

natural law, 43, 50–1
Newton, Isaac, 52
Nietzsche, F., 228
Norman, Richard, 7

Oedipus, 184–5
Oppenheimer, Robert, 53–4
oracles, 8, 17–21, 24
'ought', 76, 81–2, 158–64, 170, 200–2, 204, 206

Pareto, V., 10–11, 17
Parkin, Molly, 141, 144
patience, 205–6
penitance, 198–9, 218–20
Peter, Saint, 207
Philips, D. Z., 49, 208
Plato, 15, 68, 173, 175–6, 187–8, 190, 193, 200, 211, 226
Polanyi, Michael, 64–5
Popper, Karl, 50–2, 55–6
prayer, 39, 194–7
Prichard, H. A., 130–1, 133–9, 142, 176, 193
Protagoras, 11, 164
punishment, 145, 173, 194–5, 197–201, 208, 210–14, 217–28

rationality, 9, 16, 25, 27–31, 33–5, 42, 45, 55, 60–1, 69, 154, 164, 179
reality, 11–14, 22–3, 27, 123
Reinhardt, Lloyd, 208
relativism, 42, 73
remorse, 146, 167–8, 185, 225–6
retribution, 213
reward, 210–12, 214–16, 222–3, 225, 227
Rhees, Rush, viii, 40–1, 72, 74–5, 150, 202, 204, 209, 228
Rousseau, J.-J., 3, 90–5, 97–100, 102–4, 107–9
Rovere, Richard, 68

Russell, Bertrand, 26

Sartre, J.-P., 177–8
self-pity, 145–6
sexual relations, 43–4, 46–7
Shakespeare, William, 194–6
Shaw, Irwin, 71
Sidgwick, Henry, 151–4, 159, 161, 163, 165–7, 170, 176
Simmel, Georg, 49
Singer, Marcus, 159–60, 170
Snow, C. P., 59
Socrates, 15, 68, 193, 195, 202–3, 226
Sophists, 51, 81
Sophocles, 185
Spencer, B., 45
Spinoza, B., 117
state, 6, 90–1, 100, 103–4
Stocks, J. L., 187
Swift, Jonathan, 66–7

Thibon, Gustave, 209

Tilghman, B. R., 150
Tolstoy, L., 187–92
truthfulness, 4–5, 61–70
Twain, Mark, 194–6

Utilitarianism, 4, 174, 179, 213

Vico, Giambattista, 43, 47, 49, 92

Weil, Simone, 42, 49, 107–8, 150, 181, 183–4, 207, 209, 219–20, 222, 226
will, 6–7, 46, 100–4, 107–8, 110–30, 134, 137–8, 178–80, 182, 203, 205, 207, 211–12; *see also* free will; general will
Wisdom, John, 66–7, 72
witchcraft, *see* magic and witchcraft
Wittgenstein, L., 6–7, 22–3, 25–6, 40, 46, 48, 61, 69, 110–30, 132, 134, 138, 142, 154–5, 180, 194–5, 201–6, 208–11, 213, 220–1, 223, 225–6, 228